T0256559

A Textbook of Data Structures and Algorithms 3

One of the greatest lessons I have learnt in my life is
to pay as much attention to the means of work as to its end…
I have been always learning great lessons from that one principle,
and it appears to me that all the secret of success is there;
to pay as much attention to the means as to the end….
Let us perfect the means; the end will take care of itself.

– Swami Vivekananda
(Lecture Delivered at Los Angeles, California, January 4, 1900)

A Textbook of Data Structures and Algorithms 3

Mastering Advanced Data Structures and Algorithm Design Strategies

G A Vijayalakshmi Pai

WILEY

First published 2022 in Great Britain and the United States by ISTE Ltd and John Wiley & Sons, Inc.

Previous edition published in 2008 as "Data Structures and Algorithms: Concepts, Techniques and Applications" by McGraw Hill Education (India) Pvt Ltd. © McGraw Hill Education (India) Pvt Ltd. 2008

ISTE Ltd
27-37 St George's Road
London SW19 4EU
UK

www.iste.co.uk

John Wiley & Sons, Inc.
111 River Street
Hoboken, NJ 07030
USA

www.wiley.com

Library of Congress Control Number: 2022947642

British Library Cataloguing-in-Publication Data
A CIP record for this book is available from the British Library
ISBN 978-1-78630-892-4

Contents

Preface

Efficient problem solving using computers, irrespective of the discipline or application, calls for the design of efficient algorithms. The inclusion of appropriate data structures is of critical importance to the design of efficient algorithms. In other words, *good algorithm design must go hand in hand with appropriate data structures for an efficient program design to solve a problem.*

Data structures and algorithms is a fundamental course in computer science, which most undergraduate and graduate programs in computer science and other allied disciplines in science and engineering offer during the early stages of the respective programs, either as a core or as an elective course. The course enables students to have a much-needed foundation for efficient programming, leading to better problem solving in their respective disciplines.

Most of the well-known text books/monographs on this subject have discussed the concepts in relation to a programming language – beginning with Pascal and spanning a spectrum of them such as C, C++, C#, Java, Python and so on, essentially calling for ample knowledge of the language, before one proceeds to try and understand the data structure. There does remain a justification in this. The implementation of data structures in the specific programming language need to be demonstrated or the algorithms pertaining to the data structures concerned need a convenient medium of presentation and when this is the case, why not a programming language?

Again, while some authors have insisted on using their books for an advanced level course, there are some who insist on a working knowledge of the specific programming language as a prerequisite to using the book. However, in the case of a core course, as it is in most academic programs, it is not uncommon for a novice or a sophomore to be bewildered by the "miles of code" that demonstrate or explain a data structure, rendering the subject difficult to comprehend. In fact, the efforts that one needs to put in to comprehend the data structure and its applications are distracted by the necessity to garner sufficient programming knowledge to follow the code. It is indeed ironic that while a novice is taught data structures to appreciate programming, in reality it turns out that one learns programming to appreciate data structures!

In my decades-old experience of offering the course to graduate programs, which admits students from diverse undergraduate disciplines, with little to no strong knowledge of programming, I had several occasions to observe this malady. In fact, it is not uncommon in some academic programs, especially graduate programs which, due to their shorter duration, have a course in programming and data structures running in parallel in the same semester, much to the chagrin of the novice learner! That a novice is forced to learn data structures through their implementation (in a specific programming language), when in reality it ought to be learning augmented with the implementation of the data structures, has been the reason behind the fallout.

A solution to this problem would be to

i) Frame the course such that the theory deals with the concepts, techniques and applications of data structures and algorithms, not taking recourse to any specific programming language, but instead settling for a pseudo-language, which clearly expounds the data structure. Additionally, supplementing the course material with illustrative problems, review questions and exercises to reinforce the students' grasp of the concepts would help them gain useful insights while learning.

ii) Augment the theory with laboratory sessions to enable the student to implement the data structure in itself or as embedded in an application, in the language of his/her own choice or as insisted upon in the curriculum. This would enable the student who has acquired sufficient knowledge and insight into the data structures to appreciate the beauty and merits of employing the data structure by programming it themself, rather than "look" for the data structure in a prewritten code.

This means that text books catering to the fundamental understanding of the data structure concepts for use as course material in the classroom are as much needed as the books that cater to the implementation of data structures in a programming language for use in the laboratory sessions. While most books in the market conform to the latter, bringing out a book to be classroom course material and used by instructors handling a course on data structures and algorithms, comprehensive enough for the novice students to benefit from, has been the main motivation in writing this book.

As such, the book details concepts, techniques and applications pertaining to data structures and algorithms, independent of any programming language, discusses several examples and illustrative problems, poses review questions to reinforce the understanding of the theory, and presents a suggestive list of programming assignments to aid implementation of the data structures and algorithms learned.

In fact, the book may either be independently used as a textbook since it is self-contained or serve as a companion for books discussing data structures and algorithms implemented in specific programming languages such as C, C++, Java, Python, and so on.

At this juncture, it needs to be pointed out that a plethora of programming resources and freely downloadable implementations of the majority of the data structures in almost all popular languages are available on the Internet, which can undoubtedly serve as good guides for the learner. However, it has to be emphasized that an earnest student of data structures and algorithms must invest a lot of time and self-effort in trying to implement the data structures and algorithms learned, in a language of one's choice, all by oneself, in order to attain a thorough grasp of the concepts.

About this edition

This edition is a largely revised and enlarged version of its predecessor, published by McGraw Hill, USA. The earlier edition published in 2008 saw 15 reprints in its life span of 13 years (ending January 2022) and was recommended as a text book for the course in several universities and colleges. It comprised 17 chapters categorized into five parts and reinforced learning through 133 illustrative problems, 215 review questions and 74 programming assignments.

The features of this new edition are as follows:

– There are 22 chapters spread across three volumes that detail sequential linear data structures, linked linear data structures, nonlinear data structures, advanced data structures, searching and sorting algorithms, algorithm design techniques and NP-completeness.

– The data structures of k-d trees and treaps have been elaborated in a newly included chapter (Chapter 15) in Volume 3.

– The data structures of strings, bit rays, unrolled linked lists, self-organizing linked lists, segment trees and k-ary trees have been introduced in the appropriate sections of the existing chapters in Volumes 1 and 2.

– The concepts of counting binary search trees and Kruskal's algorithm have been detailed in the appropriate sections of the existing chapters in Volume 2.

– Skip list search, counting sort and bucket sort have been included in the chapters on searching and sorting algorithms in Volume 3.

– The algorithm design techniques of divide and conquer, the greedy method and dynamic programming have been elaborately discussed in Chapters 19–21 in Volume 3.

– The concept of NP-completeness has been detailed in a newly included chapter, Chapter 22 in Volume 3.

– Several illustrative problems, review questions and programming assignments have been added to enrich the content and aid in understanding the concepts. The new edition thus includes 181 illustrative problems, 276 review questions and 108 programming assignments.

Organization of the book

The book comprises three volumes, namely, Volume 1: Chapters 1–7, Volume 2: Chapters 8–12 and Volume 3: Chapters 13–22.

Volume 1 opens with an *introduction to data structures* and concepts pertaining to the *analysis of algorithms*, detailed in Chapters 1 and 2, which is essential to appreciate the theories and algorithms related to data structures and their applications.

Chapters 3–5 detail sequential linear data structures, namely, *arrays*, *strings*, *bit arrays*, *stacks*, *queues*, *priority queues* and *dequeues*, and their applications. Chapters 6 and 7 elucidate linked linear data structures, namely *linked lists*, *linked stacks* and *linked queues*, and their applications.

Volume 2 details nonlinear data structures. Chapters 8 and 9 elaborate on the nonlinear data structures of *trees*, *binary trees* and *graphs*, and their applications. Chapters 10–12 highlight the advanced data structures of *binary search trees*, *AVL trees*, *B trees*, *tries*, *red-black trees* and *splay trees*, and their applications.

Volume 3 details an assortment of data structures, algorithm design strategies and their applications.

Chapters 13–15 discuss *hash tables*, *files*, *k-d trees* and *treaps*. Chapter 16 discusses the search algorithms of *linear search*, *transpose sequential search*, *interpolation search*, *binary search*, *Fibonacci search*, *skip list search* and other search techniques.

Chapter 17 elaborates on the internal sorting algorithms of *bubble sort, insertion sort, selection sort, merge sort, shell sort, quick sort, heap sort, radix sort, counting sort* and *bucket sort*, and Chapter 18 discusses the external sorting techniques of *sorting with tapes, sorting with disks, polyphase merge sort* and *cascade merge sort*.

Chapters 19–21 detail the algorithm design strategies of *divide and conquer*, the *greedy method* and *dynamic programming* and their applications.

Chapter 22 introduces the theories and concepts of *NP-completeness*.

For a full list of the contents of Volumes 1 and 2, see the summary at the end of this book.

Salient features of the book

The features of the book are as follows:

– all-around emphasis on theory, problems, applications and programming assignments;

– simple and lucid explanation of the theory;

– inclusion of several applications to illustrate the use of data structures and algorithms;

– several worked-out examples as illustrative problems in each chapter;

– list of programming assignments at the end of each chapter;

– review questions to strengthen understanding;

– self-contained text for use as a text book for either an introductory or advanced level course.

Target audience

The book could be used both as an introductory or an advanced-level textbook for undergraduate, graduate and research programs, which offer data structures and algorithms as a core course or an elective course. While the book is primarily meant to serve as a course material for use in the classroom, it could be used as a companion guide during the laboratory sessions to nurture better understanding of the theoretical concepts.

An introductory level course for a duration of one semester or 60 lecture hours, targeting an undergraduate program or first-year graduate program or a diploma program or a certificate program, could include Chapters 1–7 of Volume 1, Chapter 8 of Volume 2, Chapters 13, 16 (sections 16.1, 16.2, 16.5) and 17 (sections 17.1–17.3, 17.5, 17.7) of Volume 3 in its curriculum.

A middle-level course for a duration of one semester or 60 lecture hours targeting senior graduate-level programs and research programs such as MS/PhD could include Chapters 1–7 of Volume 1, Chapters 8–11 of Volume 2, Chapter 13 and selective sections of Chapters 16–17 of Volume 3.

An advanced level course that focuses on advanced data structures and algorithm design could begin with a review of Chapter 8 and include Chapters 9–12 of Volume 2, Chapters 14 and 15 and selective sections of Chapters 16–18, and Chapters 19–22 of Volume 3 in its curriculum based on the level of prerequisite courses satisfied.

Chapters 8–10 and Chapter 11 (sections 11.1–11.3) of Volume 2 and Chapters 13, 14 and 18 of Volume 3 could be useful to include in a curriculum that serves as a prerequisite for a course on database management systems.

To re-emphasize, all theory sessions must be supplemented with laboratory sessions to encourage learners to implement the concepts learned in an appropriate language that adheres to the curricular requirements of the programs concerned.

Acknowledgments

The author is grateful to ISTE Ltd., London, UK, for accepting to publish the book, in collaboration with John Wiley & Sons Inc., USA. She expresses her appreciation to the publishing team, for their professionalism and excellent production practices, while bringing out this book in three volumes.

The author expresses her sincere thanks to the Management and Principal, PSG College of Technology, Coimbatore, India for the support extended while writing the book.

The author would like to place on record her immense admiration and affection for her father, Late Professor G. A. Krishna Pai and her mother Rohini Krishna Pai for their unbounded encouragement and support to help her follow her life lessons and her sisters Dr. Rekha Pai and Udaya Pai, for their unstinted, anywhere-anytime-anything kind of help and support, all of which were instrumental and inspirational in helping this author create this work.

G. A. Vijayalakshmi Pai
August 2022

13

Hash Tables

13.1. Introduction

The data structures of binary search trees, AVL trees, B trees, tries, red-black trees and splay trees discussed so far in the book (Volume 2) are tree-based data structures. These are nonlinear data structures and serve to capture the hierarchical relationship that exists between the elements forming the data structure. However, there are applications that deal with linear or tabular forms of data, devoid of any superior-subordinate relationship. In such cases, employing these data structures would be superfluous. ***Hash tables*** are one among such data structures which favor efficient storage and retrieval of data elements that are linear in nature.

13.1.1. *Dictionaries*

Dictionary is a collection of data elements uniquely identified by a field called a ***key***. A dictionary supports the operations of search, insert and delete. The ***ADT of a dictionary*** is defined as a set of elements with distinct keys supporting the operations of *search, insert, delete* and *create* (which creates an empty dictionary). While most dictionaries deal with distinct keyed elements, it is not uncommon to find applications calling for dictionaries with duplicate or repeated keys. In this case, it is essential that the dictionary evolves rules to resolve the ambiguity that may arise while searching for or deleting data elements with duplicate keys.

A dictionary supports both ***sequential*** and ***random access***. Sequential access is one in which the data elements of the dictionary are ordered and accessed according to the order of the keys (ascending or descending, for example). Random access is one in which the data elements of the dictionary are accessed according to no particular order.

Hash tables are ideal data structures for dictionaries. In this chapter, we introduce the concept of hashing and hash functions. The structure and operations of the hash tables are also discussed. The various methods of **collision resolution**, for example, **linear open addressing** and **chaining** and their performance analyses are detailed. Finally, the application of hash tables in the fields of compiler design, relational database query processing and file organization are discussed.

13.2. Hash table structure

A **hash function** $H(X)$ is a mathematical function which, when given a key X of the dictionary D maps it to a position P in a storage table termed **hash table**. The process of mapping the keys to their respective positions in the hash table is called **hashing**. Figure 13.1 illustrates a hash function.

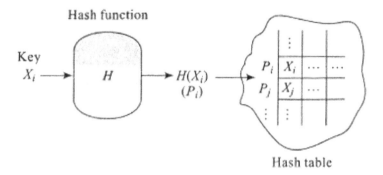

Figure 13.1. *Hashing a key*

When the data elements of the dictionary are to be stored in the hash table, each key X_i is mapped to a position P_i in the hash table as determined by the value of $H(X_i)$, that is, $P_i = H(X_i)$. To search for a key X in the hash table all that one does is determine the position P by computing $P = H(X)$ and accessing the appropriate data element. In the case of insertion of a key X or its deletion, the position P in the hash table where the data element needs to be inserted or from where it is to be deleted respectively, is determined by computing $P = H(X)$.

If the hash table is implemented using a sequential data structure, for example, arrays, then the hash function $H(X)$ may be so chosen to yield a value that corresponds to the index of the array. In such a case the hash function is a mere mapping of the keys to the array indices.

EXAMPLE 13.1.–

Consider a set of distinct keys { AB12, VP99, RK32, CG45, KL78, OW31, ST65, EX44 } to be represented as a hash table. Let us suppose the hash function H is defined as below:

$$H(XYmn) = ord(X)$$

where X, Y are the alphabetical characters, m, n are the numerical characters of the key, and $ord(X)$ is the ordinal number of the alphabet X.

The computations of the positions of the keys in the hash table are shown below:

Key *XYmn*	H(*XYmn*)	Position of the key in the hash table
AB12	*ord(A)*	1
VP99	*ord(V)*	22
RK32	*ord(R)*	18
CG45	*ord(C)*	3
KL78	*ord(K)*	11
OW31	*ord(O)*	15
ST65	*ord(S)*	19
EX44	*ord(E)*	5

The hash table accommodating the data elements appears as shown below:

1	AB12	....
2	....	
3	CG45	
4	....	
5	EX44	....
....	.....	
11	KL78	
...		
15	OW31	....
...		
18	RK32	
19	ST65	....
....		
22	VP99	....
...	...	...

In Example 13.1, it was assumed that the hash function yields distinct values for the individual keys. If this were to be followed as a criterion, then the situation may turn out of control since, in the case of dictionaries with a very large set of data elements, the hash table size can be too huge to be handled efficiently. Therefore, it is convenient to choose hash functions that yield values lying within a limited range so as to restrict the length of the table. This would consequently imply that the hash functions may yield identical values for a set of keys. In other words, a set of keys could be mapped to the same position in the hash table.

Let X_1, X_2, ...X_n be the n keys that are mapped to the same position P in the hash table. Then, $H(X_1) = H(X_2) = ...H(X_n) = P$. In such a case, X_1, X_2, ...X_n are called **synonyms**. The act of two or more synonyms vying for the same position in the hash table is known as a **collision.** Naturally, this entails a modification in the structure of the hash table to accommodate the synonyms. The two important methods of linear open addressing and chaining to handle synonyms are presented in sections 13.4 and 13.5, respectively.

13.3. Hash functions

The choice of the hash function plays a significant role in the structure and performance of the hash table. It is therefore essential that a hash function satisfies the following characteristics:

i) easy and quick to compute;

ii) even distribution of keys across the hash table. In other words, a hash function must minimize collisions.

13.3.1. *Building hash functions*

The following are some of the methods of obtaining hash functions:

i) **Folding**: The key is first partitioned into two or three or more parts. Each of the individual parts is combined using any of the basic arithmetic operations such as addition or multiplication. The resultant number could be conveniently manipulated, for example, truncated, to finally arrive at the index where the key is to be stored. Folding assures a better spread of keys across the hash table.

Example: Consider a six-digit numerical key: 719532. We choose to partition the key into three parts of two digits each, that is, 71 | 95 | 32, and merely add the numerical equivalent of each of the parts, that is, $71 + 95 + 32 = 198$. Truncating the result yields 98 which is chosen as the index of the hash table where the key 719532 is to be accommodated.

ii) **Truncation:** In this method, the selective digits of the key are extracted to determine the index of the hash table where the key needs to be accommodated. In the case of alphabetical keys, their numerical equivalents may be considered. Truncation though quick to compute does not ensure even distribution of keys.

Example: Consider a group of six-digit numerical keys that need to be accommodated in a hash table with 100 locations. We choose to select digits in positions 3 and 6 to determine the index where the key is to be stored. Thus, key 719532 would be stored in location 92 of the hash table.

iii) **Modular arithmetic:** This is a popular method and the size of the hash table L is involved in the computation of the hash function. The function makes use of modulo arithmetic. Let k be the numerical key or the numerical equivalent if it is an alphabetical key. The hash function is given by

$H(k) = k \ mod \ L$

The hash function evidently returns a value that lies between 0 and L-1. Choosing L to be a prime number has a proven better performance by way of even distribution of keys.

Example: Consider a group of six-digit numerical keys that need to be stored in a hash table of size 111. For a key 145682, $H(k) = 145682 \ mod \ 111 = 50$. Hence, the key is stored in location 50 of the hash table.

13.4. Linear open addressing

Let us suppose a group of keys is to be inserted into a hash table HT of size L, making use of the modulo arithmetic function $H(k) = k \ mod \ L$. Since the range of the hash table index is limited to lie between 0 and L-1, for a population of N ($N > L$) keys, collisions are bound to occur. Hence, a provision needs to be made in the hash table to accommodate the data elements that are synonyms.

We choose to adopt a sequential data structure to accommodate the hash table. Let HT[$0: L$-1] be the hash table. Here, the L locations of the hash table are termed **buckets.** Every bucket provides accommodation for the data elements. However, to accommodate synonyms, that is, keys that map to the same bucket, it is essential that a provision be made in the buckets. We, therefore, partition buckets into what are called **slots** to accommodate synonyms. Thus, if bucket b has s slots, then s synonyms can be accommodated in bucket b. In the case of an array implementation of a hash table, the rows of the array indicate buckets and the columns the slots. In such a case, the hash table is represented as HT[$0:L-1$, $0:s-1$]. The number of slots in a bucket needs to be decided based on the application. Figure 13.2 illustrates a general hash table implemented using a sequential data structure.

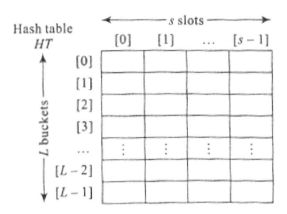

Figure 13.2. *Hash table implemented using a sequential data structure*

EXAMPLE 13.2.–

Let us consider a set of keys {45, 98, 12, 55, 46, 89, 65, 88, 36, 21} to be represented as a hash table as shown in Figure 13.2. Let us suppose the hash function H is defined as $H(X) = X \bmod 11$. The hash table, therefore, has 11 buckets. We propose three slots per bucket. Table 13.1 shows the hash function values of the keys and Figure 13.3 shows the structure of the hash table.

Key X	45	98	12	55	46	89	65	88	36	21
H(X)	1	10	1	0	2	1	10	0	3	10

Table 13.1. *Hash function values of the keys (Example 13.2)*

Observe how keys {45, 12, 89}, {98, 65, 21} and {55, 88} are synonyms mapping to the same bucket 1, 10 and 0 respectively. The provision of three slots per bucket makes it possible to accommodate synonyms.

Hash Table

HT	[0]	[1]	[2]
[0]	55	88	
[1]	45	12	89
[2]	46		
[3]	36		
[4]			
[5]			
[6]			
[7]			
[8]			
[9]			
[10]	98	65	21

Figure 13.3. *Hash table (Example 13.2)*

Now, what happens if a synonym is unable to find a slot in the bucket? In other words, if the bucket is full, then where do we find a place for the synonyms? In such a case an *overflow* is said to have occurred. All collisions need not result in overflows. But in the case of a hash table with single slot buckets, collisions mean overflows.

The bucket to which the key is mapped by the hash function is known as the *home bucket*. To tackle overflows we move further down, beginning from the home bucket and look for the closest slot that is empty and place the key in it. Such a method of handling overflows is known as *Linear probing* or *Linear open addressing* or *closed hashing*.

EXAMPLE 13.3.–

Let us proceed to insert the keys {77, 34, 43} in the hash table discussed in Example 13.2. The hash function values of the keys are {0, 1, 10}. When we proceed to insert 77 in its home bucket 0, we find a slot is available and hence the insertion is done. In the case of 34, its home bucket 1 is full and hence there is an overflow. By linear probing, we look for the closest slot that is vacant and find one in the second slot of bucket 2. While inserting 43, we find bucket 10 to be full.

The search for the closest empty slot proceeds by moving downward in a circular fashion until it finds a vacant place in slot 3 of bucket 2. Note the circular movement of searching the hash table while looking for an empty slot. Figure 13.3 illustrates the linear probing method undertaken for the listed keys. The keys which have been accommodated in places other than their home buckets are shown over grey background.

Hash Table

HT	[0]	[1]	[2]
[0]	55	48	77
[1]	45	12	89
[2]	46	34	43
[3]	36		
[4]			
[5]			
[6]			
[7]			
[8]			
[9]			
[10]	98	65	21

Figure 13.4. *Linear open addressing (Example 13.3)*

13.4.1. *Operations on linear open addressed hash tables*

Search: Searching for a key in a linear open addressed hash table proceeds on lines similar to that of insertion. However, if the searched key is available in the home bucket then the search is done. The time complexity in such a case is $O(1)$. However, if there had been overflows while inserting the key, then a sequential search has to be called which searches through each slot of the buckets following the home bucket until either (i) the key is found or (ii) an empty slot is encountered in which case the search terminates or (iii) the search path has curled back to the home bucket. In the case of (i), the search is said to be successful. In the cases of (ii) and (iii), it is said to be unsuccessful.

EXAMPLE 13.4.–

Consider the snapshot of the hash table shown in Figure 13.5, which represents keys whose first character lies between 'A' and 'I', both inclusive. The hash function used is $H(X) = ord(C)\ mod\ 10$ where C is the first character of the alphabetical key X.

Hash Table

HT	[0]	[2]
[0]	I81	I90
[1]	A12	A91
[2]	B47	I99
[3]		
[4]	D36	
[5]		
[6]	F18	F78
[7]	G64	F73
[8]	H11	F99
[9]	I54	I75
	⋮	⋮

Figure 13.5. *Illustration of search in a hash table*

The search for keys F18 and G64 is straightforward since they are present in their home buckets, which are 6 and 7, respectively. The search for keys A91 and F78 for example, are slightly more involved, in the sense that though they are available in their respective home buckets they are accessed only after a sequential search for them is done in the slots corresponding to their buckets. On the other hand, the search for I99 fails to find it in its home bucket, which is 9. This, therefore, triggers a sequential search of every slot following the home bucket until the key is found, in which case the search is successful or until an empty slot is encountered, in which case the search is a failure. I99 is indeed found in slot 2 of bucket 2! Observe how the search path curls back to the top of the hash table from the home bucket of key I99. Let us now search for the key G93. The search proceeds to look into its home bucket (7) before a sequential search for the same is undertaken in the slots following the home bucket. The search stops due to its encountering an empty slot and therefore the search is deemed unsuccessful.

Algorithm 13.1 illustrates the search algorithm for a linear open addressed hash table.

Insert: the insertion of data elements in a linear open addressed hash table is executed as explained in the previous section. The hash function, which is quite often modulo arithmetic based, determines the bucket b and thereafter slot s in which the data element is to be inserted. In the case of overflow, we search for the closest empty slot beginning from the home bucket and accommodate the key in the slot. Algorithm 13.1 could be modified to execute the insert operation. The line

```
if ( HT[i, j] = 0) then  print (" KEY not found");
```

in the algorithm is replaced by

```
if ( HT[i, j] = 0) then  HT[i, j] = X;

              /* insert X in the empty slot*/
```

Delete: the delete operation on a hash table can be clumsy. When a key is deleted it cannot be merely wiped off from its bucket (slot). A deletion leaves the slot vacant and if an empty slot is chosen as a signal to terminate a search then many of the elements following the empty slot and displaced from their home buckets may go unnoticed. To tackle this it is essential that the keys following the empty slot be moved up. This can make the whole operation clumsy.

An alternative could be to write a special element in the slot every time a delete operation is done. This special element not only serves to camouflage the empty space 'available' in the deleted slot when a search is in progress but also serves to accommodate an insertion when an appropriate element assigned to the slot turns up.

However, it is generally recommended that deletions in a hash table be avoided as much as possible due to their clumsy implementation.

13.4.2. *Performance analysis*

The complexity of the linear open addressed hash table is dependent on the number of buckets. In the case of hash functions that follow modular arithmetic, the number of buckets is given by the divisor L.

The best case time complexity of searching for a key in a hash table is given by *O(1)* and the worst case time complexity is given by *O(n)*, where *n* is the number of data elements stored in the hash table. A worst case occurs when all the *n* data elements map to the same bucket.

The time complexities when compared to those of their linear list counterparts are not in any way less. The best and worst case complexity of searching for an element in a linear list of n elements is respectively, $O(1)$ and $O(n)$. However, on average, the performance of the hash table is much more efficient than that of the linear lists. It has been shown that the average case performance of a linear open addressed hash table for an unsuccessful and successful search is given by

$$U_n \sim \frac{1}{2}\left(1 + \frac{1}{(1-\alpha)^2}\right)$$

$$S_n \sim \frac{1}{2}\left(1 + \frac{1}{(1-\alpha)}\right)$$

where U_n and S_n are the number of buckets examined on an average during an unsuccessful and successful search respectively. The average is considered over all possible sequences of the n keys X_1, X_2, ...X_n. α is the **loading factor** of the hash table and is given by $\alpha = \frac{n}{b}$ where b is the number of buckets. The smaller the loading factor better is the average case performance of the hash table in comparison to that of linear lists.

13.4.3. *Other collision resolution techniques with open addressing*

The drawbacks of linear probing or linear open addressing could be overcome to an extent by employing one or more of the following strategies:

i) **Rehashing**

A major drawback of linear probing is **clustering** or **primary clustering** wherein the hash table gives rise to long sequences of records with gaps in between the sequences. This leads to longer sequential searches especially when an empty slot needs to be found. The problem could be resolved to an extent by resorting to what is known as **rehashing**. In this, a second hash function is used to determine the slot where the key is to be accommodated. If the slot is not empty, then another function is called for, and so on.

Thus, rehashing makes use of at least two functions H, H' where $H(X)$, $H'(X)$ map keys X to any one of the b buckets. To insert a key, $H(X)$ is computed and the key X is accommodated in the bucket if it is empty. In the case of a collision, the second hash function $H'(X)$ is computed and the search sequence for the empty slot proceeds by computing,

$$h_i = (H(X) + i.\ H'(X))\ mod\ b,\ i = 1,\ 2,\ ....$$

```
procedure LOP_HASH_SEARCH(HT, b, s  X)
/*  HT[0:b-1, 0:s-1] is the hash table implemented as a
two dimensional array. Here b is the number of buckets
and s is the number of slots. X is the key to be
searched in the hash table. In case of unsuccessful
search,  the procedure prints the message  "KEY not
found" otherwise prints "KEY found"*/

  h = H(X); /* H(X) is the hash function computed
                                       on X  */
  i = h; j =0; /* i, j are the indexes for the
                  bucket and slot respectively*/
  while ( HT[i, j] ≠ 0  and  HT[i, j] ≠  X ) do
     j = j + 1;       /* search for X in the slots*/
     if (j > (s-1)) then j = 0;
                /* reset slot index to 0 to continue
                     searching in the next bucket*/

     if (j == 0) then { i = (i+1) mod  b;
                    /* continue searching in the
                 next bucket in a circular manner*/

     if (i == h) then  {print ( "Key not found");
                        exit();}
  endwhile
  if ( HT[i, j]== X) then print (" KEY found");
  if ( HT[i, j] = 0) then print (" KEY not found");

end LOP_HASH_SEARCH
```

Algorithm 13.1. *Procedure to search for a*
key X in a linear open addressed hash table

Here, h_1, h_2, ... is the search sequence before an empty slot is found to accommodate the key. It needs to be ensured that $H'(X)$ does not evaluate to 0, since there is no way this would be of help. A good choice for $H'(X)$ is given by $M - (X \bmod M)$ where M is chosen to be a prime smaller than the hash table size (see illustrative problem 13.6)

ii) **Quadratic probing**

This is another method that can substantially reduce clustering. In this method when a collision occurs at address h, unlike linear probing which probes buckets in locations $h+1$, $h+2$ .... and so forth, the technique probes buckets at locations $h+1$, $h+4$, $h+9$,.... and so forth. In other words, the method probes buckets at locations $(h + i^2)\ mod\ \ b$, $\ i = 1, 2, \ ....$, where h is the home bucket and b is the number of buckets. However, there is no guarantee that the method gives a fair chance to probe all locations in the hash table. Though quadratic probing reduces primary clustering, it may result in probing the same set of alternate cells. Such a case known as **secondary clustering** occurs especially when the hash table size is not prime.

If b is a prime number then quadratic probing probes exactly half the number of locations in the hash table. In this case, the method is guaranteed to find an empty slot if the hash table is at least half empty (see illustrative problems 13.4 and 13.5).

iii) **Random probing**

Unlike quadratic probing where the increment during probing was definite, random probing makes use of a random number generator to obtain the increment and hence the next bucket to be probed. However, it is essential that the random number generator function generates the same sequence. Though this method reduces clustering, it can be a little slow when compared to others.

13.5. Chaining

In the case of linear open addressing, the solution of accommodating synonyms in the closest empty slot may contribute to a deterioration in performance. For example, the search for a synonym key may involve sequentially going through every slot occurring after its home bucket before it is either found or unfound. Also, the implementation of the hash table using a sequential data structure such as arrays limits its capacity (b × s slots). While increasing the number of slots to minimize overflows may lead to wastage of memory, containing the number of slots to the bare minimum may lead to severe overflows hampering the performance of the hash table.

An alternative to overcome this malady is to keep all synonyms that are mapped to the same bucket chained to it. In other words, every bucket is maintained as a singly linked list with synonyms represented as nodes. The buckets continue to be represented as a sequential data structure as before, to favor the hash function computation. Such a method of handling overflows is called **chaining** or **open hashing** or **separate chaining**. Figure 13.6 illustrates a chained hash table.

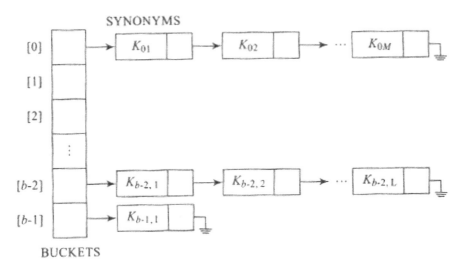

Figure 13.6. *A chained hash table*

In the figure, observe how the buckets have been represented sequentially and each of the buckets is linked to a chain of nodes which are synonyms mapping to the same bucket.

Chained hash tables only acknowledge collisions. There are no overflows *per se* since any number of collisions can be handled provided there is enough memory to handle them!

EXAMPLE 13.5.–

Let us consider the set of keys {45, 98, 12, 55, 46, 89, 65, 88, 36, 21} listed in Example 13.2, to be represented as a chained hash table. The hash function H used is $H(X) = X \bmod 11$. The hash function values for the keys are shown in Table 13.1. The structure of the chained hash table is shown in Figure 13.7.

Observe how each of the groups of synonyms for example, {45, 12, 89}, {98, 65, 21} and {55, 88} are represented as singly linked lists corresponding to the buckets 1, 10 and 0 respectively. In accordance with the norms pertaining to singly linked lists, the link field of the last synonym in each chain is a null pointer. Those buckets which are yet to accommodate keys are also marked null.

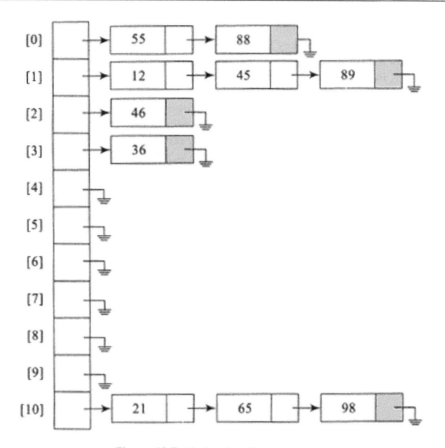

Figure 13.7. *Hash table (Example 13.5)*

13.5.1. *Operations on chained hash tables*

Search: The search for a key X in a chained hash table proceeds by computing the hash function value $H(X)$. The bucket corresponding to the value $H(X)$ is accessed and a sequential search along the chain of nodes is undertaken. If the key is found then the search is termed successful otherwise unsuccessful. If the chain is too long maintaining the chain in order (ascending or descending) helps in rendering the search efficient.

Algorithm 13.2 illustrates the procedure to undertake a search in a chained hash table.

Insert: To insert a key X into a hash table, we compute the hash function $H(X)$ to determine the bucket. If the key is the first node to be linked to the bucket then all that it calls for is a mere execution of a function to insert a node in an empty singly linked list. In the case of keys that are synonyms, the new key could be inserted either at the beginning or the end of the chain leaving the list unordered. However, it would be prudent and less expensive too, to maintain each of the chains in the ascending or descending order of the keys. This would also render the search for a specific key among its synonyms to be efficiently carried out.

EXAMPLE 13.6.–

Let us insert keys {76, 48} into the chained hash table shown in Figure 13.7. Since 76 already has three synonyms in its chain corresponding to bucket 10, we choose to insert it in order in the list. On the other hand, 48 is the first key in its bucket, which is 4. Figure 13.8 illustrates the insertion.

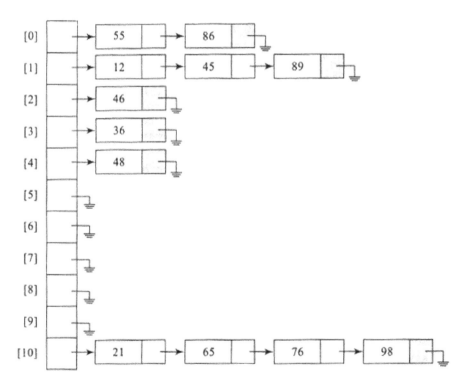

Figure 13.8. *Inserting keys into a chained hash table*

```
procedure CHAIN_HASH_SEARCH(HT, b, X)
/*    HT[0:b-1] is the hash table implemented as a one
dimensional array of pointers to buckets. Here b is the number
of buckets. X is the key to be searched in the hash table. In
case of unsuccessful search, the procedure prints the message
"KEY not found" otherwise prints "KEY found"*/

  h = H(X); /* H(X) is the hash function computed on X */

  TEMP = HT[h];      /* TEMP is the pointer to the first
                                node in the chain*/
  while (DATA(TEMP) ≠ X  and TEMP ≠ NIL ) do
                /* search for the key down the chain*/
    TEMP = LINK(TEMP);
  endwhile


  if ( DATA(TEMP)== X) then print (" KEY found");
  if ( TEMP == NIL) then print (" KEY not found");

end CHAIN_HASH_SEARCH.
```

Algorithm 13.2. *Procedure to search*
for a key X in a chained hash table

Algorithm 13.2 could be modified to insert a key. It merely calls for the insertion of a node in a singly linked list that is unordered or ordered.

Delete: Unlike that of linear open addressed hash tables, the deletion of a key X in a chained hash table is elegantly done. All that it calls for is a search for X in the corresponding chain and deletion of the respective node.

13.5.2. *Performance analysis*

The complexity of the chained hash table is dependent on the length of the chain of nodes corresponding to the buckets. The best case complexity of a search is $O(1)$. A worst case occurs when all the n elements map to the same bucket and the length of the chain corresponding to that bucket is n, with the searched key turning out to be the last in the chain. The worst-case complexity of the search in such a case is $O(n)$.

On an average, the complexity of the search operation on a chained hash table is given by

$$U_n \sim \frac{(1+\alpha)}{2}, \alpha \geq 1$$

$$S_n \sim 1 + \frac{\alpha}{2}$$

where U_n and S_n are the number of nodes examined on an average during an unsuccessful and successful search respectively. α is the loading factor of the hash table and is given by $\alpha = \frac{n}{b}$ where b is the number of buckets.

The average case performance of the chained hash table is superior to that of the linear open addressed hash table.

13.6. Applications

In this section, we discuss the application of hash tables in the fields of compiler design, relational database query processing and file organization.

13.6.1. *Representation of a keyword table in a compiler*

In section 10.4.1, (Volume 2) the application of binary search trees and AVL trees for the representation of symbol tables in a compiler was discussed. Hash tables find applications in the same problem as well.

A *keyword table* which is a *static symbol table* is best represented by means of a hash table. Each time a compiler checks out a string to be a keyword or a user-id, the string is searched against the keyword table. An appropriate hash function could be designed to minimize collisions among the keywords and yield the bucket where the keyword could be found. A successful search indicates that the string encountered is a keyword and an unsuccessful search indicates that it is a user-id. Considering the significant fact that but for retrievals, no insertions or deletions are permissible on a keyword table, hash tables turn out to be one of the best propositions for the representation of symbol tables.

EXAMPLE 13.7.–

Consider a subset of a keyword set commonly used in programming languages, for example, { while, repeat, and, or, not, if, else, begin, end, function, procedure, int, float, Boolean}. For simplicity, we make use of the hash function $H(X) = ord(C)$ -1 where C is the first character of the keyword X. Figure 13.9 illustrates a linear open addressed hash table with two slots per bucket (HT[*0..25, 0..1*]) and a chained hash table representation for the keyword set. Considering the efficient retrievals promoted by the hash table, the choice of the data structure for the symbol table representation contributes to the efficient performance of a compiler as well.

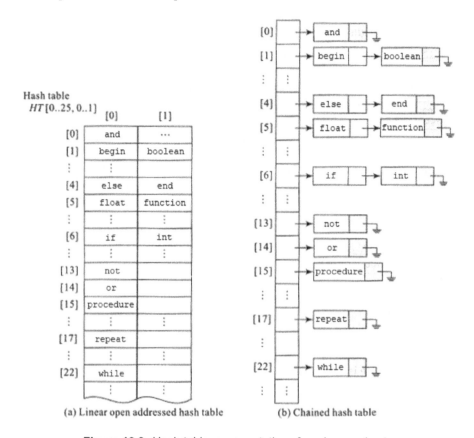

(a) Linear open addressed hash table   (b) Chained hash table

Figure 13.9. *Hash table representations for a keyword set*

13.6.2. *Hash tables in the evaluation of a join operation on relational databases*

Relational databases support a selective set of operations, for example, *selection, projection, join (natural join, equi-join)* and so on, which aid query processing. Of these, the *natural join* operation is most commonly used in *relational database management systems*. As indicated by the notation ⋈, the operation works on two *relations* (databases) to combine them into a single relation. Given two relations R and S, a natural join operation of the two databases is indicated as

R ⋈ S. The resulting relation is a combination of the two relations based on *attributes* common to the two relations.

EXAMPLE 13.8.–

Consider the two relations ITEM_DESCRIPTION and VENDOR shown in Figure 13.10(a). The ITEM_DESCRIPTION relation describes the items and the VENDOR relation contains details about the vendors supplying the items. The relation ITEM_DESCRIPTION contains the attributes ITEM_CODE and ITEM_NAME. The VENDOR relation contains the attributes ITEM_CODE, VENDOR _NAME and ADDRESS (city).

A query pertaining to who the vendors are for a given item code calls for joining the two relations. The join of the two relations yields the relation shown in Figure 13.10(b). Observe how the natural join operation combines the two relations on the basis of their common attribute ITEM_CODE. Those *tuples* (rows) of the two relations having a common *attribute value* in the ITEM_CODE field are "joined" together to form the output relation.

Relation: ITEM_DESCRIPTION

ITEM_CODE	ITEM_NAME
P402	Pump.hp4-5-6
M636	Motor.621P
S706	Stabilizer.VA500

Relation: VENDOR

ITEM_CODE	VENDOR_NAME	ADDRESS
P402	Premier Electricals	Pune
M636	Bharath Electronics	Coimbatore
S706	India Electricals	Kolkata

(a)

Relation: ITEM-DESCRIPTION ⋈ VENDOR

ITEM_CODE	ITEM_NAME	VENDOR_NAME	ADDRESS
P402	Pump.hp4-5-6	Premier Electricals	Pune
M636	Motor.621P	Bharath Electronics	Coimbatore
S706	Stabilizer.VA500	India Electricals	Kolkata

(b)

Figure 13.10. *Natural join of two relations*

One method of evaluating a join is to use the *hash method*. Let $H(X)$ be the hash function where X is the attribute value of the relations. Here $H(X)$ is the address of the bucket which contains the attribute value and a pointer to the appropriate tuple corresponding to the attribute value. The pointer to the tuple is known as *Tuple Identifier* (TID). TIDs in general, besides containing the physical address of the tuple of the relation also hold identifiers unique to the relation. The hash tables are referred to as hash indexes in relational database terminology.

A natural join of the two relations R and S over a common attribute ATTRIB, results in each bucket of the hash indexes recording the attribute values of ATTRIB along with the TIDs of the tuples in relations R and S whose R.ATTRIB = S.ATTRIB.

When a query associated with the natural join is to be answered all that it calls for is to access the hash indexes to retrieve the appropriate TIDs associated with the query. Retrieving the tuples using the TIDs satisfies the query.

EXAMPLE 13.9.–

Figure 13.11(a) shows a physical view of the two relations ITEM_DESCRIPTION and VENDOR. Figure 13.11(b) shows the hash function values based on which the hash table (Figure 13.11(c)) has been constructed. The hash function used is not discussed. Each bucket of the hash index records the TIDs of the attribute values mapped to the bucket. Thus, TIDs corresponding to ITEM_CODE = P402 of both the relations, are mapped to bucket 16 and so on.

Assume that a query "List the vendor(s) supplying the item P402" is to be processed. To process this request, we first compute H("P402") which as shown in Figure 13.11(b) yields the bucket address 16. Accessing bucket 16 we find the TID corresponding to the relation VENDOR is 7001. To answer the query all that needs to be done is to retrieve the tuple whose TID is 7001.

A general query such as "List the vendors supplying each of the items" may call for sequentially searching each of the hash indexes corresponding to each attribute value of ITEM_CODE.

ITEM_DESCRIPTION

TID	ITEM_CODE	ITEM_NAME
4001	P402	Pump.hp4-5-6
4002	M636	Motor.621P
4003	S706	Stabilizer.VA500

VENDOR

TID	ITEM_CODE	VENDOR_NAME	ADDRESS
7001	P402	Premier Electricals	Pune
7002	M636	Bharath Electronics	Coimbatore
7003	S706	India Electricals	Kolkata

(a) A physical view of the relations ITEM_DESCRIPTION and VENDOR

X	P402	M636	S706
$H(X)$	16	5	14

(b) Hash function values of the ITEM_CODE attribute values

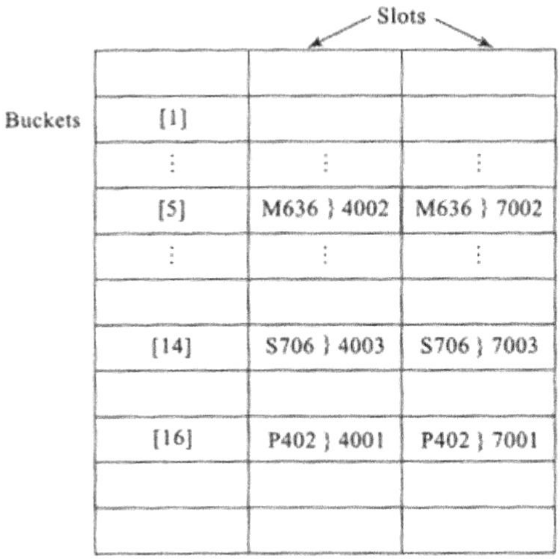

Buckets		Slots	
[1]			
⋮	⋮	⋮	
[5]	M636 } 4002	M636 } 7002	
⋮	⋮	⋮	
[14]	S706 } 4003	S706 } 7003	
[16]	P402 } 4001	P402 } 7001	

(c) Hash table

Figure 13.11. *Evaluation of natural join operation using hash indexes*

13.6.3. *Hash tables in a direct file organization*

File organization deals with methods and techniques to structure data in *external* or *auxiliary storage* devices such as tapes, disks, drums and so forth. A *file* is a collection of related data termed *records*. Each record is uniquely identified by what is known as a *key*, which is a datum or a portion of data in the record. The major concern in all these methods is regarding the access time when records pertaining to the keys (*primary* or *secondary*) are to be retrieved from the storage devices to be updated or inserted or deleted. Some of the commonly used file organization schemes are *sequential file organization, serial file organization, indexed sequential access file organization* and *direct file organization*. Chapter 14 elaborately details files and their methods of organization.

The *direct file organization* (see section 14.8) which is a kind of file organization method, employs hash tables for the efficient storage and retrieval of records from the storage devices. Given a file of records, $\{ f_1, f_2, f_3, \ldots\ldots f_N \}$ with keys $\{ k_1, k_2, k_3, \ldots k_N \}$ a hash function $H(k)$ where k is the record key, determines the storage address of each of the records in the storage device. Thus, direct files undertake direct mapping of the keys to the storage locations of the records with the records of the file organized as a hash table.

Summary

– Hash tables are ideal data structures for dictionaries. They favor efficient storage and retrieval of data lists which are linear in nature.

– A hash function is a mathematical function which maps keys to positions in the hash tables known as buckets. The process of mapping is called hashing. Keys which map to the same bucket are called as synonyms. In such a case a collision is said to have occurred. A bucket may be divided into slots to accommodate synonyms. When a bucket is full and a synonym is unable to find space in the bucket then an overflow is said to have occurred.

– The characteristics of a hash function are that it must be easy to compute and at the same time minimize collisions. Folding, truncation and modular arithmetic are some of the commonly used hash functions.

– A hash table could be implemented using a sequential data structure such as arrays. In such a case, the method of handling overflows where the closest slot that is vacant is utilized to accommodate the synonym key is called linear open addressing or linear probing. However, over the course of time, linear probing can lead to the problem of clustering thereby deteriorating the performance of the hash table to a mere sequential search!

– The other alternative methods of handling overflows are rehashing, quadratic probing and random probing.

– A linked implementation of a hash table is known as chaining. In this all the synonyms are chained to their respective buckets as a singly linked list. On an average, a chained hash table is superior in performance when compared to that of a linear probed hash table.

– Hash tables have found applications in the design of symbol tables in compiler design, query processing in relational database management systems and direct file organizations.

13.7. Illustrative problems

PROBLEM 13.1.–

Insert the following data into a hash table implemented using linear open addressing. Assume that the buckets have three slots each. Make use of the hash function $h(X) = X \bmod 9$.

{17, 09, 34, 56, 11, 71, 86, 55, 22, 10, 4, 39, 49, 52, 82, 13, 40, 31, 35, 28, 44}

Solution:

The linear open addressed hash table is shown in Figure P13.1 Those keys not accommodated in their home buckets are shown over a grey shaded background.

	Slots		
HT	[0]	[1]	[2]
[0]	9	44	
[1]	55	10	82
[2]	56	11	28
[3]	39		
[4]	22	4	49
[5]	86	13	40
[6]	31		
[7]	34	52	
[8]	17	71	35

Buckets

Figure P13.1. *The hash table implemented using linear open addressing, for the data listed in illustrative problem 13.1*

PROBLEM 13.2.–

For the set of keys listed in illustrative problem 13.1, trace a chained hash table making use of the same hash function.

Solution:

The chained hash table is shown in Figure P13.2. The nodes in the chain are inserted in ascending order of the key values.

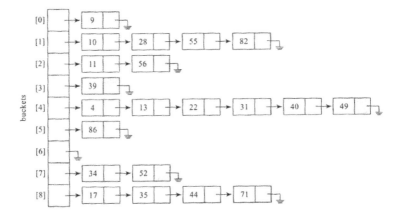

Figure P13.2. *The hash table implemented using chaining for the data listed in illustrative problem 13.1*

PROBLEM 13.3.–

Comment on the statement: "To minimize collisions in a linear open addressed hash table it is recommended that the ratio of the number of buckets in a hash table to the number of keys to be stored in the hash table is made bigger".

Solution:

No, this is illogical since increasing the number of buckets will only lead to the wastage of space.

PROBLEM 13.4.–

For the set of keys {17, 9, 34, 56, 11, 4, 71, 86, 55, 10, 39, 49, 52, 82, 31, 13, 22, 35, 44, 20, 60, 28} obtain a hash table HT[0..8, 0..2] following quadratic probing. Make use of the hash function $H(X) = X \bmod 9$. What are your observations?

Solution:

Quadratic probing employs the function $(h + i^2) \bmod n$ $i = 1, 2, ...,$ where $n = 9$, to determine the empty slot during collisions. Here h is the address of the home bucket given by the hash function $H(X)$, where X is the key. The quadratic probed hash table is shown in Figure P13.4.

HT	[0]	[1]	[2]
[0]	9	44	
[1]	55	10	82
[2]	56	11	20
[3]	39		
[4]	4	49	31
[5]	86	13	22
[6]	60		
[7]	34	52	
[8]	17	71	35

28 fails to find
an empty slot

Figure P13.4. *The hash table following quadratic probing and using the hash function h(X) = X mod 9, for the keys listed in illustrative problem 13.4*

Note how during the insertion of keys 13 and 22, their home buckets, which is 4 is full. To handle this collision, quadratic probing begins searching buckets 4+1 mod 9,

$4+2^2$ mod 9, …. Since the first searched bucket 5 has empty slots the keys find accommodation there. However in the case of key 44, to handle its collision with bucket 8, quadratic probing searches for an empty slot as ordered by the sequence, $8+1$ mod 9, $8+2^2$ mod 9, … The search for an empty slot is successful when the bucket $8+1^2$ mod 9 is encountered. 44 is accommodated in slot 2 of bucket 0.

The case of inserting key 28 is interesting for, despite the hash table containing free slots, quadratic probing is unable to find an empty slot to accommodate the key. The sequence searched for is $1+1$ mod 9, $1+2^2$ mod 9, $1+3^2$ mod 9, …….

An important observation regarding quadratic probing is that there is no guarantee of finding an empty slot in a quadratic probed hash table if the hash table size is not prime. In this example, the hash table size is not prime.

PROBLEM 13.5.–

For the set of keys listed in illustrative problem 13.4, obtain a hash table following quadratic probing and employing the hash function $H(X) = X \bmod 11$. What are your observations?

Solution:

The quadratic probed hash table for the given set of keys using the hash function is shown in Figure P13.5.

HT	[0]	[1]	[2]
[0]	11	55	22
[1]	34	56	44
[2]	13	35	
[3]			
[4]	4		
[5]	71	49	82
[6]	17	39	60
[7]	28		
[8]	52		
[9]	9	86	31
[10]	10	20	

Figure P13.5. *The hash table following quadratic probing and using the hash function h(X) = X mod 11, for the keys listed in illustrative problem 13.4*

An important observation regarding this example is that quadratic probing can always find an empty slot to insert a key if the hash table size is prime and the table is at least half empty.

PROBLEM 13.6.–

For the set of keys {11, 55, 13, 35, 71, 52, 61, 9, 86, 31, 49, 85, 70} obtain the hash table HT[0..8, 0..1] which employs rehashing for collision resolution. Assume the hash function to be $H(X) = X \bmod 9$ and the rehashing function to be $H'(X) = 7- (X \bmod 7)$. The collision resolution function is given by $h_i = (H(X)+ i. H'(X)) \bmod b$, $i=1, 2, ...$, where b is the number of buckets.

Solution:

The hash table for the problem is shown in Figure P13.6.

HT	[0]	[1]
[0]	9	
[1]	55	85
[2]	11	49
[3]		
[4]	13	31
[5]	86	70
[6]		
[7]	52	61
[8]	35	71

Figure P13.6. *The hash table employing rehashing for collision resolution, for the set of keys listed in illustrative problem 13.6*

Observe how during the insertion of key 49 a collision occurs and its bucket 4 ($H(49)= 49 \bmod 9 = 4$) is found to be full. Rehashing turns to the next hash function $H'(49) = 7- (49 \bmod 7)$ to help obtain the empty slot to accommodate the key. The slot searched is $h1 = (H(49) + 1. H'(49)) \bmod 9 = 2$. Since the bucket contains a vacant slot, key 49 is accommodated in the slot.

In the case of key 85 which once again collides with the keys in bucket 4, rehashing computes $H'(85) = 6$ and $h_1 = (H(85) + 1. H'(85)) \bmod 9 = 1$. Key 85 is accommodated in bucket 1 slot 2. Finally, following similar lines, key 70 is accommodated in bucket 5.

PROBLEM 13.7.–

Assume a chained hash table in which each of the chains is implemented as a binary search tree rather than a singly linked list. Build such a hash table for the keys {9, 10, 6, 20, 14, 16, 5, 40, 4, 2, 7, 3, 8} using the hash function $H(X)= X\ mod\ 5$ where X is the key. What are the advantages of adopting this system?

Solution:

A chained hash table with each of the chains implemented as a binary search tree is shown in Figure P13.7.

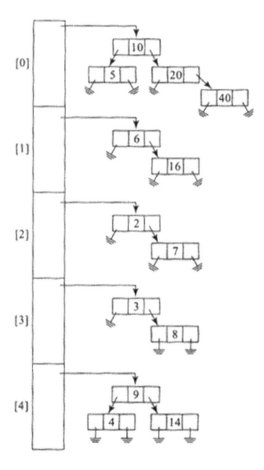

Figure P13.7. *The chained hash table with the chains implemented as binary search trees, for the data listed in illustrative problem 13.7*

The advantage is that during the search operation, the binary search tree-based chains would record *O(log n)* performance. In contrast, a linear chain would report *O(n)* complexity on an average.

PROBLEM 13.8.–

Fill in Table P13.8(a) with the number of comparisons made, when the elements shown in row 1 of the table ({66, 100, 55, 3, 99, 144}) are either successfully or unsuccessfully searched over the list of elements {66, 42, 96, 100, 3, 55, 99} when the latter is represented as (i) sequential list (ii) binary search tree and (iii) linear probing based hash table with single slot buckets, using the hash function $h(X)= X \bmod 7$.

Representation of data elements	Number of comparisons					
	66	100	55	3	99	144
Sequential list						
Binary search tree						
Hash table						

Table P13.8(a). *Search comparison table for illustrative problem 13.8*

Solution:

Representing the elements of the list to be searched as a sequential list, yields {3, 42, 55, 66, 96, 99, 100}. The number of comparisons made for searching 66 is 4 and that for 144 which is an unsuccessful search is 7.

Representation of the elements in the list as a binary search tree is given below. The number of comparisons made for element 66 is 1 and that for 144 is 3.

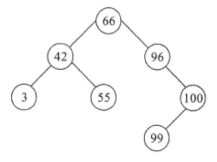

Representation of the elements as a linear probed hash table with single slot buckets is shown below. The hash function used is $h(X) = X \bmod 7$. The data element displaced from the home bucket is shown over grey background. The number of comparisons made for element 66 is 1 and that for 144 is 7.

[0]	42
[1]	99
[2]	100
[3]	66
[4]	3
[5]	96
[6]	55

The comparisons for the rest of the elements are shown in Table P13.8(b).

Representation of data elements	Number of comparisons					
	66	100	55	3	99	144
Sequential list	4	7	3	1	6	7
Binary search tree	1	3	3	3	4	3
Hash table	1	1	1	2	1	7

Table P13.8(b). *The completed search comparison table for the data listed in illustrative problem 13.8*

Review questions

1) Hash tables are ideal data structures for --------------------

a) dictionaries   b) graphs   c) trees   d) none of these

2) State whether true or false:

In the case of a linear open addressed hash table with multiple slots in a bucket,

   i) overflows always mean collisions, and

   ii) collisions always mean overflows

a) i) true ii) true   b) i) true ii) false

c) i) false ii) true   d) i) false ii) false

3) In the context of building hash functions, find the odd term out in the following list:

Folding, modular arithmetic, truncation, random probing

a) folding   b) modular arithmetic   c) truncation   d) random probing

4) In the case of a chained hash table of n elements with b buckets, assuming that a worst-case resulted in all the n elements getting mapped to the same bucket, then the worst-case time complexity of a search on the hash table would be given by

a) $O(1)$ b) $O(n/b)$ c) $O(n)$ d) $O(b)$

5) Match the following:

A) rehashing   i) collision resolution

B) folding   ii) hash function

C) linear probing

    a) (A, i))   (B, ii))   (C, ii))

    b) (A, ii))   (B, ii))   (C, i))

    c) (A, ii))   (B, i))   (C, i))

    d) (A, i))   (B, ii))   (C, i))

6) What are the advantages of using modulo arithmetic for building hash functions?

7) How are collisions handled in linear probing?

8) How are insertions and deletions handled in a chained hash table?

9) Comment on the search operation for a key K in a list L represented as a

i) sequential list, ii) chained hash table, and iii) linear probed hash table

10) What is rehashing? How does it serve to overcome the drawbacks of linear probing?

11) The following is a list of keys. Making use of a hash function $h(k) = k\ mod\ 11$, represent the keys in a linear open addressed hash table with buckets containing (i) three slots and (ii) four slots.

    090 890 678 654 234 123 245 678 900 111 453 231 112 679 238
    876 009 122 233 344 566 677 899 909 512 612 723 823 956 221
    331 441 551

12) For review problem 11, resolve collisions by means of i) rehashing that makes use of an appropriate rehashing function and ii) quadratic probing.

13) For review problem 11, implement a chained hash table.

Programming assignments

1) Implement a hash table using an array data structure. Design functions to handle overflows using i) linear probing, ii) quadratic probing and iii) rehashing. For a set of keys observe the performance when the methods listed above are executed.

2) Implement a hash table for a given set of keys using the chaining method of handling overflows. Maintain the chains in the ascending order of the keys. Design a menu-driven front-end interface, to perform the insert, delete and search operations on the hash table.

3) The following is a list of binary keys:

0011, 1100, 1111, 1010, 0010, 1011, 0111, 0000, 0001, 0100, 1000, 1001, 0011.

Design a hash function and an appropriate hash table to store and retrieve the keys efficiently. Compare the performance when the set is stored as a sequential list.

4) Store a dictionary of a limited set of words as a hash table. Implement a spell check program that, given an input text file, will check for the spelling using the hash table-based dictionary and in the case of misspelled words will correct the same.

5) Let TABLE_A and TABLE_B be two files implemented as a table. Design and implement a function JOIN (TABLE_A, TABLE_B) which will "natural join" the two files as discussed in section 13.6.2. Make use of an appropriate hash function.

14

File Organizations

14.1. Introduction

The main component of a computer system is the *memory*, also referred to as the *main memory* or the *internal memory* of the computer. Memory is a storage repository of data that is used by the CPU during its processing.

When the CPU has to process voluminous data, the computer system has to take recourse to *external memory* or *external storage* to store the data, due to the limited capacity of the internal memory. The devices which provide support for external memory are known as *external storage devices* or *auxiliary storage devices*.

Given that the main memory of the computer is the *primary memory*, the external memory is also referred to as *secondary memory* and the devices as *secondary storage devices*. Examples of secondary storage devices are magnetic tapes, magnetic disks, drums, floppies, USB flash drives and so forth. While the internal memory of a computer system is *volatile*, meaning that data may be lost when the power goes off, secondary memory is *nonvolatile*.

Each of the secondary storage devices has its distinct characteristics. Magnetic tapes, built on the principle of audio tape devices, are *sequential storage devices* that store data sequentially. On the other hand, magnetic disks, drums, floppy diskettes and USB flash drives are *random access storage devices* that can store and retrieve data both sequentially and randomly. Random-access storage devices are also known as ***direct access storage devices***. Section 18.2 elaborately discusses the structure and configuration of magnetic tapes and disks.

The growing demands for information have called for the support of what is known as **tertiary storage devices**. Though these devices are capable of storing huge volumes of data running to terabytes or petabytes, at lesser costs, they are characterized by significantly higher read/write time when compared to secondary storage devices. Examples of tertiary storage devices are optical disk jukeboxes, ad hoc tape storage and tape silos.

The organization of data in the internal memory calls for an application of both sequential and linked data structures. In the same vein, the organization of data in the secondary memory also calls for a number of strategies for their efficient storage and retrieval. **Files** are used for the organization of data in the secondary memory.

In this chapter, we discuss the concept of files and their methods of organization, for example, heap or pile files, sequential files, indexed sequential files and direct files.

14.2. Files

A file is commonly thought of as a folder that holds a sheaf of related documents arranged according to some order. In the context of secondary storage devices, *files* are used for the storage and organization of related data. In fact, a file is a *logical organization of data*. A file is technically defined to be a collection of *records*. A record is a logical collection of *fields*. A field is a collection of characters, which can be either numeric, alphabetic or alphanumeric. A file could be a collection of *fixed length records* or *variable length records*, where the *length of a record* is indicative of the number of characters that makes up a record.

Let us consider the example of a student file. The file is a logical collection of student records. A student record is a collection of fields such as `roll number`, `name`, `city`, `date of birth`, `grade` and so forth. Each of these fields could be numeric, alphabetic or alphanumeric. A sample set of student records are shown below.

Student file

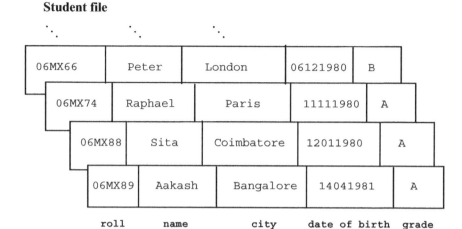

| roll number | name | city | date of birth (DDMMYYYY) | grade |

A file is a logical entity and has to be mapped onto a physical medium for its storage and access. To facilitate storage, it is essential to know the *field length* or *field size* (normally specified in bytes). Thus, every file has its *physical organization*.

For example, the student file stored on a magnetic tape would have the records listed above occurring sequentially, as shown in Figure 14.1. In such a case the processing of these records would only call for the application of sequential data structures. In fact, in the case of magnetic tapes, the logical organization of the records in the files and their physical organization when stored in the tape, are one and the same.

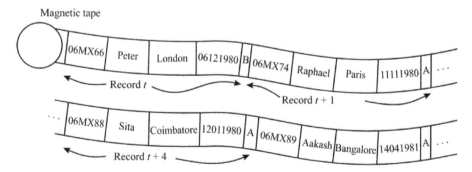

Figure 14.1. *Physical organization of the student file on a magnetic tape*

On the other hand, the student file could be stored either sequentially or non-sequentially (random access) on a magnetic disk, as called for by the applications using the file. In the case of random access, the records are physically stored in various portions of the disk where space is available. Figure 14.2 illustrates a snapshot of the student file storage in the disk. The logical organization of the records in the file is kept track of by physically linking the records through pointers. The processing of such files would call for linked data structures. Thus, in the case of magnetic disks, for files that have been stored in a non-sequential manner, the logical and physical organizations need not coincide.

Magnetic Disk

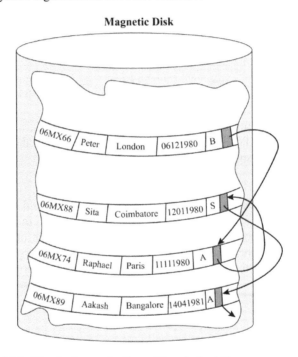

Figure 14.2. *Physical organization of the student file on a magnetic disk*

The physical organization of the files is designed and ordered by the *File Manager* of the operating system.

14.3. Keys

In a file, one or more fields could serve to *uniquely identify* the records for efficient retrieval and storage. These fields are known as ***primary keys*** or commonly, **keys**. For example, in the student file discussed above, the roll number could be designated as the primary key as it uniquely identifies each student and hence the record too.

If additional fields were added to the primary key, the combination would still continue to uniquely identify the record. Such a combination of fields is referred to as a **super key**. For example, the combination of roll number and name would still continue to uniquely identify records in the student file. A primary key can therefore be described as a **minimal super key**.

It is possible to have more than one combination of fields that can serve to uniquely identify a record. These combinations are known as **candidate keys**. It now depends on the file administrator to choose any one combination as the primary key. In such a case, the rest of the combinations are called **alternate keys**. For example, consider an employee file shown below.

Employee file

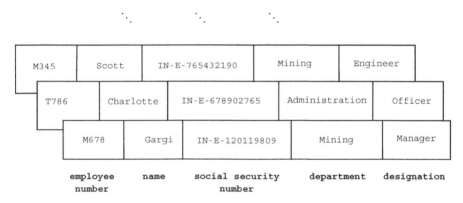

employee number	name	social security number	department	designation
M345	Scott	IN-E-765432190	Mining	Engineer
T786	Charlotte	IN-E-678902765	Administration	Officer
M678	Gargi	IN-E-120119809	Mining	Manager

Here, both the fields, employee number and social security number could act as the primary keys since both would serve to uniquely identify the record. Thus, we term them candidate keys. If we chose to have an employee number as the primary key then the social security number would be referred to as an alternate key.

A field or a combination of fields that may not be a candidate key, but can serve to classify records based on a particular characteristic, are called **secondary keys**. For example in the employee file, department could be a secondary key to classifying employees based on the department.

14.4. Basic file operations

Some of the basic file operations are:

i) *open,* which prepares the files concerned, for reading or writing. Commonly, a file pointer is opened and set at the beginning of the file that is to be read or written;

ii) *read,* when the contents of the record pointed to by the file pointer, are read;

iii) *insert,* when new records are added to the file;

iv) *delete*, when existing records are removed from the file;

v) *update*, when data in one or more fields in the existing records of the files are modified;

vi) *reset*, when the file pointer is set to the beginning of the file;

vii) *close*, when the files that were opened for operations are closed for access.

Commercial implementations of programming languages provide a variety of other file operations. However, from a data structure standpoint, the operations of insert, delete and update are considered significant and therefore we shall restrict our discussion to these operations alone.

In the case of deletion, the operation could be executed logically or physically, as determined by the application. In the case of *physical deletion*, the records are physically removed from the file. On the other hand, in the case of *logical deletion*, the record is either "flagged" or "marked" to indicate that it is not in use. Every record has a bit or a byte called the *deletion marker* which is set to some value indicating deletion of the record. Though the records are physically available in the file, they are logically excluded from consideration during file processing. The logical deletion also facilitates the restoration of the deleted records, which could be done by "unflagging" or "unmarking" the records.

In the case of the student file, the addition of details pertaining to new students could call for the insertion of appropriate student records. Students opting to drop out of the program could have their records 'logically' or 'physically' deleted. Again, a change of address or a change in grades after revaluation could call for the relevant fields of the record to be updated.

14.5. Heap or pile organization

The *heap or pile organization* is one of the simplest file organizations. These are non-keyed sequential files. The records are maintained in no particular order. The insert, delete and update operations are undertaken as described below. This unordered file organization is basically suitable for instances where records are to be collected and stored for future use.

14.5.1. *Insert, delete and update operations*

Insert: To insert records into the heap or pile, the records are merely appended to the file.

Delete: To delete records, either a physical deletion or logical deletion is done. In the case of physical deletion, either the record is physically deleted or the last record is brought forward to replace the deleted one. This indeed calls for several accesses.

Update: To retrieve a record to update it, a linear search of the file is needed, which in the worst case, could call for a search from the beginning to the end of the file.

14.6. Sequential file organization

Sequential files are ordered files maintained in a logical sequence as primary keys. The organization was primarily meant to satisfy the characteristics of magnetic tapes which are sequential devices.

14.6.1. *Insert, delete and update operations*

A sequential file is stored in the same logical sequence as its records, on the tape. Thus, the physical and logical organization of sequential files are one and the same. Since random access is difficult on a tape, the handling of insert, delete and update operations could turn out to be expensive if they are handled on an individual basis. Therefore a batched mode of these operations is undertaken.

For a sequential file *S*, the records which are to be inserted, deleted or updated are written onto a separate tape as a sequential file *T*. The file *T*, known as the *transaction file*, is ordered according to its primary keys. Here, *S* is referred to as the *master file*. With both *S* and *T* ordered according to their primary keys, a maintenance program reads the two files and while undertaking a "merge" operation, executing the relevant operation (insert/delete/update), in parallel. The updated file is available on an output tape.

During the merge operation, in the case of an insert operation, the new records merely get copied onto the output tape in the primary key ordering sequence. In the case of a delete operation, the corresponding records are stopped from getting copied onto the output tape and are just skipped. For update operation, the appropriate fields are updated and the modified records are copied onto the output tape. Figure 14.3 illustrates the master maintenance procedure.

The new file that is available on the output tape is referred to as the **new master file** S^{new}. The advantage of this method is that it leaves a backup of the master file before it is updated. The file S at this point gets referred to as the **old master file**. In fact, it is common to retain an ancestry of backup files depending on the needs of the application. In such a case, while the new master file would be referred to as the **son file**, the old master file would be referred to as the **father file** and the older master file as the **grandfather file**, and so on.

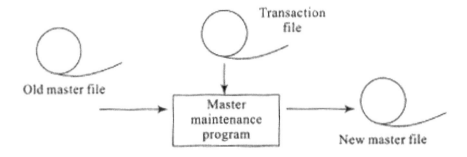

Figure 14.3. *Master file maintenance*

14.6.2. *Making use of overflow blocks*

Since the updating of the file calls for the creation of a new file each time, an alternative could be to store the records in blocks with 'holes' in them. The 'holes' are vacant spaces at the tail end of the blocks.

Insertions are accommodated in these 'holes'. If there is no space to accommodate insertions in the appropriate blocks, the records are accommodated in special blocks called **overflow** blocks.

Although this method renders insert operations efficient, retrievals could call for a linear search of the whole file. In the case of deletions, it would be prudent to adopt logical deletions. However, when the number of logical deletions increases or when the overflow blocks fill up fast, it is advisable to reorganize the entire file.

14.7. Indexed sequential file organization

While sequential file organizations provide efficient sequential access to data, random access to records is quite cumbersome. *Indexed sequential file organizations* are hybrid organizations that provide efficient sequential, as well as random access to data. The method of storage and retrieval, known as the *indexed sequential access method* (**ISAM**) makes use of *indexes* to facilitate random access of data, while the data themselves are maintained in *sequential* order. The files following the ISAM method of storage and retrieval are also known as *ISAM files*.

14.7.1. *Structure of the ISAM files*

An ISAM file consists of:

i) a *primary storage area*, where the data records of the file are sequentially stored;

ii) a *hierarchy of indexes*, where an *index* is a directory of information pertaining to the physical location of the records;

iii) *overflow area(s)* or *block(s)*, where new records to be added to the file and which could not be accommodated in the primary storage area, are stored.

Though ISAM files provide efficient retrieval of records, the operations of insertion and deletion can get quite involved and need to be efficiently handled. There are many methods to maintain indexes and efficiently handle insertions and deletions in the primary storage, as well as overflow areas.

The primary storage area is divided into *blocks* where each block can store a definite number of records. The data records of the ISAM file are distributed onto the blocks in the logical order of their sequence, one block after the other. Thus, all of the keys of the records stored in block B_t have to be greater than or equal to those of the records stored in the previous block B_{t-1}.

The index is a two-dimensional table with each entry indicative of the physical location of the records. An index entry is commonly a *key-address pair*, $(K, B\uparrow)$ where K is the key of the record and $B\uparrow$ is a pointer to the block containing the record or sometimes a pointer to the record itself. An index is always maintained in the sorted order of the keys K. If the index maintains an entry for each record of the file then the index is an $N \times 2$ table where N is the size of the file. In such a case the index is said to be a *dense index*. In the case of large files, the processing time of dense indexes can be large due to the huge amount of entries in them. To reduce the processing time, we could devise strategies so that only one entry per block is made in the index. In such a case, the index is known as a *sparse index*. Commonly, the entry could pertain to a special record in the block, known as the *block anchor*. The block anchor could be either the first record (smallest key) or the last record (largest key) of the block. If the file occupies b blocks the size of the index would be $b \times 2$.

EXAMPLE 14.1.–

Figure 14.4 illustrates a schematic diagram of a naïve ISAM file. The records of the file are stored sequentially in the ascending order of their primary keys. The file occupies 10 blocks, each comprising 100 records. The last record of each block is chosen as the block anchor. Observe how the index maintains entries for each of the block anchors alone. The entries in the index are sorted according to the key values.

14.7.2. Insert, delete and update operations for a naïve ISAM file

The insert, delete and update operations for a naïve ISAM file are introduced here. However, it needs to be recollected that a variety of methods exist for maintaining indexes, each of which commands its exclusive methods of operations.

Insert: To insert records, the records are first inserted in the primary storage area. The existing records in a block may have to be moved to make space for the new records. This, in turn, may call for a change in the index entries, especially if the block anchors shift due to the insertions.

A simple solution would be to provide 'holes' in the blocks where new records could be inserted. However, the possibility of blocks overflowing cannot be ruled out. In such a case the new records are pushed into the overflow area, which merely maintains the records as an unordered list. Another option would be to maintain an overflow area for each block, as a sorted linked list of records.

Delete: The most convenient way to handle deletions is to undertake logical deletions by making use of deletion markers.

Update: A retrieval of records for update is quite efficiently done in an ISAM file. To retrieve a record with key K', we merely undertake a linear search (or even binary search discussed in section 16.5 of Chapter 16) of the index table to find the entry $(K, B\Uparrow)$, such that $K' \leq K$. Following the pointer $B\Uparrow$, we linearly search the block of records to retrieve the desired record. However, in the case of the record being available in the overflow blocks, the search procedure can turn out to be a bit more complex.

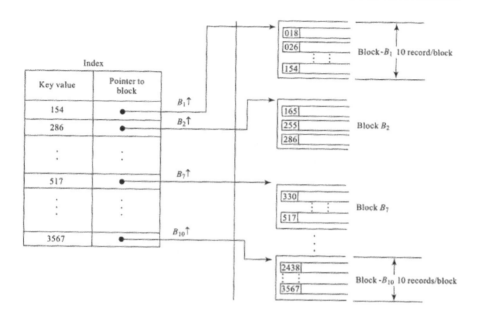

Figure 14.4. *Schematic diagram of a naïve ISAM file*

For example, in the ISAM file structure shown in Figure 14.4, to retrieve the record with key 255, we merely search the index to find the appropriate entry $(286, B_2\uparrow)$, where $B_2\uparrow$ is the pointer to the block B_2. A linear search of the key 255 in block B_2 retrieves the desired record.

14.7.3. *Types of indexing*

There are many methods of indexing files. Commonly, all methods of indexes make use of a single key field on which the index entries are maintained. The key field is known as the ***indexing field***. A few of the indexing techniques are detailed here.

14.7.3.1. *Primary indexing*

This is one of the most common forms of indexing. The file is sorted according to its primary key. The ***primary index*** is a sparse index that contains the pair $(K, B\uparrow)$ as its entries, where K is the primary key of the block anchor and $B\uparrow$ is the pointer to the block concerned. The indexing method used in the ISAM file illustrated in example 14.1, is in fact primary indexing. The general operations of insert, delete and update discussed in section 14.7.2 hold true for primary indexing-based ISAM files.

14.7.3.2. Multilevel indexing

In the case of voluminous files, despite employing sparse indexes, searching through the index can itself become an overhead due to a large number of entries in the index. In such a case, to cut down the search time, a hierarchy of indexes also known as *multilevel indexes* is constructed. Multilevel indexes are indexes over indexes.

Example 14.2 discusses an ISAM file based on multilevel indexing. It can be seen that while the lowest level index points to the physical location of the blocks, the rest of the indexes point to their lower level indexes. To retrieve a record with key K, we begin from the highest level index and work our way down the indexes until the appropriate block is reached. A linear search of the block yields the record.

EXAMPLE 14.2.–

Figure 14.5 illustrates an ISAM file with multilevel indexing. The file has 10,000 records and is stored in a sequential fashion. 400 blocks, each holding 25 records, make up the primary storage area. The file organization shows three levels of indexing. Observe how each of the higher level indexes are indexes over the lower level indexes. To search for a key K we begin from the highest level index and follow the pointers to the lower level indexes. At the lowest level index, we obtain the block address from which the record could be searched out.

14.7.3.3. Cluster indexing

Typically, ISAM files have their records ordered sequentially according to the primary key values. It is possible that the records are ordered sequentially according to some non-key field that can carry duplicate values. In such a case, the indexing field, which is the non-key field, is called the *clustering field* and the index is called the *cluster index*.

A cluster index is a sparse index. As with all other sparse indexes, a cluster index is also made up of entries of the form $(I, B\uparrow)$, where I is the clustering field value and $B\uparrow$ is the block address of the appropriate record. For a group of records with the same value for I, $B \uparrow$ indicates the block address of the first record in the group. The rest of the records in the group may be easily accessed by making a forward search in the block concerned, since the records in the primary storage area are already sorted according to the non-key field.

However, in the case of cluster indexing, the insert/delete operations, as before, can become complex, since the data records are physically ordered. A straightforward strategy for efficient handling of insert/delete operations would be to maintain the block or cluster of blocks in such a way that all records holding the same value for their clustering field are stored in the same blocks or cluster of blocks.

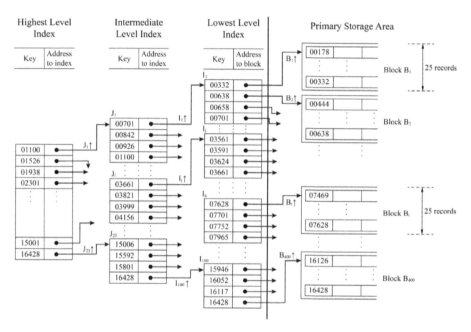

Figure 14.5. *An ISAM file based on multilevel indexing*

EXAMPLE 14.3.–

An ISAM file based on cluster indexing is illustrated in Figure 14.6. We consider the record structure of the employee file discussed in Section 14.3. department is used as the clustering field. Observe the duplicate values of the clustering field in the records. The blocks are maintained in such a way that records holding the same value for the clustering field are stored in the same block or cluster of blocks.

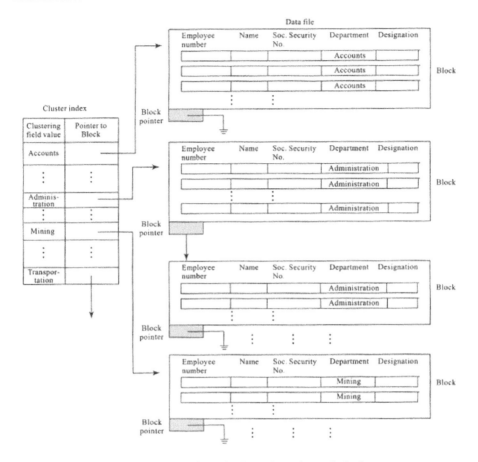

Figure 14.6. *An ISAM file based on cluster indexing*

14.7.3.4. *Secondary indexing*

Secondary indexes are built on files for which some primary access already exists. In other words, the data records in the prime storage area are already sorted according to the primary key and available in blocks. The secondary indexing may be on a field that may be a candidate key (distinct values) or on a non-key field (duplicate values).

In the case of the secondary key field having distinct values, the index is a dense index with one entry $(K, B\uparrow)$, where K is the secondary key value and $B\uparrow$ is the block address, for every record. The $(K, B\uparrow)$ entries are however ordered on the key K, to facilitate binary search on the index during retrievals of data. To retrieve the record with secondary key value K, the entire block of records pointed to by $B\uparrow$ is transferred to the internal memory and a linear search is done to retrieve the record.

In the case of the secondary key field having duplicate values, there are various options available to construct a secondary index. The first is to maintain a dense index of $(K, B\uparrow)$ pairs, where K is the secondary key value and $B\uparrow$ is the block address, for every record. In such a case the index could carry several entries of $(K, B\uparrow)$ pairs, for the same value of K. The second option would be to maintain the index as consisting of variable length entries. Each index entry would be of the form $(K, B_1\uparrow, B_2\uparrow, B_3\uparrow, \ldots\ldots B_t\uparrow)$, where $B_i\uparrow$s are block addresses of the various records holding the same value for the secondary key K. The third option is a modification of the second where $B_i\uparrow$s are maintained as a linked list of block pointers and the index entry is just $(K, T\uparrow)$, where $T\uparrow$ is a pointer to the linked list.

A file could have several secondary indexes defined on it. Secondary indexes find significant applications in query-based interfaces to databases.

EXAMPLE 14.4.–

Figure 14.7 illustrates a secondary indexing-based file. The secondary index implements its entries as a tuple comprising the secondary key value and the list of block addresses of the records with the particular key value. The sequential file available in the primary storage area is already sorted on its primary key.

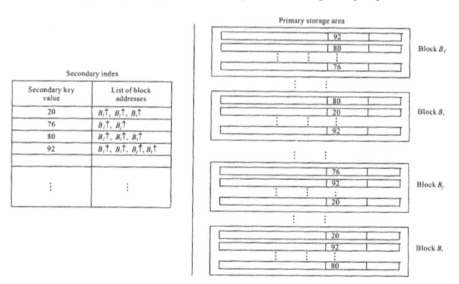

Figure 14.7. *Secondary indexing of a file*

14.8. Direct file organization

Direct file organizations make use of techniques to directly map the key values of their records to their respective physical location addresses. Commonly, the techniques employ some kind of arithmetic or mathematical functions to bring about the mapping. The direct mapping of the keys with their addresses paves the way for efficient retrievals and storage.

Hash functions are prominent candidates used by direct files to bring about the mapping between the keys and the addresses. Hash functions and hashing were elaborately discussed in Chapter 13. The application of hashing for the storage of files in the external memory is known as *external hashing*.

Given a file of records $\{R_1, R_2, R_3, \ldots \ldots R_N\}$ with keys $\{k_1, k_2, k_3, \ldots k_N\}$, a hash function H is employed to determine the storage address of each of the records in the storage device. Given a key k, $H(k)$ yields the storage address. Unlike other file organizations where indexes are maintained to track the storage address area, direct files undertake direct mapping of the keys to the storage locations of the records. In practice, the hash function $H(k)$ yields a bucket number which is then mapped to the absolute block address in the disk.

Buckets are designed to handle collisions amongst keys. Thus, a group of synonyms shares the same bucket. In the case of overflow of a bucket, a common solution employed is to maintain overflow buckets with links to their original buckets. Severe overflows to the same bucket may call for multiple overflow buckets linked to one another. This may however deteriorate the performance of the file organization during a retrieval operation. If a deletion leaves an overflow bucket empty, then the bucket is removed and perhaps could be inserted into a linked list of empty overflow buckets for future use.

EXAMPLE 14.5.–

Figure 14.8 illustrates the overall structure of a direct file organization. Each bucket records the synonym keys and the pointers to their storage locations. The storage area is divided into blocks that hold a group of records. Note the overflow buckets which take care of synonyms that overflowed from their respective buckets.

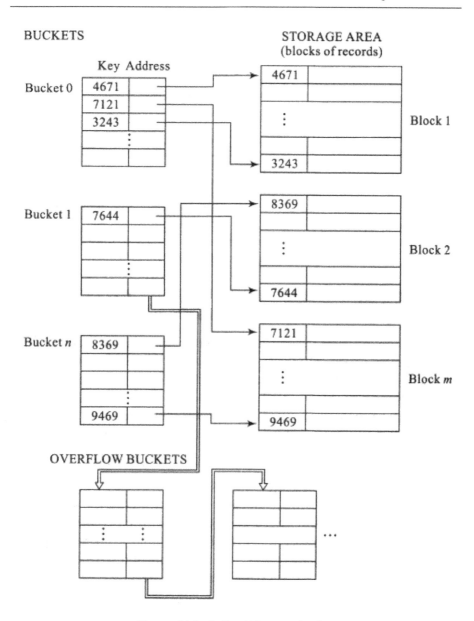

Figure 14.8. *A direct file organization*

Summary

– The internal memory or the primary memory of a computer is limited in capacity. To handle voluminous data, a computer system resorts to external memory or secondary memory.

– A file is a collection of records and a record is a collection of fields. File organizations are methods or strategies for the efficient storage and retrieval of data. While the organization of records in a file refers to its logical organization, the storage of the records on the secondary storage device refers to its physical organization.

– A primary key or a key, is a field or a collection of fields that uniquely identifies a record. Candidate keys, super keys, secondary keys and alternate keys are other terms associated with the keys of a file.

– Files support a variety of operations such as open, close, read, insert, delete, update and reset.

– A heap or pile organization is a non-keyed file where records are not maintained in any particular order.

– A sequential file organization maintains its records in the order of its primary keys. The insert, delete and update operations are carried out in a batched mode, leading to the creation of transaction and new master files. The operations could also be handled by making use of overflow blocks.

– Indexed sequential files offer efficient sequential and random access to its data records. The random access is made possible by making use of indexes. A variety of indexing based file organizations are possible by employing various types of indexing. Primary indexing, multilevel indexing, cluster indexing and secondary indexing are some of the important types of indexing.

– Direct file organizations make use of techniques to map their keys to the physical storage addresses of the records. Hash functions are a popular choice to bring about this mapping.

14.9. Illustrative problems

PROBLEM 14.1.–

The primary keys of a sample set of records are listed below. Assuming that the primary storage area accommodates seven records/a block and that the first record of the block is chosen as the block anchor, outline a schematic diagram for an ISAM file organization of the records built on primary indexing.

007 024 116 244 356 359 386 451 484 496 525 584 591 614 622 646 678 785 981 991 999 1122 1466 2468 3469 4567 8907

Solution:

The schematic diagram of the ISAM file organization based on primary indexing is shown in Figure P14.1.

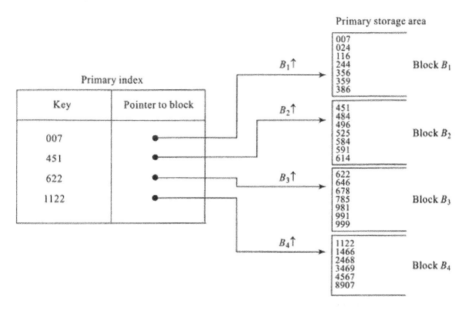

Figure P14.1. *A schematic diagram of an ISAM file organization built on primary indexing, for the data listed in illustrative problem 14.1*

PROBLEM 14.2.–

For the sample set of records shown in illustrative problem 14.1, design an ISAM file organization based on multilevel indexing for two levels of indexes. Assume a block size of 4 in the primary storage area and the first record of the block as the block anchor.

Solution:

The schematic diagram of the ISAM file organization based on multilevel indexing for two levels of indexes is shown in Figure P14.2.

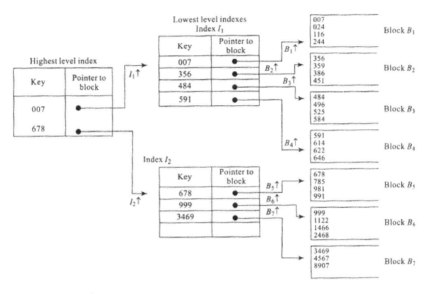

Figure P14.2. *A schematic diagram of an ISAM file organization built on multilevel indexing, for the data listed in illustrative problem 14.1*

PROBLEM 14.3.–

For the following Used car file with the record structure shown below, design a secondary indexing-based file organization, making use of the sample set of records shown in Table P14.3. Here, vehicle registration number is the primary key. Assume a block size of two records in the primary storage area. Design secondary indexes using the fields (i) year of registration and (ii) colour.

Used car record structure:

Vehicle registration number	year of registration	colour	model

vehicle registration number	year of registration	colour	model
TN4117	1990	Pearl white	Prestige
TN4623	1990	Silky silver	Pride

TN5724	1991	Metallic blue	Pride
TN6234	1994	Silky silver	Sarathi
TN7146	1994	Metallic blue	Sarathi
TN7245	1994	Pearl white	Pride
TN8436	1995	Black	Prestige
TN8538	1996	Pearl white	Flight

Table P14.3. *Sample records of the* `Used car` *file*

Solution:

The schematic diagram for the secondary indexing of the `Used car` file is shown in Figure P14.3. Both of the indexes are shown in the same figure. Observe how the data records are ordered according to the primary key in the primary storage area.

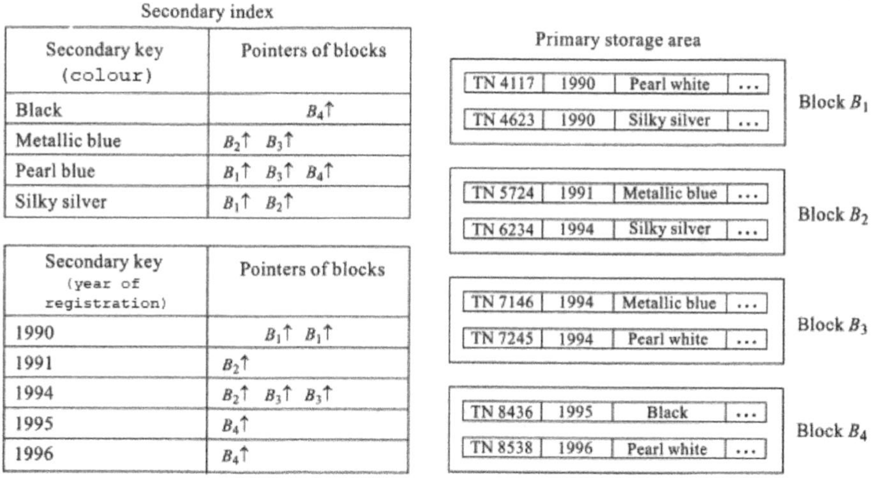

Figure P14.3. *The schematic diagram for the secondary indexing of the* `Used car` *file*

PROBLEM 14.4.–

For the `Used car` file discussed in illustrative problem 14.3, design a cluster index-based file organization on the non-key field `year of registration`. Assume that the blocks in the primary storage area can hold up to two records each.

Solution:

Figure P14.4 illustrates the schematic diagram for the cluster index-based file organization for the Used car file.

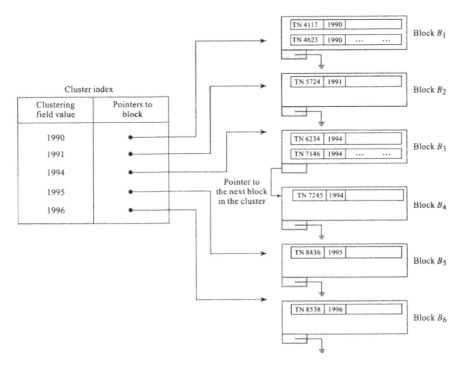

Figure P14.4. *Schematic diagram for the cluster index-based file organization for the* Used car *file*

PROBLEM 14.5.–

Design a direct file organization using a hash function, to store an item file with item number as its primary key. The primary keys of a sample set of records of the item file are listed below. Assume that the buckets can hold two records each and the blocks in the primary storage area can accommodate a maximum of four records each. Make use of the hash function $h(k) = k\ mod\ 8$, where k represents the numerical value of the primary key (item number).

369 760 692 871 659 975 981 115 620 208 821 111 554 781 181 965

Solution:

Figure P14.5 represents the schematic diagram of the direct file organization of the `item` file using a hash function. Table P14.5 represents the hash function values of the primary keys.

Primary key (k)	369	760	692	871	659	975	981	115	620	208	821	111	554	781	181	965
Hash function value ($h(k)$)	1	0	4	7	3	7	5	3	4	0	5	7	2	5	5	5

Table P14.5. *Hash function values of the primary keys of the* `item` *file*

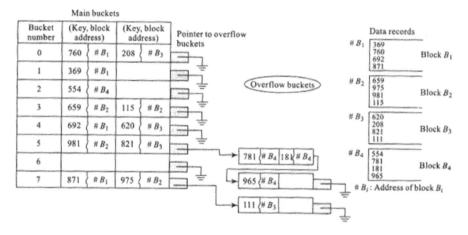

Figure P14.5. *Schematic diagram of the direct file organization using the hash function, for the* `item` *file*

PROBLEM 14.6.–

For the direct file organization of the `item` file constructed in illustrative problem 14.5, undertake the following operations independently:

i) Insert item records with primary keys 441 and 805.

ii) Delete the records with primary keys 369 and 111.

Solution:

Figure P14.6(a) illustrates the insertion of the keys 441 and 805 into the direct file. Figure P14.6(b) illustrates the deletion of the keys 369 and 111. The delete operations are undertaken independent of the insert operations. The affected portions of the file alone are shown in the figures.

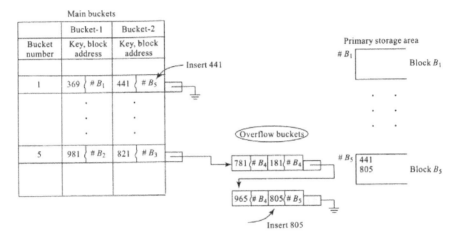

Figure P14.6(a). *Insertion of keys 441 and 805 into the direct file shown in Figure P14.5*

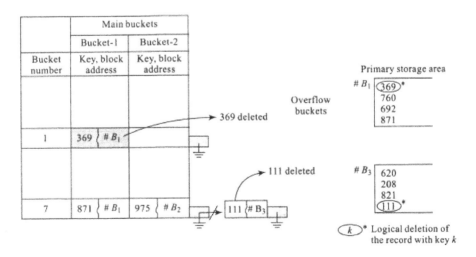

Figure P14.6(b). *Deletion of keys 369 and 111 from the direct file shown in Figure P14.5*

It can be observed how the deletion of key 111 empties the overflow bucket, as a result of which the entire empty bucket gets removed.

Review questions

1) A minimal super key is in fact a -------------------

a) secondary super key   b) primary key

c) non-key   d) none of these

2) State whether true or false:

i) A cluster index is a sparse index

ii) A secondary key field with distinct values yields a dense index

a) i) true ii) true   b) i) true ii) false

c) i) false ii) true   d) i) false ii) false

3) An index consisting of variable length entries where each index entry would be of the form $(K, B_1 \uparrow, B_2 \uparrow, B_3 \uparrow, \ldots\ldots B_t \uparrow)$, where $B_i \uparrow$s are block addresses of the various records holding the same value for the secondary key K, can occur only in

a) primary indexing   b) secondary indexing

c) cluster indexing   d) multilevel indexing

4) Match the following:

A) heap file organization   i) transaction file

B) sequential file organization   ii) non keyed

C) ISAM file organization   iii) hash function

D) direct file organization   iv) indexing

a) (A, i))   (B, iv))   (C, iii))   (D, ii))

b) (A, ii))   (B, iv))   (C, iii))   (D, i))

c) (A, ii))   (B, i))   (C, iv))   (D, iii))

d) (A, iii))   (B, i))   (C, ii))   (D, iv))

5) Find the odd term out in the context of basic file operations, from the following list:

open   close   update   delete   evaluate   read

a) close   b) read   c) open   d) evaluate

6) Distinguish between primary memory and secondary memory.

7) Give examples for i) super key ii) primary key iii) secondary key and iv) alternate key.

8) How are insertions and deletions carried out in a pile?

9) Distinguish between logical and physical deletion of records.

10) Compare the merits and demerits of a heap file with that of a sequential file organization.

11) How do ISAM files ensure random access to data?

12) What is the need for multilevel indexing in ISAM files?

13) When are cluster indexes used?

14) How are secondary indexes maintained?

15) What is external hashing?

16) A file comprises the following sample set of primary keys. The block size in the primary storage area is 2. Design an ISAM file organization based on i) primary indexing and ii) multilevel indexing (level = 3).

    090 890 678 654 234   123   245   678 900 111 453   231 112 679 238
    876 311 433 544 655 766 877 988 009 122 233 344 566 677 899 909
    512 612 723 823 956

17) Making use of the hash function $h(k) = k \bmod 11$, where k is the key, design a direct file organization for the sample file (list of primary keys) shown in review problem 16. Assume that the bucket size is 3 and the block size is 4.

18) Assume that the sample file (list of primary keys) shown in review problem 16, had a field called `category` which carries the character 'A' if the primary key is odd and 'B' if the primary key is even. Design a cluster index-based file organization built on the field `category`. Assume a block size of 4.

Programming assignments

1) Implement the `used car` file discussed in illustrative problem 14.3, in a programming language of your choice that supports the data structures of files and records. Experiment with the basic operations of a file. What other operations does the language support to enhance the use of the file? Write a menu-driven program to implement the operations.

2) Assume that the used car file discussed in illustrative problem 14.3, was implemented as a sequential file. Simulate the batched mode of updating the sequential file by creating a transaction file of insertions (details of cars that are brought in for sale) and deletions (cars that were sold out), to update the existing master file.

3) A movie file has the following record structure:

name of the movie	producer	director	type	production cost

Assume that the name of the movie is the primary key of the file. The field type refers to the type of the movie, for example, drama, sci-fi, horror, crime thriller, comedy and so forth. Input a sample set of records of your choice into the movie file.

i) Implement a primary index-based ISAM file organization.

ii) Implement secondary indexes on director, type and production cost.

iii) How could the secondary index-based file organization in Programming Assignment 3 (ii), be used to answer a query such as "Who are the directors who have directed films of the comedy or drama type, who have incurred the highest production cost?"

4) A company provides reimbursement of mobile phone subscription charges to its employees belonging to the managerial cadre and above. The following record structure captures the details. employee number, which is designated as the primary key, is a numerical 3-digit key. type refers to a post-paid or pre-paid class of subscription to the mobile service. subscription charges refer to the charges incurred by the employee at the end of every month.

employee number	designation	mobile number	type	Subscription charges

For a sample set of records implement the file as

a) an array of records (block size = 1), and

b) an array of pointers to records (assume that each pointer to a record is a linked list of two nodes, each representing a record. In other words, each block is a linked list of two nodes (block size = 2)).

Make use of an appropriate hash function to design a direct file organization for the said file. Write a menu-driven program, which

i) inserts new records when recruitments or promotions to the managerial cadre is made,

ii) deletes records when the employees concerned relinquish duties or terminate mobile subscriptions due to various reasons,

iii) updates records regarding the `subscription charges` at the end of every month, changes if any, in `type` and `designation` fields and so forth.

5) Make use of a random number generator to generate a list of 500 three-digit numbers. Create a sequential list FILE of the 500 numbers. Artificially implement storage blocks on the sequential list with every block containing a maximum of 10 numbers only. Open an index INDX over the sequential list FILE which records the highest key in each storage block and the address of the storage block. Implement Indexed Sequential search to look for keys K in FILE. Compare the number of comparisons made by the search with that of the sequential search for the same set of keys.

Extend the implementation to include an index over the index INDX.

15

k-d Trees and Treaps

15.1. Introduction

k-d trees and ***Treaps*** are binary trees that are built on the principle of binary search trees, which was elaborated in Chapter 10 (Volume 2). While *k*-d trees are adept in handling multi-dimensional keys, Treaps are randomized binary search trees and are good at handling data sets in which each of the data elements has priorities attached to them.

The structure, operations and applications of the two data structures are detailed in the ensuing sections.

15.2. *k*-d trees: structure and operations

k-dimensional trees or ***k-d trees*** invented by Jon Louis Bentley in 1975 (Bentley 1975) are ***multi-dimensional binary search trees***, which can undertake query-based searches such as ***range search***, ***nearest-neighbor search*** and ***fast retrieval of a key***, efficiently.

k-d trees handle multi-dimensional keys, $K_i = (a_{i,1}, a_{i,2}, \dots a_{i,k}), i = 1, 2, \dots N$ (dimensionality *k*), organize them in *k*-dimensional space as ***points*** and partition them into non-overlapping regions. Therefore, the regions partitioning the *k*-dimensional space hold ***disjoint subsets*** of the set of keys K_i, *i = 1, 2, ...N*. On account of this property, *k*-d trees are termed as ***space-partitioning*** data structures. It is this space-partitioning principle that is responsible for the efficient behavior of *k*-d trees. However, despite handling *k*-dimensional keys using the space-partitioning principle, *k-d trees in structure, look only like binary trees.*

So, who partitions them in *k*-dimensional space?

The non-leaf nodes! Each non-leaf node can be thought of as a *hyperplane* that partitions the space into two *half-spaces*. Keys (points) in the left half-space will group together as the left subtree and those on the right as the right subtree, of the node.

The key is k-dimensional, so where is the partitioning done?

k-d trees follow various methods to partition the keys at each non-leaf node. A simple procedure is discussed here.

A simple and straightforward method is to assign partitioning based on dimension 1 to the root or level 0 of the tree, partitioning based on dimension 2 to level 1 of the tree, partitioning based on dimension 3 to level 2 of the tree and so on until partitioning based on dimension k is assigned to level $k-1$. Remember, partitioning needs to proceed until the leaf nodes, whose left and right child nodes are empty nodes, are arrived at.

In the event of the partitioning still being incomplete, the dimensions are cycled once again through the rest of the levels of the tree. Thus, partitioning based on dimension 1 will be assigned to level k, dimension 2 to level $k+1$ and so on until the leaf nodes are arrived at.

To undertake this task of cyclical partitioning based on the dimensions of the key, each node is assigned a *discriminator* (**DISC**) which computes the dimension based on which partitioning needs to be done at that node. A node in level i of the tree would have its DISC as *(i mod k) + 1* and all nodes on a given level i would have the same DISC. Thus, it can be seen that the root node which is at level 0, will have its partitioning based on dimension *(0 mod k) + 1* which is 1, and nodes at level 1 based on *(1 mod k) + 1* which is 2 and so on.

EXAMPLE 15.1.–

A k-d tree for $k = 2$, constructed using the keys {P: (3,5), Q: (2, 6), R: (5, 8), S: (1, 7), T: (5, 4) , U: (4, 5)} is shown in Figure 15.1. It can be seen that the k-d tree looks like a binary tree in structure with the empty child nodes represented as empty squares/rectangles and the discriminant DISC for nodes in the tree cycling over {1, 2} for nodes in each level. In other words, the DISC cycles over the axes {x, y} notionally, given the two-dimensional nature of the keys.

Nodes Q and R have positioned themselves as the left and right child nodes of P since DISC (node P) = 1 (x-axis) and therefore like binary search trees, the comparison of the keys Q: (2, 6) and R: (5, 8) with P: (3, 5) were made on the basis of the first component of the keys. Since 2 < 3, Q stays as the left child node and since 5 > 3, R stays as the right child node.

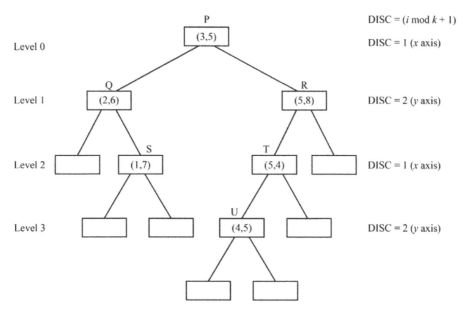

Figure 15.1. *An example k-d tree for* k = 2

In the case of T, note that due to DISC (P) = 1 it moves to the right subtree of P, since comparison of the first components yields 5 > 3 and since DISC (R) = 2 (*y*-axis) and comparison of the second components yields 4 < 8, T positions itself as the left child node of R.

Following a similar explanation, in the case of node U, DISC (node P) = 1 pushes it right (since 4 > 3), DISC (node R) = 2, pushes it left (since 5 < 8) and finally, DISC (node T) = 1 pushes it left (since 4 < 5).

Figure 15.2 illustrates the space-partitioning principle of *k*-d trees which contributes to its efficiency in executing query-based searches. The keys {P, Q, R, S, T, U} have been represented as points in *k*-dimensional space (*k* = 2). Each non-leaf node in the *k*-d tree represents a hyperplane that partitions the *k*-dimensional space into two half-spaces. The points to the left of the hyperplane form the left subtree and those on the right form the right subtree of the node. The hyperplane is drawn perpendicular to the axis represented by the dimension.

Following the above, it can be seen that node P which is the root and divides the whole k-d tree into left and right subtrees, has its hyperplane drawn perpendicular to its axis which is the x-axis. Observe S, Q on the left half space and R, T, U on the right half space of the hyperplane described by node P. Let us consider U since its hyperplane is perpendicular to the y axis, but the node itself occurs on the right half-space of node P and on the left half-spaces of both R and T, the hyperplane is drawn as shown in the figure. All hyperplanes for nodes whose DISC = 1 have been shown in broken lines and those for nodes whose DISC = 2 have been shown in solid lines.

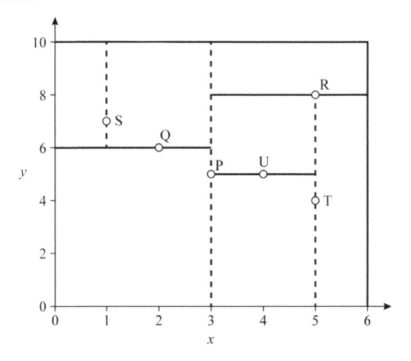

Figure 15.2. *Space-partitioning principle of* k-d *tree shown in Figure 15.1*

EXAMPLE 15.2.–

A k-d tree for $k = 3$, constructed using the keys {A: (5, 7, 8), B: (4, 6, 3), C: (8, 5, 1), D: (2, 6, 4), E: (3, 5, 6), F: (1, 7, 2), G: (4, 8, 3)} is shown in Figure 15.3. Observe how despite the three-dimensional keys, the k-d tree looks like a binary tree. Also, note that B and C have positioned themselves on the left and right subtrees of A respectively since the comparison was based on the first components of the keys because of DISC = 1 at node A. Similarly, F must have moved left of A for DISC = 1 at node A, then moved right of B for DISC = 2 and finally moved to the left of D for DISC = 3. Observe how G cycles through the dimensions, DISC = 1, 2, 3, 1 of the nodes in its search path, before it inserts itself in the right subtree of F. The empty nodes are shown as empty squares/rectangles.

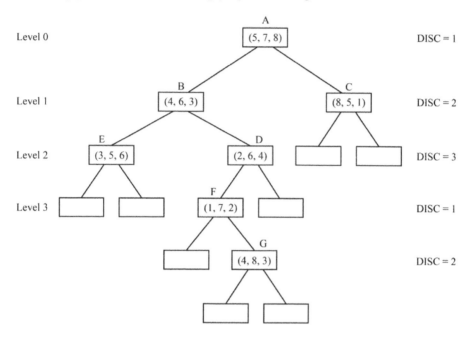

Figure 15.3. *An example k-d tree for* k = 3

15.2.1. *Construction of a k-d tree*

There are different ways of constructing *k*-d trees, given a set of *k*-dimensional keys, $K_i = (a_{i,1}, a_{i,2}, \dots a_{i,k}), i = 1, 2, \dots N$. Two canonical methods of construction are discussed here:

i) The first method deals with building the tree node by node, considering the keys in the order of their appearance and inserting them one by one in the fashion of how a binary search tree gets constructed.

The construction of the *k*-d tree begins by making the first key K_1 the root node, with its left and right child nodes set as empty nodes. The *DISC* field of the root node is set to *(0 mod k) +1* which is 1. The second key K_2 now proceeds to insert itself into the tree. To undertake this K_2 compares itself with K_1 and since *DISC(K_1)* is 1, the partitioning is done based on the respective first components of K_1 and K_2 (dimension 1) which let us suppose are (a_{11}, a_{21}). Thus, based on whether

$a_{21} < a_{11}$ or $a_{21} \geq a_{11}$, key K_2 is inserted as the left child or the right child of node K_1.

In general, to insert key K_i in the k-d tree, each of the components $a_{i,j}$ of the key K_i, compare themselves with the respective components of the keys in the nodes, beginning with the root node, as dictated by the DISC of the nodes and move down level by level, either left or right until the rightful place is reached at which point the key is inserted as a node. It is quite possible that to insert a key, it has to cycle through the dimensions as dictated by the DISC of the nodes it encountered on its search path, as explained earlier.

EXAMPLE 15.3.–

The construction of the k-d tree for $k = 2$, using the aforementioned method, for the list of keys {P: (3, 5), Q: (2, 6), R: (5, 8), S: (1, 7), T: (5, 4), U: (4, 5)} discussed in Example 15.1 is demonstrated here.

Figure 15.4 illustrates the snapshots of the construction of the tree. The keys are handled in the order of their appearance. Therefore, P becomes the root with its DISC (node P) = 1 as shown in Step 1 of the figure. In Step 2, Q gets inserted as the left child of P since for DISC (node P) = 1, comparing Q with P yields 2 < 3. In Step 3, R gets inserted as the right child of P for a similar reason. In Step 4, S compares itself with P and since DISC (node P) = 1, it gets pushed to the left subtree. There it encounters Q and since DISC (node Q) = 2, the comparison yields 7 > 6 and therefore Q gets pushed to the right and settles as the right child of Q. Proceeding in this way, finally when U (4, 5) is to be inserted, it moves right of P, left of R and lastly left of T, based on the respective comparisons, as dictated by DISC of the respective nodes. Node U settles down as the left child of node T.

ii) In the second method, each node on level i, which has been assigned the task of partitioning the list of keys based on its discriminator $DISC = i$, finds the ***median*** M of the ith components of the keys allotted to it. Median is the middle most key of the list of keys when it is sorted according to its ith component key values.

Thus, if there are N keys, then the middle most key is the one occupying a position $\left\lceil \frac{N}{2} \right\rceil$ in the *sorted list*. The key which holds the median element is set as the node and those keys whose i^{th} components are less than median M are moved to the left subtree and those which are greater than median M are moved to the right subtree of the node. This method yields a balanced k-d tree in which each leaf node has the same path length from the root node.

Keys: {P: (3,5), Q: (2,6), R: (5,8), S: (1,7), T: (5,4), U: (4,5)}

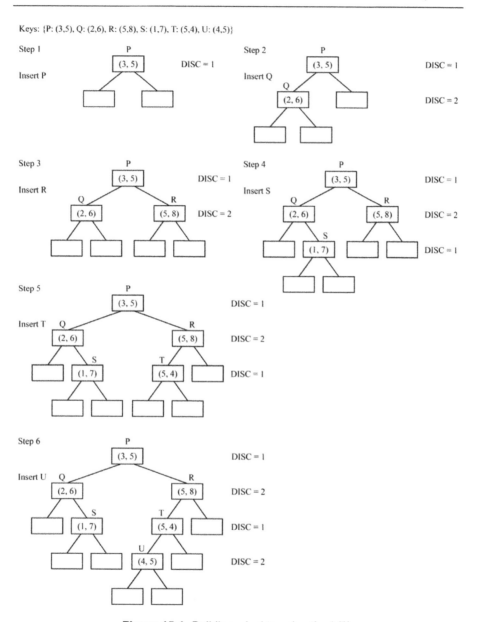

Figure 15.4. *Building a k-d tree (method (i))*

EXAMPLE 15.4.–

The construction of the k-d tree for $k = 2$, using the median element of the keys, for the list of keys {P: (3, 5), Q: (2, 6), R: (5, 8), S: (1, 7), T: (5, 4), U: (4, 5)} discussed in Example 15.1 is demonstrated here.

Keys: {P: (3,5), Q: (2,6), R: (5,8), S: (1,7), T: (5,4), U: (4,5)}

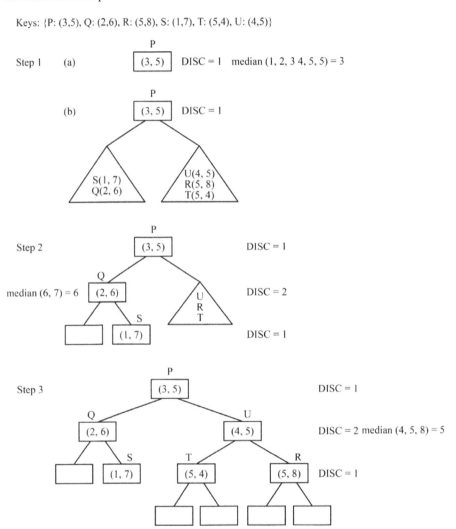

Figure 15.5. *Building a k-d tree (method (ii))*

Figure 15.5 illustrates the snapshots of the construction of the tree. In Step 1, since the root node has DISC = 1, the median of the first components of the keys is computed which is *median* (1, 2, 3, 4, 5, 5) = element occupying position $\left\lceil\frac{6}{2}\right\rceil$ = 3. Therefore, P: (3, 5) becomes the root node and keys S and Q get pushed to the left subtree, and keys U, R and T to the right subtree. The process repeats for each of the subtrees. Thus, for the right subtree as shown in Step 3, the median of U, R, T for DISC = 2, yields *median* (4, 5, 8) = element occupying position $\left\lceil\frac{3}{2}\right\rceil$ = 2. Therefore U: (4, 5) is chosen as the root of the right subtree and since there is only one key left on either side of the median, T: (5, 4) settles as the left child and R: (5, 8) as the right child of U.

15.2.2. *Insert operation on k-d trees*

Inserting a node in a *k*-d tree progresses in a similar way as the node was inserted while building the tree, discussed in method (i) of section 15.2.1. **procedure** kd_INSERT (Algorithm 15.1) illustrates a recursive pseudocode description of the insert operation on a *k*-d tree. Here, x is the key to be inserted into the *k*-d tree, T is the pointer to the *k*-d tree and DISC is the discriminator.

```
procedure kd_INSERT( x, NODE T,  DISC)
/* x:      the new key x to be inserted into the k-d tree
   NODE T: the node in the k-d tree which holds the key
           as DATA(T) and pointers LEFT(T) and RIGHT(T)
           to its left and right child nodes.   T points
           to the k-d tree
   DISC: Discriminator for the node
   k:    dimension of the key     */


if (T == NIL)
then T = new NODE(x);   /* create new node for x
          which is the root of the k-d tree */

if (x == DATA(T)) then exit; /* duplicate key -
                                exit */
if (x[DISC] < DATA(T)[DISC])
                /* x[DISC] and DATA(T)[DISC] are   the
                components of the key to be inserted
                and key stored in the node
                respectively, for the dimension
                indicated by DISC*/
```

```
then
    LEFT(T)=kd_INSERT(x, LEFT(T),(DISC mod k) +1);
else
    RIGHT(T)=kd_INSERT(x, RIGHT(T),(DISC mod k)+1);

return(T)
```

end kd_INSERT

Algorithm 15.1. *Inserting a key into a k-d tree*

However, such insertions can imbalance the k-d tree rendering the query-based searches computationally expensive. So, in such a case a rebalancing of the tree might have to be done.

15.2.3. *Find minimum operation on k-d trees*

The find minimum operation (FIND MIN) finds the minimum element of the multi-dimensional keys, in a given dimension d. This operation is significant in a k-d tree since the deletion of nodes in a k-d tree involves FIND MIN operations extensively. In a binary search tree, the FIND MIN operation would merely involve a recursive traversal through the left subtrees beginning with the root node, until the minimum key was found as a leaf node in the left subtree of the root node. Such a procedure cannot be followed in its totality over k-d trees since k-d trees cycle through dimensions of the keys as dictated by the DISC of the node at each level of the tree.

The strategy adopted by the FIND MIN operation when it traverses the k-d tree to find the minimum element MIN in dimension d is as described below:

F1: If the dimension d is the same as the DISC of the node CURRENT at the current level of its traversal, then the minimum element is in the left subtree of the node CURRENT if a left subtree exists for the node. Recursively traverse the left subtree until the minimum element MIN_LEFT is found. Return the minimum of the dth dimension element of the key in node CURRENT and MIN_LEFT as the minimum element MIN.

F2: If the dimension d is different from the DISC of the node CURRENT at the current level of its traversal, then the minimum element may lie either in the left subtree or the right subtree of node CURRENT. Therefore, recursively traverse both the left subtree and right subtree of CURRENT to obtain the minimum elements MIN_LEFT and MIN_RIGHT of the left and right subtrees of CURRENT, respectively. The ultimate minimum element MIN is the minimum of the dth dimension element of the key in node CURRENT, MIN_LEFT and MIN_RIGHT.

Needless to say, the *k-d* tree alternates between norms **F1** and **F2**, while recursively traversing the tree to obtain the final minimum element MIN.

procedure kd_FINDMIN (Algorithm 15.2) illustrates a recursive pseudocode description of finding the minimum element over a dimension *d*, in a *k*-d tree.

```
procedure kd_FINDMIN(NODE T, dim, DISC)
/* NODE T:  the node in the k-d tree which holds the key
            as DATA(T) and pointers LEFT(T) and RIGHT(T)
            to its left and right child nodes
   dim:     dimension of the minimum element
   DISC:    Discriminator for the node
   k:       dimension of the key
*/

   if (T == NIL)
   then return(T);                      /* empty k-d tree*/

   if (dim == DISC)
   then
       if ( LEFT(T) == NIL )
       then return (DATA(T)[dim]);
       else
       return (min(DATA(T)[dim],
           kd_FINDMIN(LEFT(T),dim,(DISC mod k)+1)));
   else
       return (min( DATA(T)[dim],
           kd_FINDMIN(LEFT(T),dim,(DISC mod k)+1),
           kd_FINDMIN(RIGHT(T),dim,(DISC mod k)+1)));

end kd_FINDMIN
```

Algorithm 15.2. *Finding the minimum element over a dimension d, in a k-d tree*

EXAMPLE 15.5.–

Consider the *k-d* tree shown in Step 3 of Figure 15.5, constructed out of two dimensional keys {P: (3, 5), Q: (2, 6), R: (5, 8), S: (1, 7), T: (5, 4), U: (4, 5)}. The aim is to find the minimum elements MIN1 and MIN2 across dimensions 1 and 2, respectively. At the end of the FIND MIN operation, MIN1 would be set to 1 and MIN2 would be set to 4.

To obtain MIN1, FIND MIN begins with the root node P: (3, 5). Since node P has DISC = 1, which is the same as the dimension of MIN1, FIND MIN proceeds to recursively traverse the left subtree of P, adopting norm **F1**, trying to look for an element that is lesser than 3. Thus, MIN1 would be **min** (3, FIND MIN(node Q)). Since node Q: (2, 6) has DISC = 2 which is different from the dimension of MIN1, FIND MIN (node Q) adopting norm **F2**, proceeds to obtain the minimum elements of the left subtree and right subtree of node Q and returning the result of **min** (2, FIND MIN (right subtree of node Q), FIND MIN (left subtree of node Q)). FIND MIN (left subtree of node Q) returns **NIL** and FIND MIN (right subtree of node Q) returns the minimum element as 1, adopting norm **F1** since node S: (1, 7) has its DISC =1 which is the same as the dimension of MIN1. Backtracking the recursive calls, FIND MIN (node Q) computes **min** (2, **NIL**, 1) and returns 1 to FIND MIN (node P) which computes **min** (3, FIND MIN(node Q) = 1) and outputs MIN1 = 1.

In the case of obtaining MIN2, FIND MIN begins with root node P whose DISC = 1, which is not the same as the dimension of MIN2. Therefore adopting norm **F2**, it proceeds to traverse both left and right subtrees of node P recursively, to obtain the respective minimum elements and compute **min** (5, FIND MIN (node Q), FIND MIN (node U)) to return the value of MIN2. Following a similar discussion, FIND MIN (node Q) computes **min** (6, **NIL**) and returns 6, while FIND MIN (node U) returns 4. Finally, MIN2 is set as **min** (5, 6, 4) = 4.

15.2.4. *Delete operation on k-d trees*

Delete operation makes use of the FIND MIN operation discussed in the earlier section. The delete operation is carried out as follows:

D1: If the node NODE to be deleted in the *k*-d tree is a leaf node, then delete NODE.

D2: If the node NODE to be deleted has DISC = *i*, and has a right subtree, then call FIND MIN, to obtain the node RIGHT_MIN, which has the minimum element along dimension *i* in the right subtree and replace NODE with RIGHT_MIN. Recursively delete RIGHT_MIN from the right subtree.

D3: If the node NODE to be deleted has DISC = *i*, and has a left subtree, then call FIND MIN to obtain the node LEFT_MIN, which has the minimum element along dimension *i* in the left subtree and replace NODE with LEFT_MIN. Recursively delete LEFT_MIN from the left subtree. Move the revised left subtree as the right child of the current node.

procedure kd_DELETE (Algorithm 15.3) illustrates a recursive pseudocode description of the delete operation in a *k*-d tree.

```
procedure kd_DELETE (x, NODE T, DISC)
/* x:        key to be deleted
   NODE T: the node in the k-d tree which holds the key
           as DATA(T) and pointers LEFT(T) and RIGHT(T)
           to its left and right child nodes
   DISC:    Discriminator for the node
   k:       dimension of the key
*/
  NEXT_DISC = (DISC mod k)+1;
  if (T == NIL) then exit();   /* key not found*/

  if (x == DATA(T))         /* node T represents the
                              key  to be deleted*/
  then
     if (RIGHT(T) != NIL)

     then
           {DATA(T) =
           kd_FINDMIN(RIGHT(T),DISC,NEXT_DISC);
           RIGHT(T) =
           kd_DELETE(DATA(T),RIGHT(T),NEXT_DISC);}
     else
         if (LEFT(T) != NIL)
         then
           {DATA(T) =
           kd_FINDMIN(LEFT(T), DISC, NEXT_DISC);
           RIGHT(T) =
           kd_DELETE(DATA(T),LEFT(T),NEXT_DISC);}
         else T = NIL;   /* remove leaf node */

  else /* find the node to delete*/
     if ( x[DISC] < DATA(T)[DISC])
     then
           LEFT(T) =
           kd_DELETE(x, LEFT(T), NEXT_DISC);
     else
           RIGHT(T) =
           kd_DELETE(x, RIGHT(T), NEXT_DISC);
  return(T)

end kd_DELETE
```

Algorithm 15.3. *Delete operation in a k-d tree*

EXAMPLE 15.6.–

Figure 15.6 illustrates deletions undertaken over k-d trees. Figure 15.6(a) shows that Delete Q on the k-d tree given, where Q is a leaf node merely deletes the node, illustrating norm **D1** discussed above.

In Figure 15.6(b), Delete P calls for replacing node P whose DISC = 1, with the node containing the minimum element along dimension 1, in its right subtree. This is in accordance with norm **D2** discussed above. The FIND MIN operation on the right subtree of node P yields node U as the RIGHT_MIN element and hence node P is replaced with node U. Following norms, node U is recursively deleted which results in node R replacing node U. Node R being a leaf node is deleted following norm **D1**, to yield the k-d tree shown.

Figure 15.6(c) illustrates Delete P for the root node P, whose DISC = 1, in the k-d tree shown. Since the right subtree of node P is empty, following norm **D3**, the FIND MIN operation works to obtain LEFT_MIN, the node containing the minimum element along dimension 1 in the left subtree of node P. Node S is chosen as LEFT_MIN and node P is replaced by node S. Node S is recursively deleted and since it is a leaf node the deletion of node S is trivially done following norm **D1**. Finally, the revised left subtree is moved to the right of node S.

15.2.5. *Complexity analysis and applications of k-d trees*

Since a k-d tree is a multi-dimensional binary search tree in structure, the average case complexity of undertaking an insert, delete or retrieval operation is $O(log\ n)$ and the worst case complexity for the same is $O(n)$.

k-d trees have found wide use in search-based applications. Thus, *range search*, where data elements lying between two limits, *a, b* are to be retrieved, finds a congenial data structure in k-d trees, to efficiently retrieve the elements in the range. The characteristic of k-d trees to split the data sets into ordered halves at each level of the tree helps to undertake range searches efficiently.

The *nearest neighbor (NN) search* where the data point closest to the given data point needs to be found out from the data set, or its generalization, viz., *k-nearest neighbor (kNN) search,* where the k best points which are the nearest neighbors of the given data point need to be found out, can be efficiently implemented over k-d trees.

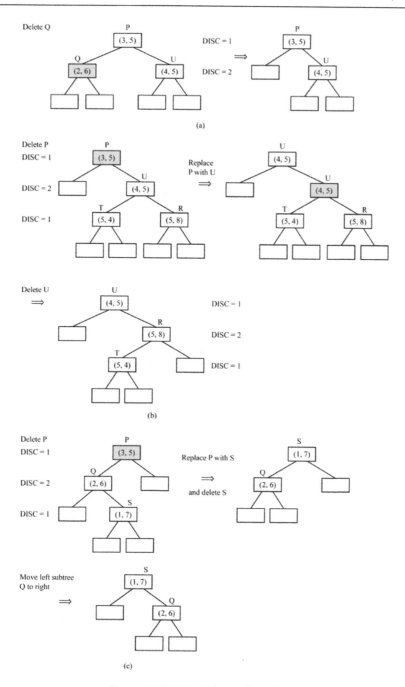

Figure 15.6. *Deletions in a* k-d *tree*

15.3. Treaps: structure and operations

A **Treap** (randomized binary search tree) is a portmanteau of *Tree* and *Heap* and was first described by Raimund Seidel and Cecilia R Aragon in 1989 (Aragon and Seidel 1989).

"Tree" primarily refers to a binary tree. A **heap** is a **complete binary tree** in which the keys of every parent node are greater than or equal to those of their child nodes, which eventually implies that the root node of a heap would hold the largest amongst all the keys represented by the heap. Such a heap is referred to as a **max-heap**. It is also possible to define a heap where the keys of every parent node are smaller than or equal to those of their child nodes, which ultimately renders the root node of the heap to hold the smallest of all the keys represented by the heap. In such a case, the heap is referred to as a **min-heap**. Details about complete binary trees can be found in section 8.4 of Chapter 8 (Volume 2) and those about heaps can be found in section 17.8 of Chapter 17.

15.3.1. Treap structure

The treap is a binary tree that organizes data sets that comprise **keys**, each of which has a random **priority** factor attached to it. Thus, every node in the treap has a structure as shown in Figure 15.7. The key is written on the top and the priority factor is written at the bottom, to describe a **treap node**.

Figure 15.7. *Structure of a node in a treap*

The characteristics of the binary tree describing a treap are as follows:

i) The keys follow the standard ordering of binary search trees and therefore, *from the stand point of keys, the treap is a binary search tree.*

ii) The random priority factors follow the ordering of a heap (*max-heap*, for instance) and therefore, *from the stand point of priorities, the treap is a max-heap.* It is also possible to construct a treap following the *min-heap* principle for ordering priorities.

EXAMPLE 15.7.–

For a dataset comprising keys and their random priorities, as shown below, Figure 15.8 illustrates a treap.

Keys: 500   308   670   204   440

Priorities: 7   3   4   1   2

Observe how the keys have ordered themselves as a binary search tree and the priorities have ordered themselves as a max-heap.

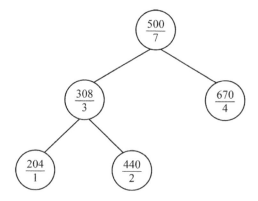

Figure 15.8. *An example treap*

15.3.2. *Operations on treaps*

The Retrieval, Insert and Delete operations on a Treap are described below.

15.3.2.1. *Retrieval from a treap*

The retrieval of a key along with its priority proceeds just as one does while retrieving a key from a binary search tree (see section 10.2 in Chapter 10 (Volume 2) for information regarding the insertion, deletion and retrieval operations of a binary search tree).

15.3.2.2. *Insertion into a treap*

The insertion of a (key, priority) pair into a treap, initially proceeds just as one would insert a key into a binary search tree. Having inserted the (key, priority) pair at its appropriate place, the binary search tree ordering of the keys is no doubt satisfied, but there may be a possibility of violation of the max-heap ordering of the priorities. To set this right, treap undertakes **rotations** as detailed below.

15.3.2.3. *Rotations*

The rotations are of two types: **left rotation** and **right rotation**. Figure 15.9 illustrates the same. Observe that the left and right rotations are mirror images of one another. The rotations not just merely helping to set right the max-heap ordering of the keys in the treap, but also ensuring that the binary search tree ordering of the keys in the treap remains undisturbed. While *s* and *t* denote nodes that are directly involved in the rotations, *T1, T2* and *T3* denote subtrees that are indirectly affected due to the rotations. Note how subtree *T2* changes its parent node after rotation, to ensure that the binary search tree ordering of the treap is kept intact.

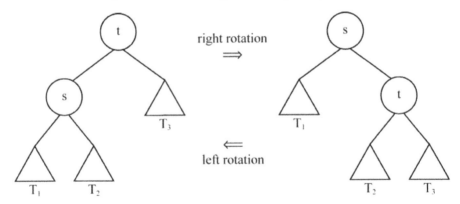

Figure 15.9. *Rotations in a treap*

EXAMPLE 15.8.–

Let us insert (717, 6) into the treap shown in Figure 15.8, where 717 is the key and 6 is the priority accorded to the key. Figure 15.10(a) illustrates the normal insertion of key 717 into the treap preserving its binary search tree ordering. However, the violation of the max-heap ordering of the priorities is visible. Figure 15.10(b) illustrates the left rotation undertaken by the treap to preserve its max-heap ordering of the priorities.

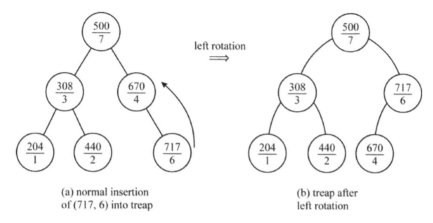

(a) normal insertion
of (717, 6) into treap

(b) treap after
left rotation

Figure 15.10. *Insertion into a treap that calls for rotation*

15.3.2.4. *Deletion from a treap*

If the node NODE to be deleted, is a leaf node then NODE is merely pulled off the treap. On the other hand, if the node NODE to be deleted is a non-leaf node, then first initialize the priority of NODE to -∞. Now proceed to set right the violation of the max-heap ordering that has taken place on account of this initialization, by means of a series of rotations (left and/or right) as the case demands, until the NODE whose revised priority is -∞, gets pushed down as a leaf node. Lastly, delete the leaf node NODE.

EXAMPLE 15.9.–

Let us undertake the operations i) delete (440, 2) and ii) (500, 7) independently, on the treap illustrated in Figure 15.8.

Observe that deletion of (440, 2) is trivial since key 440 is a leaf node in the treap. It is a rotation-free deletion. The treap continues to preserve its characteristics even after the deletion. Figure 15.11(a) illustrates the deletion of (440, 2) from the treap.

In the case of deletion of (500, 7), since key 500 is a non-leaf node (root node rather), the deletion procedure is a tad involved. Let us first initialize the priority of key 500 to -∞. Figure 15.11(b) shows the treap after revision of priority of key 500 to -∞. The violation of the max-heap ordering of the priorities is glaringly visible. Now, we proceed to make a series of rotations, left - right - right, to push (500, -∞) to a leaf node, before it is finally pulled out of the treap, following the norm of deleting a leaf node.

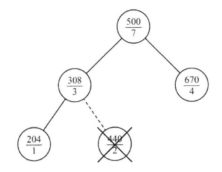

(a) Deletion of (440,2), a leaf node of a treap
(rotation free deletion)

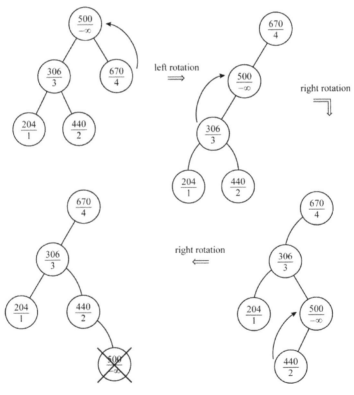

(b) Deletion of (500,7), a non-leaf node of the treap
(deletion with rotation)

Figure 15.11. *Deletions from a treap (with and without rotations)*

EXAMPLE **15.10.–**

Build a treap using the (key, priority) data set {(86, 5), (41, 7), (32, 2), (98,1), (74, 3), (56, 6)}.

Figure 15.12 illustrates the building of the treap.

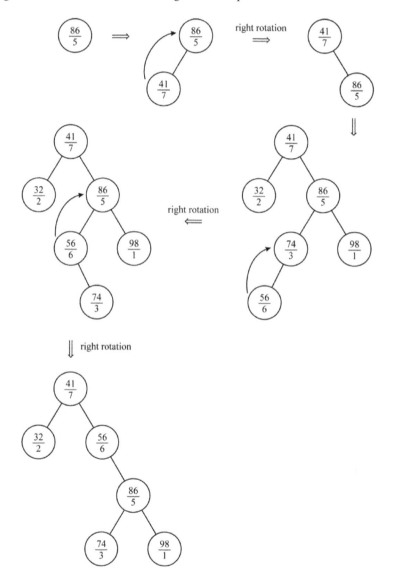

Figure 15.12. *Building a treap*

15.3.3. *Complexity analysis and applications of treaps*

A treap in principle is a binary search tree. Hence, an insert, delete and retrieval operation over a treap reports $O(log\ n)$ average case complexity and $O(n)$ worst-case complexity.

Since treaps involve paired data, comprising a key and a priority accorded to it, it can be used in applications where a priority-based service is scheduled. For example, to put it very generally, if a process manager or a job scheduler has to manage processes or jobs that arrive and depart with varying priorities, then there is no better data structure than treaps. The keys could describe the process id or job id and the priority could represent the process or job priority. The max-heap ordering would ensure that the process or job with the highest priority moves to the root node. Once the process or job terminates, deletion of the root node could be done, which automatically entails the next high priority job request to be designated as the root node, after restructuring the treap, and so on and so further, until all the process or job requests have been attended to and the treap turns null.

Summary

– *k*-d trees are multi-dimensional binary search trees, which can undertake query-based searches over a data set efficiently.

– *k*-d trees handle multi-dimensional keys and partition them into non-overlapping regions holding disjoint subsets of the keys and therefore are known as space-partitioning data structures. However, despite their complex characteristics, *k*-d trees look like plain binary trees.

– The space partitioning is effected by the non-leaf nodes based on the dimension of the key components denoted as the discriminator (DISC) and the levels of the binary tree.

– *k*-d trees can be constructed by inserting the keys one by one in the order of their appearance in the data set, or by making use of the median of the key components dictated by DISC at every level of the tree.

– The insert, delete and find-min operations on a *k*-d tree report $O(log\ n)$ time complexity in the average case and $O(n)$ time complexity in the worst case.

– Treaps in principle are a combination of binary search trees and heaps, which handle data sets that are (key, priority) pairs.

– The keys in the (key, priority) pairs follow a binary search tree ordering and priorities follow a max-heap/min-heap ordering.

– Treaps call for rotations to restructure the tree if the max-heap/min-heap principle is violated during insertions or deletions.

– Treaps report *O(log n)* average case complexity and *O(n)* worst case complexity for the insert, delete and retrieval operations.

15.4. Illustrative problems

PROBLEM 15.1.–

Build a *k*-d tree, *k* = 2, for the keys {P: (5, 6), Q: (2, 7), U: (6, 1), S: (3, 9), T: (9, 4), R: (1, 8)}

Solution:

Figure P15.1(a) illustrates the *k*-d tree built using the method i) and Figure P15.1(b) illustrates the steps to build the same using method ii), as discussed in section 15.2.1.

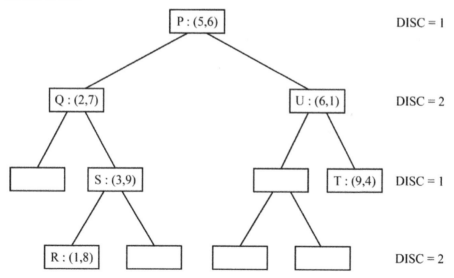

Figure P15.1(a). *Building a k-d tree node by node, for the keys listed in illustrative problem 15.1 (method (i), section 15.2.1)*

Step 1: Median (1, 2, 3, 5, 6, 9) = 3

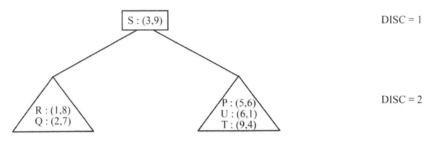

Step 2: Median (7, 8) = 7   Median (1, 4, 6) = 4

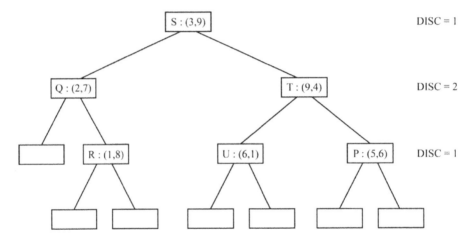

Figure P15.1(b). *Building a k-d tree by finding the medians, for the keys listed in illustrative problem 15.1 (method (ii), section 15.2.1)*

PROBLEM 15.2.–

For the *k*-d tree shown in Figure 15.5, i) insert W: (3, 2), and ii) insert G: (6, 4).

Solution:

Figure P15.2 illustrates the insertions of W: (3, 2) and G: (6, 4).

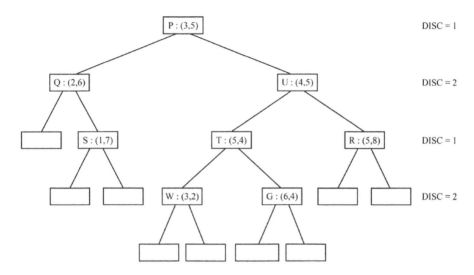

Figure P15.2. *Insertions of W: (3, 2) and G: (6, 4) in the* k-d *tree shown in Figure 15.5*

PROBLEM 15.3.–

For the *k*-d tree shown in Figure P15.2, i) delete S: (1, 7) and ii) delete P: (3, 5)

Solution:

Figure P15.3(a) illustrates the deletion of S. Since S is a leaf node the deletion is trivial satisfying norm **D1** discussed in section 15.2.4.

Deletion of P involves following norms **D1** and/or **D2** discussed in section 15.2.4.

Thus, node P needs to be replaced by the node RIGHT_MIN which holds the minimum element along dimension 1, in the right subtree of node P. FIND MIN helps trace the node RIGHT_MIN, by working over norms **F1** and **F2** discussed in section 15.2.3. The node RIGHT_MIN arrived at is W: (3, 2). Delete W which is a leaf node, and replace P with W. Figure P15.3(b) illustrates the final *k*-d tree after deletion of P.

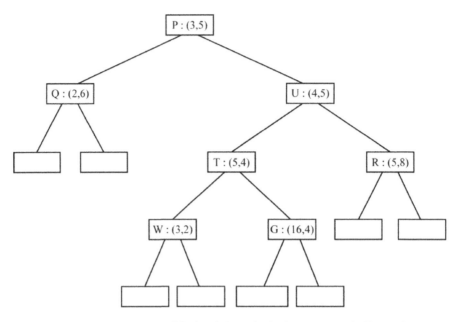

Figure P15.3(a). *Deletion of S: (1, 7) from the* k-d *tree shown in Figure P15.2*

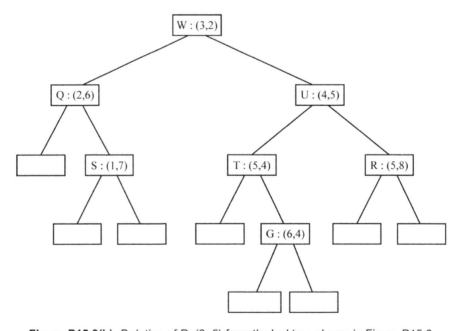

Figure P15.3(b). *Deletion of P: (3, 5) from the* k-d *tree shown in Figure P15.2*

PROBLEM 15.4.–

For the data set {(ai, 6), (ml, 7), (ds, 3), (os, 1), (se, 2)} build a treap. Perform deletion of (ml, 7) over the treap and insert (ps, 7) into the deleted treap.

Solution:

Figure P15.4(a) illustrates the treap built out of the data set. Figure P15.4(b) and (c), show the treaps, after the delete and insert operations respectively.

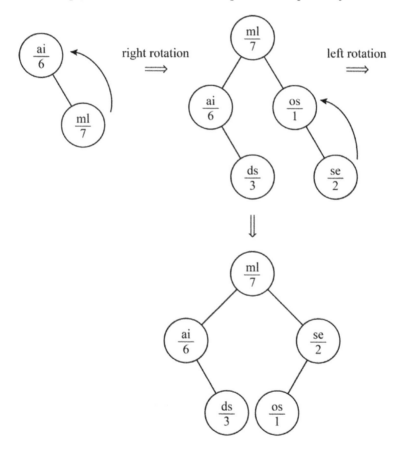

(a) Building the treap

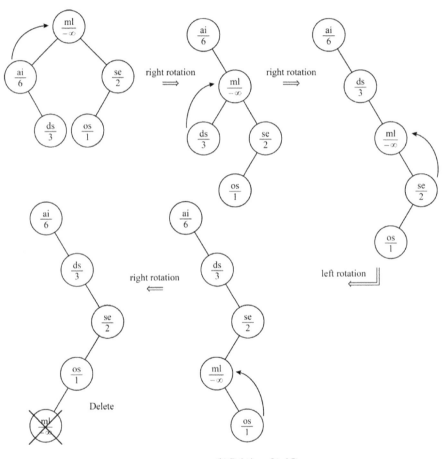

(b) Deletion of (ml,7)

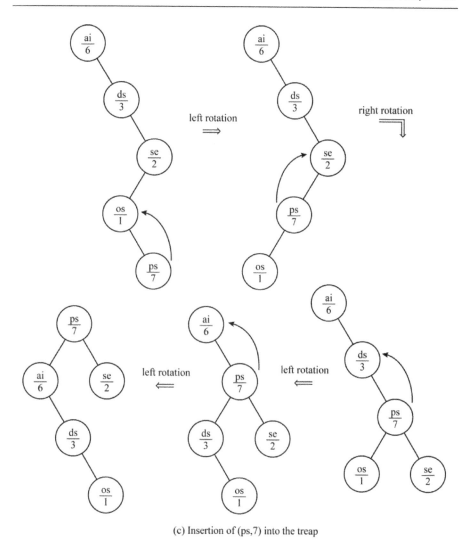

(c) Insertion of (ps,7) into the treap

Figure P15.4. *Building and maintaining the treap for the data set listed in illustrative problem 15.4*

PROBLEM 15.5.–

A job scheduler receives job requests with a priority of execution attached to it, in the following sequence. The higher the priority value, the higher the priority of job execution.

Job ID:	464	212	110	840	976	343
Priority:	3	2	3	1	2	2

Build a treap for the jobs scheduled for execution. How would the treap look when the highest priority jobs have completed execution and therefore have quit the treap?

Solution:

Figure P15.5(a) shows the treap after all the job requests were received. Insertion of jobs (110, 3) and (976, 2) called for right and left rotations respectively.

Figure P15.5(b) shows the treap soon after the highest priority jobs of (464, 3) and (110, 3) have been completed and therefore were deleted from the treap.

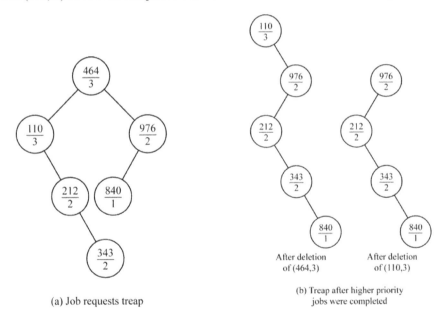

(a) Job requests treap

(b) Treap after higher priority jobs were completed

Figure P15.5. *Building and maintaining a treap for a job scheduler*

Review questions

1) Compare and contrast a binary search tree with a *k*-d tree.

2) How does one construct a *k*-d tree? Construct a *k*-d tree (*k* = 4) for the following keys: A: (5, 2, 1, 8), B: (3, 1, 6, 5), C: (8, 8, 4, 6), D: (1, 7, 6, 4), E: (7, 7, 3, 2), F: (4, 5, 1, 7), G: (3, 1, 2, 9).

3) How does one find the minimum element along dimension *i*, of a data set represented as a *k*-d tree? Find the minimum element of the data set listed in review question 2, using the *k*-d tree constructed for the same.

4) Perform deletions of data elements C and G in the *k*-d tree constructed for the list of elements shown in review question 2.

5) What are the characteristics of a treap?

6) Construct a treap for the data set: {(K, 8), (A, 7), (G, 4), (C, 1), (M, 9), (S, 5)}. Insert (F, 5) into the treap and delete (M, 9) from the treap.

7) Assume that a treap follows the *min-heap* principle with regard to its ordering of priorities. Construct such a treap for the data listed in illustrative problem 15.4. Demonstrate deletions of (os, 1) and (se, 2) from the treap.

Programming assignments

1) Given a multi-dimensional data set, implement a program in a language of your choice that supports the pointer data structure, to construct a *k*-d tree for the same.

2) Write a program that will undertake a range search of all elements lying within limits *a, b* along a dimension *i* of the multidimensional data set, represented as a *k*-d tree.

For example, given the data set {(7, 5), (4, 2), (6, 8), (1, 4), (3, 5), (2, 4), (3, 7), (9, 1), (6, 6), (5, 1)} represented as a *k*-d tree (*k* = 2), a range search of data elements lying within (*a* = 3, *b* = 7) along dimension *i* = 2 yields {(7, 5), (1, 4), (3, 5), (3, 7), (6, 6)}.

3) Implement a treap and demonstrate the insert, delete and find operations on it.

16

Searching

16.1. Introduction

Search (or *searching*) is a commonplace occurrence in everyday life. Searching for a book in the library, searching for a subscriber's telephone number in the telephone directory and searching for one's name in the electoral rolls are some examples.

In the discipline of computer science, the problem of search has assumed enormous significance. It spans a variety of applications or rather disciplines, beginning from searching for a key in a list of data elements to searching for a solution to a complex problem in its *search space* amidst constraints. Innumerable problems exist where one searches for patterns – images, voice, text, hypertext, photographs and so forth – in a repository of data or patterns, for the solution of the problems concerned. A variety of search algorithms and procedures appropriate to the problem and the associated discipline exist in the literature.

In this chapter, we enumerate search algorithms pertaining to the problem of looking for a key K in a list of data elements. When the list of data elements is represented as a linear list, the search procedures of *linear search* or *sequential search*, *transpose sequential search*, *interpolation search*, *binary search* and *Fibonacci search* are applicable.

When the list of data elements is represented using nonlinear data structures such as binary search trees or AVL trees or B trees and so forth, the appropriate *tree search* techniques unique to the data structure representation may be applied.

Hash tables also promote efficient searching. Search techniques such as *breadth first search* and *depth first search* are applicable on graph data structures. In the case of data representing an index of a file or a group of ordered elements, *indexed sequential search* may be employed. This chapter discusses all the above-mentioned search procedures.

16.2. Linear search

A *linear search* or *sequential search* is one where a key K is searched for in a linear list L of data elements. The list L is commonly represented using a sequential data structure such as an array. If L is ordered then the search is said to be an *ordered linear search* and if L is unordered then it is said to be *unordered linear search*.

16.2.1. Ordered linear search

Let $L = \{K_1, K_2, K_3, \ldots K_n\}$, $K_1 < K_2 < \ldots K_n$ be the list of ordered elements. To search for a key K in the list L, we undertake a linear search comparing K with each of the K_i. So long as $K > K_i$ comparing K with the data elements of the list L progresses. However, if $K \leq K_i$, then if $K = K_i$ the search is done, otherwise the search is unsuccessful, implying K does not exist in the list L. It is easy to see how ordering the elements renders the search process to be efficient.

Algorithm 16.1 illustrates the working of ordered linear search.

EXAMPLE 16.1.–

Consider an ordered list of elements $L[0:5] = \{16, 18, 56, 78, 90, 100\}$. Let us search for the key $K = 78$. Since K is greater than 16, 18, and 56, the search terminates at the fourth element when $K \leq (L[3] = 78)$ is true. At this point, since $K = L[3] = 78$, the search is successfully done. However in the case of searching for key $K = 67$, the search progresses until the condition $K \leq (L[3] = 78)$ is reached. At this point, since $K \neq L[3]$, we deem the search to be unsuccessful.

Ordered linear search reports a time complexity of $O(n)$ in the worst case and $O(1)$ in the best case, in terms of key comparisons. However, it is essential that the elements are ordered before the search process is undertaken.

16.2.2. Unordered linear search

In this search, a key K is looked for in an unordered linear list $L = \{K_1, K_2, K_3, \ldots K_n\}$ of data elements. The method obviously of the "brute force" kind, merely calls for a sequential search down the list looking for the key K.

Algorithm 16.2 illustrates the working of the unordered linear search.

EXAMPLE 16.2.–

Consider an unordered list $L[0:5]$ = {23, 14, 98, 45, 67, 53} of data elements. Let us search for the key K = 53. Obviously, the search progresses down the list comparing key K with each of the elements in the list until it finds it as the last element in the list. In the case of searching for the key K = 110, the search progresses but falls off the list thereby deeming it to be an unsuccessful search.

Unordered linear search reports a worst case complexity of $O(n)$ and a best case complexity of $O(1)$ in terms of key comparisons. However, its average case performance in terms of key comparisons can only be inferior to that of ordered linear search.

```
procedure LINEAR_SEARCH_ORDERED(L, n, K)

/*L[0:n-1] is a linear ordered list of data elements.  K
is the key to be searched for in the list. In case of
unsuccessful search,  the procedure prints the message
"KEY not found" otherwise prints "KEY found" and returns
the index i*/


    i = 0;
    while (( i < n) and (K > L[i])) do  /* search for
                                      X down the list*/
        i = i + 1;

    endwhile

    if ( K = L[i])

    then {print (" KEY found");

            return (i);}        /*  Key K found.
                                    Return index i */
    else

            print (" KEY not found");
end LINEAR_SEARCH_ORDERED.
```

Algorithm 16.1. *Procedure for ordered linear search*

procedure LINEAR_SEARCH_UNORDERED(L, n, K)

*/*L[0:n-1] is a linear unordered list of data elements.
K is the key to be searched for in the list. In case of
unsuccessful search, the procedure prints the message
"KEY not found" otherwise prints "KEY found" and returns
the index i*/*

```
  i = 0;
  while (( i < n) and ( L[i]≠K)) do   /* search for
                                  X down the list*/
    i = i + 1;
  endwhile
  if ( L[i]= K)
  then {print (" KEY found");
        return (i);}              /* Key K found.
                                  Return index i */
  else
        print (" KEY not found");
end LINEAR_SEARCH_UNORDERED.
```

Algorithm 16.2. *Procedure for unordered linear search*

16.3. Transpose sequential search

Also known as ***self organizing sequential search***, *transpose sequential search* searches a list of data items for a key, checking itself against the data items one at a time in a sequence. If the key is found, then it is swapped with its predecessor and the search is termed successful. The swapping of the search key with its predecessor, once it is found, favors a faster search when one repeatedly looks for the key. The more frequently one looks for a specific key in a list, the faster the retrievals take place in transpose sequential search since the found key moves towards the beginning of the list with every retrieval operation. Thus, a transpose sequential search is most successful when a few data items are repeatedly looked for in a list.

Algorithm 16.3 illustrates the working of transpose sequential search.

procedure TRANSPOSE_SEQUENTIAL SEARCH(L, n, K)

/ L[0:n-1] is a linear unordered list of data elements.
K is the key to be searched for in the list. In case of
unsuccessful search, the procedure prints the message
"KEY not found" otherwise prints "KEY found" and swaps
the key with its predecessor in the list */*

```
i = 0;
while (( i < n) and ( L[i]≠K)) do      /*search for
                                    X down the list*/
    i = i + 1;
endwhile

if (L[i]= K)
then
      {print (" KEY found"); /* key K found*/
      swap(L[i], L[i-1]);}    /* swap key with its
                            predecessor in the list*/
  else
      print (" KEY not found");

end TRANSPOSE_SEQUENTIAL SEARCH.
```

Algorithm 16.3. *Procedure for transpose sequential search*

EXAMPLE 16.3.–

Consider an unordered list $L = \{34, 21, 89, 45, 12, 90, 76, 62\}$ of data elements. Let us search for the following elements in the order of their appearance:

90, 89, 90, 21, 90, 90

Search key	List L before search	Number of element comparisons made during the search	List L after search
90	{34, 21, 89, 45, 12, 90, 76, 62}	6	{34, 21, 89, 45, **90, 12**, 76, 62}
89	{34, 21, 89, 45, 90, 12, 76, 62}	3	{34, **89, 21**, 45, 90, 12, 76, 62}
90	{34, 89, 21, 45, 90, 12, 76, 62}	5	{34, 89, 21, **90, 45**, 12, 76, 62}
21	{34, 89, 21, 90, 45, 12, 76, 62}	3	{34, **21, 89**, 90, 45, 12, 76, 62}
90	{34, 21, 89, 90, 45, 12, 76, 62}	4	{34, 21, **90, 89**, 45, 12, 76, 62}
90	{34, 21, 90, 89, 45, 12, 76, 62}	3	{34, **90, 21**, 89, 45, 12, 76, 62}

Table 16.1. *Transpose sequential search of {90, 89, 90, 21, 90, 90} in the list L= {34, 21, 89, 45, 12, 90, 76, 62}*

Transpose sequential search proceeds to find each key by the usual process of checking it against each element of L one at a time. However, once the key is found it is swapped with its predecessor in the list. Table 16.1 illustrates the number of comparisons made for each key during its search. The list L before and after the search operation are also illustrated in the table. The swapped elements in the list L after the search key is found is shown in bold. Observe how the number of comparisons made for the retrieval of 90 which is repeatedly looked for in the search list, decreases with each search operation.

The worst case complexity in terms of comparisons for finding a specific key in the list L is $O(n)$. In the case of repeated searches for the same key, the best case would be $O(1)$.

16.4. Interpolation search

Some search methods employed in every day life can be interesting. For example, when one looks for the word "beatitude" in the dictionary, it is quite common for one to turn over pages occurring at the beginning of the dictionary, and when one looks for "tranquility", to turn over pages occurring towards the end of the dictionary. Also, it needs to be observed how during the search we turn sheaves of pages back and forth, if the word that is looked for occurs before or beyond the page that has just been turned. In fact, one may look askance at anybody who 'dares' to undertake sequential search to look for "beatitude" or "tranquility" in a dictionary!

Interpolation search is based on this principle of attempting to look for a key in a list of elements, by comparing the key with specific elements at "calculated" positions and ensuring if the key occurs "before" it or "after" it until either the key is found or not found. The list of elements *must be ordered* and we assume that they are uniformly distributed with respect to requests.

Let us suppose we are searching for a key K in a list $L = \{K_1, K_2, K_3, \ldots K_n\}$, $K_1 < K_2 < \ldots K_n$ of numerical elements. When it is known that K lies between K_{low} and K_{high}, that is, $K_{low} < K < K_{high}$, then the next element that is to be probed for key comparison is chosen to be the one that lies $\frac{(K - K_{low})}{(K_{high} - K_{low})}$ of the way between K_{low} and K_{high}. It is this consideration that has made the search be termed interpolation search.

During the implementation of the search procedure, the next element to be probed in a sub list $\{K_i, K_{i+1}, K_{i+2}, \ldots K_j\}$ for comparison against the key K is given by K_{mid} where *mid* is given by $mid = i + (j - i).\frac{(K - K_i)}{(K_j - K_i)}$. The key comparison results in any one of the following cases:

If $(K = K_{mid})$ then the search is done.

If $(K < K_{mid})$ then continue the search in the sublist $\{K_i, K_{i+1}, K_{i+2}, \ldots K_{mid-1}\}$.

If $(K > K_{mid})$ then continue the search in the sublist $\{K_{mid+1}, K_{mid+2}, K_{mid+3}, \ldots K_j\}$.

Algorithm 16.4 illustrates the interpolation search procedure.

```
procedure INTERPOLATION_SEARCH(L, n, K)
/*L[1:n] is a linear ordered list of data elements.   K
is the key to be searched for in the list. In case of
unsuccessful search,   the procedure prints the message
"KEY not found" otherwise prints "KEY found". */
    i = 1;
    j = n;

    if ( K < L[i]) or (K > L[j])
    then { print("Key not found");
           exit();}        /* if the key K does not
                              lie within the list then
                              print "key not found"*/
    found = false;
    while (( i ≤ j) and (found = false))do
```
$$mid = i + (j - i) . \frac{(K - L[i])}{(L[j] - L[i])};$$
```
        case
          :K = L[mid]:   { found = true;
                           print ("Key found");}
          :K < L[mid]:   j = mid -1;
          :K > L[mid]:   i = mid + 1;

        endcase

    endwhile

    if (found = false)
    then
        print (" Key not found"); /*Key K not found
                                     in the list L*/
end INTERPOLATION_SEARCH.
```

Algorithm 16.4. *Procedure for interpolation search*

EXAMPLE 16.4.–

Consider a list $L = \{24, 56, 67, 78, 79, 89, 90, 95, 99\}$ of ordered numerical elements. Let us search for the set of keys $\{67, 45\}$. Table 16.2 illustrates the trace of Algorithm 16.4 for the set of keys. The algorithm proceeds with its search since both the keys lie within the list.

Search key K	i	j	found	mid	$K \begin{array}{c} < \\ = \\ > \end{array} L[mid]$
67	1	9	false	$1 + (9 - 1).\dfrac{(67 - 24)}{(99 - 24)} = \lfloor 5.58 \rfloor$ $= 5$	$67 < (L[5] = 79)$
	1	4	false	3	$67 = (L[3] = 67)$
			true	Key found	
45	1	9	false	$1 + (9 - 1).\dfrac{(45 - 24)}{(99 - 24)} = \lfloor 3.24 \rfloor$ $= 3$	$45 < (L[3] = 67)$
	1	2	false	1	$45 > (L[1] = 24)$
	2	2	false	2	$45 < (L[2] = 56)$
	2	1	false	Key not found	

Table 16.2. Trace of Algorithm 16.4
during the search for keys 67 and 45

In the case of key 67, the search was successful. However in the case of key 45, as can be observed in the last row of the table, the condition $(i \leq j)$, that is, $(2 \leq 1)$ failed in the **while** loop of the algorithm and hence the search terminates signaling "Key not found".

The worst case complexity of interpolation search is $O(n)$. However, on average the search records a brilliant $O(log_2\ log_2\ n)$ complexity.

16.5. Binary search

In the previous section we discussed interpolation search which works on ordered lists and reports an average case complexity of $O(log_2\ log_2\ n)$. Another efficient search technique that operates on ordered lists is the **binary search** also known as **logarithmic search** or **bisection**.

A binary search searches for a key K in an ordered list $L = \{K_1, K_2, K_3, \ldots K_n\}$, $K_1 < K_2 < \ldots K_n$ of data elements, by halving the search list with each comparison until the key is either found or not found. The key K is first compared with the median element of the list, for example, K_{mid}. For a sublist $\{K_i, K_{i+1}, K_{i+2}, \ldots K_j\}$, K_{mid} is obtained as the key occurring at the position mid which is computed as $mid = \left\lfloor \frac{(i+j)}{2} \right\rfloor$. The comparison of K with K_{mid} yields the following cases:

If $(K = K_{mid})$ then the binary search is done.

If $(K < K_{mid})$ then continue binary search in the sub list $\{K_i, K_{i+1}, K_{i+2}, \ldots K_{mid-1}\}$.

If $(K > K_{mid})$ then continue binary search in the sub list $\{K_{mid+1}, K_{mid+2}, K_{mid+3}, \ldots K_j\}$.

During the search process, each comparison of key K with K_{mid} of the respective sub lists results in the halving of the list. In other words, with each comparison the search space is reduced to half its original length. It is this characteristic that renders the search process efficient. Contrast this with a sequential list where the entire list is involved in the search!

Binary search adopts the **Divide and Conquer** method of algorithm design. Divide and Conquer is an algorithm design technique where to solve a given problem, the problem is first recursively divided (*Divide*) into sub problems (smaller problem instances). The sub problems that are small enough are easily solved (*Conquer*) and the solutions are combined to obtain the solution to the whole problem. Divide and Conquer has turned out to be a successful algorithm design technique with regard to many problems. Chapter 19 details the Divide and Conquer method of algorithm design.

In the case of binary search, the divide-and-conquer aspect of the technique breaks the list (problem) into two sub lists (sub problems). However, the key is searched for only in one of the sub lists hence with every division a portion of the list gets discounted.

Algorithm 16.5 illustrates a recursive procedure for binary search.

16.5.1. Decision tree for binary search

The binary search for a key K in the ordered list $L = \{K_1, K_2, K_3, \ldots K_n\}$, $K_1 < K_2 < \ldots K_n$ traces a **binary decision tree**. Figure 16.1 illustrates the decision tree for

$n = 15$. The first element to be compared with K in the list $L = \{K_1, K_2, K_3, \ldots K_{15}\}$ is K_8, which becomes the root of the decision tree. If $K < K_8$ then the next element to be compared is K_4, which is the left child of the decision tree. For the other cases of comparisons, it is easy to trace the tree by making use of the following characteristics:

i) The indexes of the left and the right child nodes differ by the same amount from that of the parent node

For example, in the decision tree shown in Figure 16.1 the left and right child nodes of the node K_{12}, for example, K_{10} and K_{14} differ from their parent key index by the same amount.

This characteristic renders the search process to be ***uniform*** and therefore binary search is also termed as ***uniform binary search***.

ii) For n elements where $n = 2^t - 1$, the difference in the indexes of a parent node and its child nodes follows the sequence $2^0, 2^1, 2^{2\cdots}$ from the leaf upwards.

For example, in Figure 16.1 where $n = 15 = 2^4\text{-}1$, the difference in index of all the leaf nodes from their respective parent nodes is 2^0. The difference in index of all the nodes in level 3 from their respective parent nodes is 2^1 and so on.

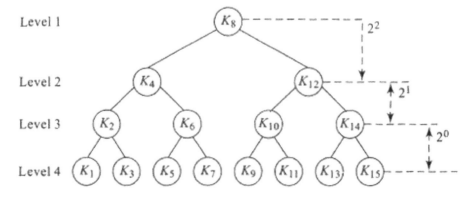

Figure 16.1. *Decision tree for binary search*

EXAMPLE 16.5.–

Consider an ordered list $L = \{K_1, K_2, K_3, \ldots K_{15}\} = \{12, 21, 34, 38, 45, 49, 67, 69, 78, 79, 82, 87, 93, 97, 99\}$. Let us search for the key $K = 21$ in the list L. The search process is illustrated in Figure 16.2. K is first compared with $K_{mid} = K_{\lfloor\frac{1+15}{2}\rfloor} = K_8 = 69$.

Since $K < K_{mid}$, the search continues in the sublist {12, 21, 34, 38, 45, 49, 67}. Now, K is compared with $K_{mid} = K_{\lfloor\frac{1+7}{2}\rfloor} = K_4 = 38$. Again $K < K_{mid}$, shrinks the search list to {12, 21, 34}. Now finally when K is compared with $K_{mid} = K_{\lfloor\frac{1+3}{2}\rfloor} = K_2 = 21$, the search is done. Thus, in three comparisons we are able to search for the key $K = 21$.

Search Key K : 21

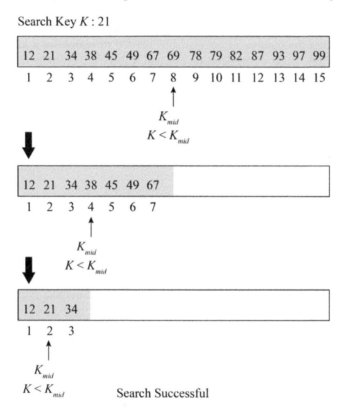

Figure 16.2. *Binary search process (Example 16.5)*

Let us now search for the key $K = 75$. Proceeding in a similar manner, K is first compared with $K_8 = 69$. Since $K > K_8$, the search list is reduced to {78, 79, 82, 87, 93, 97, 99}. Now $K < (K_{12} = 87)$, hence the search list is reduced further to {78, 79, 82}. Comparing K with K_{10} reduces the search list to {78} which obviously yields the search to be unsuccessful.

In the case of Algorithm 16.5, at this step of the search, the recursive call to BINARY_SEARCH would have both low = high = 9, resulting in *mid* = 9. Comparing K with K_{mid} results in the call to binary_search(L, 9, 8, K). Since (low > high) condition is satisfied, the algorithm terminates with the 'Key not found' message.

Considering the decision tree associated with binary search, it is easy to see that in the worst case the number of comparisons needed to search for a key would be determined by the height of the decision tree and is therefore given by $O(log_2 n)$.

16.6. Fibonacci search

The *Fibonacci number sequence* is given by {0, 1, 1, 2, 3, 5, 8, 13, 21,.....} and is generated by the following recurrence relation:

$$F_0 = 0$$
$$F_1 = 1$$
$$F_i = F_{i-1} + F_{i-2}$$

It is interesting to note that the Fibonacci sequence finds an application in a search technique termed *Fibonacci search*. While binary search selects the median of the sub list as its next element for comparison, the Fibonacci search determines the next element of comparison as dictated by the Fibonacci number sequence.

Fibonacci search works only on ordered lists and for convenience of description we assume that the number of elements in the list is one less than a Fibonacci number, that is, $n = F_k - 1$. It is easy to follow Fibonacci search once the decision tree is traced, which otherwise may look mysterious!

procedure binary_search(L, low, high, K)

```
/* L[low:high] is a linear ordered sublist of data
elements. Initially low is set to 1 and high to n.     K
is the key to be searched in the list. */

  if ( low > high)
  then   { binary_search =0;
           print("Key not found");
           exit();}              /*  key K  not found*/
```

```
    else
    {
        mid = ⌊low+high/2⌋;
        case
          : K = L[mid] : {  print ("Key found");
                            binary_search = mid;
                            return L[mid] ;}

          : K < L[mid] :  binary_search =
                  binary_search(L, low, mid -1, K);

          : K > L[mid] :    binary_search =
                  binary_search(L, mid +1, high, K);

        endcase
    }
end binary_search.
```

$$mid = \left\lfloor \frac{low+high}{2} \right\rfloor;$$

Algorithm 16.5. *Procedure for binary search*

16.6.1. *Decision tree for Fibonacci search*

The decision tree for Fibonacci search satisfies the following characteristics:

If we consider a grandparent, parent and its child nodes and if the difference in index between the grandparent and the parent is F_k then:

i) if the parent is a left child node then the difference in index between the parent and its child nodes is F_{k-1}, whereas;

ii) if the parent is a right child node then the difference in index between the parent and the child nodes is F_{k-2}.

Let us consider an ordered list $L = \{K_1, K_2, K_3, \ldots K_n\}$, $K_1 < K_2 < \ldots K_n$ where $n = F_k - 1$. The Fibonacci search decision tree for $n = 20$ where $20 = (F_8 - 1)$ is shown in Figure 16.3.

The root of the decision tree which is the first element in the list to be compared with key K during the search is that key K_i whose index i is the closest Fibonacci sequence number to n. In the case of $n = 20$, K_{13} is the root since the closest Fibonacci number to $n = 20$ is 13.

If $(K < K_{13})$ then the next key to be compared is K_8. If again $(K < K_8)$ then it would be K_5 and so on. Now it is easy to determine the other decision nodes making use of the characteristics mentioned above. Since child nodes differ from their parent by the same amount, it is easy to see that the right child of K_{13} should be K_{18} and that of K_8 should be K_{11} and so on. Consider the grandparent-parent combination, K_8 and K_{11}, respectively, since K_{11} is the right child of its parent and the difference between K_8 and K_{11} is F_4, the same between K_{11} and its two child nodes should be F_2 which is 1. Hence the two child nodes of K_{11} are K_{10} and K_{12}. Similarly, considering the grandparent and parent combination of K_{18} and K_{16} where K_{16} is the left child of its parent and their difference is given by F_3, the two child nodes of K_{16} are given by K_{15} and K_{17} (difference is F_2), respectively.

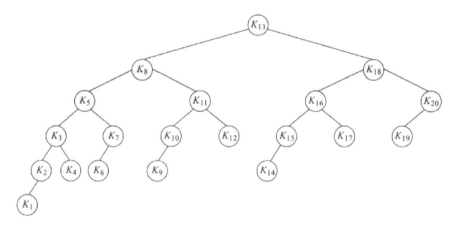

Figure 16.3. *Decision tree*
for Fibonacci search

Algorithm 16.6 illustrates the procedure for Fibonacci search. Here n, the number of data elements is such that:

i) $F_{k+1} > (n+1)$; and

ii) $F_k + m = (n +1)$ for some $m \geq 0$, where F_{k+1} and F_k are two consecutive Fibonacci numbers.

procedure FIBONACCI_SEARCH(L, n, K)

/* L[1:n] is a linear ordered (non decreasing) list of data elements. n is such that $F_{k+1} > (n+1)$. Also, $F_k + m = (n+1)$. K is the key to be searched in the list. */

Obtain the largest Fibonacci number F_k closest to n+1;

p = F_{k-1};
q = F_{k-2};
r = F_{k-3};
m = (n+1) - (p+q);

if (K > L[p]) **then** p = p+m;
found = **false**;

while ((p≠0) **and** (**not** found)) **do**

    case
       : K = L[p] : {**print** ("key found");
                   found = **true**;} */* key found*/*

      : K < L[p] : **if** (r = 0) **then** p = 0
               else
                   {p = p-r;
                    t = q;
                    q = r;
                    r = t-r;}

      : K > L[p] : **if** (q = 1) **then** p = 0
               else {p = p+r;
                    q = q-r;
                    r = r-q}
    endcase

  endwhile

  if (found = **false**) **then** **print** ("key not found");
end FIBONACCI_SEARCH.

Algorithm 16.6. *Procedure for Fibonacci search*

EXAMPLE 16.6.–

Let us search for the key $K = 434$ in the ordered list $L = \{2, 4, 8, 9, 17, 36, 44, 55, 81, 84, 94, 116, 221, 256, 302, 356, 396, 401, 434, 536\}$. Here n the number of elements is such that (i) $F_9 > (n+1)$ and (ii) $F_8 + m = (n+1)$ where $m = 0$ and $n = 20$.

The algorithm for Fibonacci search first obtains the largest Fibonacci number closest to $n+1$, that is, F_8 in this case. It compares $K = 434$ with the data element with index F_7, that is, $L[13] = 221$. Since $K > L[13]$, the search list is reduced to $L[14: 20] = \{256, 302, 356, 396, 401, 434, 536\}$. Now K compares itself with $L[18] = 401$. Since $K > L[18]$ the search list is further reduced to $L[19:20] = \{434, 536\}$. Now K is compared with $L[20] = 536$. Since $K < L[20]$ is true it results in the search list $\{434\}$ which when searched yields the search key. The key is successfully found.

Following a similar procedure, searching for 66 in the list yields an unsuccessful search.

The detailed trace of Algorithm 16.6 for the search keys 434 and 66 is shown in Table 16.3.

An advantage of Fibonacci search over binary search is that while binary search involves division which is computationally expensive, during the selection of the next element for key comparison, Fibonacci search involves only addition and subtraction.

16.7. Skip list search

Skip lists, invented in 1990 by Bill Pugh (Pugh 1990), are a good data structure for a *dictionary* ADT, which supports the operations of insert, delete and search. An ordered list of keys represented as a linked list would require $O(n)$ time on an average, while searching for a key K. The search proceeds sequentially from the beginning of the list following the links one after another, until key K is found in the event of a successful search. Thus, there is no provision for a search to fast-forward itself, by skipping elements in the list and thereby speeding up search, before it finds key K or otherwise.

Search key K	$K \begin{smallmatrix}<\\=L[p]\\>\end{smallmatrix}$	t	p	q	r	Remarks
434			13	8	5	$n = 20$ $m = 0$ since $F_8 + 0 = n + 1$
	$K > L[13] = 221$		13	8	5	Since $K > L[p]$, $p = p+m$
	$K > L[13] = 221$		18	3	2	
	$K > L[18] = 401$		20	1	1	
	$K < L[20] = 536$	1	19	1	0	
	$K = L[19] = 434$					*Key found*
66			13	8	5	$n = 20$ $m = 0$
	$K < L[13] = 221$	8	8	5	3	
	$K > L[8] = 55$		11	2	1	
	$K < L[11] = 94$	2	10	1	1	
	$K < L[10] = 84$	1	9	1	0	
	$K < L[9] = 81$					Since $(r = 0)$, p is set to 0. *Key not found*

Table 16.3. *Trace of Algorithm 16.6 (FIBONACCI SEARCH)*
for the search keys 434 and 66

Skip lists, on the other hand, build layers of lists above the original list of keys, comprising selective keys from the original list, which act as "express lanes" for the keys in the immediately lower list, while searching for a key K. Each list in the layers has a **header node** and a **sentinel node** to signal the beginning and end of the list and comprises an **ordered** set of selective keys as nodes. The lower most list is the *complete list of ordered keys* in the original list, opening with a head node and ending with a sentinel node.

While searching for a key K in the list of keys, skip list search begins from the head node of the top most layer of the list, moving horizontally across the "express lane" comparing key K with the nodes in the list and stopping at a node whose *next node* has a key value greater than or equal to K. If the next node value equals K then the search is done. If not, the search drops down to the node in the *immediate lower layer* of the list, right underneath its present position, once again moving horizontally through the lower "express lane" looking for a node whose next node is greater than or equal to K. Eventually, if the key K did not match any of the nodes in the higher layers, then following the same principle of dropping down, the search finally reaches the original list of ordered keys in the lowermost layer and after a short sequential search, will find key K if it is successful search or would not find K in the case of unsuccessful search.

If S_0 is the lowest layer comprising the original list of key values $K_1, K_2, K_3, ... K_n$, and $S_1, S_2 ... S_h$ are the higher layers of lists which act as "express lanes", then the *height* of the skip list is h. Also, to favor comparison of node values with key K as the search progresses through the layers, it would be prudent to set the header node and sentinel node values of each list in the layers, to $-\infty$ and $+\infty$, respectively.

The selective nodes in the layers $S_1, S_2 ... S_h$ are *randomly* selected, quite often governed by a probability factor of ½ associated with the flipping of a coin! To build layer S_i, each node entry in layer S_{i-1} after it makes its appearance in layer S_{i-1}, flips a coin as it were and if it is "heads", includes the same node entry in layer S_i as well, and if it is "tails" discards making the entry in layer S_i. The replication of node entries from lower layers to higher layers continues so long as the randomization process continues to flip "heads" for each layer. The moment the randomization process flips "tails" in any one of the layers, the replication of the node entries in the higher layer is stopped.

The skip list therefore can be viewed as a data structure with layers and **towers**, where each tower comprises replicated data entries over layers. In other words, a tower is made up of a single data value that is replicated across layers and therefore has different links to its predecessor and successor in each of the layers. If the lower most layer S_0 had n node entries, then layer S_1 could be *expected* to have $n/2$ node entries, layer S_2 to have $n/2^2$ entries, generalizing, layer i could be expected to have $n/2^i$ node entries. In such a case, the height of the skip list could be expected to be *O(log n)*. The average case time complexity of search in a skip list constructed such as this is, therefore, *O(log n)*.

EXAMPLE 16.7.–

Consider a set of ordered keys $\{K_1, K_2, K_3, ... K_{10}\} = \{$ 27, 38, 41, 49, 53, 62, 76, 80, 88, 97$\}$. Figure 16.4 illustrates a skip list data structure that was constructed for the data list. Observe how the bottom-most layer S_0 holds the original list of data elements, and the subsequent higher layers S_1, S_2 and S_3 hold approximately $n/2^i$ node entries $(i = 1,2,3)$, respectively, after a random selection of entries in their respective lower layers determined by a flipping of a coin, so to say. The header nodes hold a value of $-\infty$ and sentinel nodes a value of $+\infty$ to assist the process of searching through the layers. The towers comprising replicated values of a data entry across layers of the skip list, have been marked out using broken line rectangles. We defer discussing the construction of the skip list for now and focus on the search process.

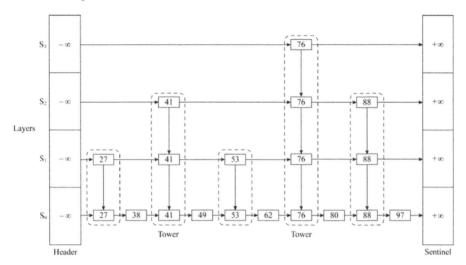

Figure 16.4. *An example skip list with an illustrative structure, for searching a key K*

To search for key $K = 97$, the procedure begins from the header node of layer S_3 and stops at node 76 since the next node which is the sentinel node has a value $+\infty$, which is greater than K. Thus, the search has moved through the S_3 "express lane" skipping all the elements in the list whose value is less than 76. The search now descends to layer S_2 and proceeds horizontally from node 76 until it stops at node 88. The search again descends to layer S_1 and unable to proceed further horizontally stops at node 88 and descends one last time to layer S_0. In layer S_0, it moves horizontally from node 88, undertaking a sequential search and finds key $K = 97$ in the very next node. Thus, had it been an ordinary linked list, searching for key K should have taken 10 comparisons. On the other hand, the given skip list was able to fast track search and retrieve the key in half the number of comparisons.

To search for $K = 53$, the procedure begins from the header node of layer S_3 and stops at the header node since the next node holds a value 76 which is greater than K. The search descends to the layer S_2 and beginning with the header node, moves horizontally until it stops itself at node 41. The search descends to layer S_1 and proceeds to move horizontally from node 41. The next node 53 is equal to key K and hence the search successfully terminates in layer S_1 itself.

16.7.1. *Implementing skip lists*

The skip list diagram shown in Figure 16.4 is only illustrative of its structure. A skip list, in reality, could be implemented using a variety of ways innovated over a linked data structure. A straightforward implementation could call for a multiply-linked data structure to facilitate forward and backward, upward and downward movements. The availability of functions such as **next**(p), **previous**(p), **above**(p) and **below**(p), where p is the current position in the skip list, to undertake forward, backward, upward and downward movements, respectively, can help manage the operations of insert, delete and retrieval on a skip list. Alternate representations could involve opening variable sized nodes for each of the layers or opening nodes with a distinct node structure for the towers in the skip list and so on.

Algorithm 16.7 illustrates the search procedure on a skip list *S* for a key *K*. The algorithm employs functions **next**(p) and **below**(p) to undertake the search.

```
procedure Skiplist_Search (S, K)
/* S  denotes the start position of the skip list and
key(p) denotes the key value of the node at position p */

    position = S;    /* initialize position to
                        start position of the skip list*/

    while below(position) ≠ NIL  do
        position = below(position);
                        /* descend to the lower layer*/

        while K ≥ key(next(position)) do
            if (K = key(next(position)))
            then
                {print("successful search");
                 exit}
              position = next(position);
                        /* traverse horizontally*/
        endwhile

    endwhile

    print( "unsuccessful search");
end Skiplist_Search
```

Algorithm 16.7. *Procedure for skip list search*

16.7.2. *Insert operation in a skip list*

To insert a key K into a skip list S, the procedure begins as if it were trying to search for a key K in the skip list S. Since the search would be unsuccessful, the lower most layer S_0 which holds the original linked list of entries and most importantly the position where the key K needs to be inserted would be automatically arrived at since the condition $K \geq$ `key(next(position))` would have failed at that point. A new node with key K is inserted at that position. However, the problem does not end there.

It needs to be decided if the node K will find a place in the upper layers S_1, S_2, S_3 and so forth, using randomization. Using the analogy of flipping a coin to illustrate randomization, "Heads" could mean insert K in the upper layer and "Tails" could mean discard insertion of key K in the upper layer as well in those above. If K is inserted in a higher layer, the randomization process continues to decide if it can be inserted in the next higher layer and so on, until a decision based on "Tails" discards its insertion in the next layer and above, once and for all. As can be observed, successive insertions of a key K in the upper layers of the skip list beginning with S_0, in the event of a sequence of "Heads" decisions, results in building a tower for key K. The average time complexity of an insert operation in a skip list is $O(log\ n)$.

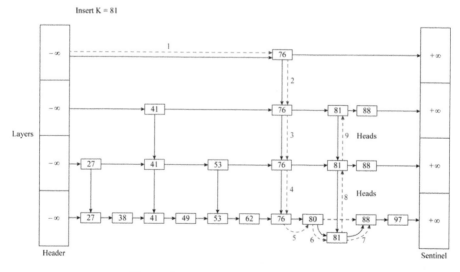

Figure 16.5. *Insertion of key K = 81 in the skip list shown in Figure 16.4*

EXAMPLE 16.8.–

Figure 16.5 illustrates the insertion of key $K = 81$ in the skip list illustrated in Figure 16.4. The procedure for insertion proceeds as if it were trying to search for key K beginning with layer S_3 and eventually descends to S_0 and inserts key $K = 81$ as the successor of node 80. Assuming that the randomization decisions for inserting the key in layers S_1 and S_2 met with "Heads", the tower for key $K = 81$ gets formed. The trail of operations carried out during the insertion is shown in broken lines in the figure and has been numbered to show the sequence of operations. While sequence numbers 1–5 of the operations illustrate descending the skip list and fixing the position where the new node is to be inserted, sequence numbers 6 and 7 illustrate inserting the new node for key $K = 81$ and finally the sequence numbers 8 and 9 show the building of the tower for key $K = 81$ assuming that the randomization process triggered "Heads" for layers S_1 and S_2 and "Tails" for S_3.

16.7.3. Delete operation in a skip list

The delete operation on a skip list is easier than an insert operation. To delete key K, which let us assume is available in the skip list, the procedure proceeds as if it were searching for key K. Key K may be found in the top most layer of its tower if such a tower was built during the insertion of key K or may only be found in layer S_0 as a node, in the absence of a tower.

In the case of a tower existing for key K, deletion only means deleting each of the nodes in its tower while moving downwards and appropriately resetting the links of its predecessor nodes to point to its successor nodes in all the layers covered by the tower. In the absence of a tower, it merely calls for deleting a single node in layer S_0 and appropriately resetting the link of its predecessor node to point to its successor node. The average time complexity of a delete operation in a skip list is $O(log\ n)$.

EXAMPLE 16.9.–

Figure 16.6 illustrates the deletion of key 41 from the skip list shown in Figure 16.4. The delete process begins as if it were searching for key $K = 41$ and descends to layer S_2 only to find that key $K = 41$ is in its tower. The procedure deletes node 41 in layer S_2 while redirecting its predecessor (header) to point to its successor which is node 76. The procedure now moves down the tower deleting all the replicative nodes in the respective layers and appropriately redirecting the links of the respective predecessor nodes to point to the respective successor nodes, as shown in the figure.

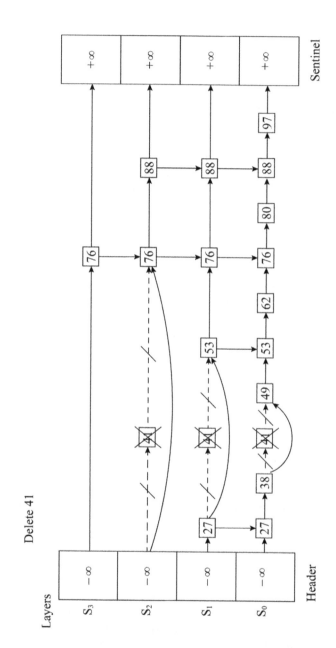

Figure 16.6. *Deletion of key K = 41 from the skip list shown in Figure 16.4*

16.8. Other search techniques

16.8.1. *Tree search*

The tree data structures of AVL trees (section 10.3 of Chapter 10, Volume 2), *m*-way search trees, B trees and tries (Chapter 11, Volume 2), Red-Black trees (section 12.1 of Chapter 12, Volume 2) and so forth, are also candidates for the solution of search-related problems. The inherent search operation that each of these data structures support can be employed for the problem of searching.

The techniques of sequential search, interpolation search, binary search and Fibonacci search are primarily employed for files or groups of records or data elements that can be accommodated within the high speed internal memory of the computer. Hence, these techniques are commonly referred to as *internal searching* methods. On the other hand, when the file size is too large to be accommodated within the memory of the computer one has to take recourse to external storage devices such as disks or drums to store the file (Chapter 14). In such cases when a search operation for a key needs to be undertaken, the process involves searching through blocks of storage spanning across storage areas. Adopting internal searching methods for these cases would be grossly inefficient. The search techniques as emphasized by *m*-way search trees, B trees, tries and so on are suitable for such a scenario. Hence, these search techniques are referred to as *external searching* methods.

16.8.2. *Graph search*

The graph data structure and its traversal techniques of Breadth first traversal and Depth first traversal (section 9.4 of Chapter 9, Volume 2) can also be employed for search-related problems. If the search space is represented as a graph and the problem involves searching for a key *K* which is a node in the graph, any of the two traversals may be undertaken on the graph to look for the key. In such a case we term the traversal techniques as Breadth first search (see illustrative problem 16.6) and Depth first search (see illustrative problem 16.7).

16.8.3. *Indexed sequential search*

The indexed sequential search (section 14.7 of Chapter 14) is a successful search technique applicable on files that are too large to be accommodated in the internal memory of the computer. Also known as the *Indexed Sequential Access Method* (*ISAM*), the search procedure and its variants have been successfully applied to database systems.

Considering the fact that the search technique is commonly used on databases or files which span several blocks of storage areas, the technique could be deemed an external searching technique. To search for a key one needs to look into the index to obtain the storage block where the associated group of records or elements are available. Once the block is retrieved, the retrieval of the record represented by the key merely reduces to a sequential search within the block of records for the key.

Summary

– The problem of search involves retrieving a key from a list of data elements. In the case of a successful retrieval the search is deemed to be successful, otherwise unsuccessful.

– The search techniques that work on lists or files that can be accommodated within the internal memory of the computer are called internal searching methods, otherwise they are called as external searching methods.

– Sequential search involves looking for a key in a list L which may or may not be ordered. However, an ordered sequential search is more efficient than its unordered counterpart.

– A transpose sequential search sequentially searches for a key in a list but swaps it with the predecessor, once it is found. This enables efficient search of keys that are repeatedly looked for in a list.

– Interpolation search imitates the kind of search process that one employs while referring to a dictionary. The search key is compared with data elements at "calculated positions" and the process progresses based on whether the key occurs before or after it. However, it is essential that the list is ordered.

– Binary search is a successful and efficient search technique that works on ordered lists. The search key is compared with the element at the median of the list. Based on whether the key occurs before or after it, the search list is reduced and the search process continues in a similar fashion in the sub list.

– Fibonacci search works on ordered lists and employs the Fibonacci number sequence and its characteristics to search through the list.

– Skip lists are randomized and layered data structures that undertake search by skipping data elements through the list.

– Tree data structures, for example, AVL trees, tries, m-way search trees, B trees and so forth, and graphs also find applications in search-related problems. Indexed sequential search is a popular search technique employed in the management of files and databases.

16.9. Illustrative problems

PROBLEM 16.1.–

For the list CHANNELS = {AXN, ZEE, CNBC, CNN, DDN HBO, GOD, FAS, R, SONY, CAF, NGE, BBC, PRO} trace transpose sequential search for the elements in the list SELECT_CHANNEL = {DDN, R, DDN, PRO, DDN, R}. Obtain the number of comparisons made during the search for each of the elements in the list SELECT_CHANNEL.

Solution:

The trace of transpose sequential search for the search of elements in the list SELECT_CHANNEL over the list CHANNELS is presented in the following table:

Search key	List L before search	Number of element comparisons made during the search	List L after search
DDN	{AXN, ZEE, CNBC, CNN, DDN, HBO, GOD, FAS, R, SONY, CAF, NGE, BBC, PRO}	5	{AXN, ZEE, CNBC, DDN, CNN, HBO, GOD, FAS, R, SONY, CAF, NGE, BBC, PRO}
R	{AXN, ZEE, CNBC, DDN, CNN, HBO, GOD, FAS, R, SONY, CAF, NGE, BBC, PRO}	9	{AXN, ZEE, CNBC, DDN, CNN, HBO, GOD, R, FAS, SONY, CAF, NGE, BBC, PRO}
DDN	{AXN, ZEE, CNBC, DDN, CNN, HBO, GOD, R, FAS, SONY, CAF, NGE, BBC, PRO}	4	{AXN, ZEE, DDN, CNBC, CNN, HBO, GOD, R, FAS, SONY, CAF, NGE, BBC, PRO}
PRO	{AXN, ZEE, DDN, CNBC, CNN, HBO, GOD, R, FAS, SONY, CAF, NGE, BBC, PRO}	14	{AXN, ZEE, DDN, CNBC, CNN, HBO, GOD, R, FAS, SONY, CAF, NGE, PRO, BBC}
DDN	{AXN, ZEE, DDN, CNBC, CNN, HBO, GOD, R, FAS, SONY, CAF, NGE, PRO, BBC}	3	{AXN, DDN, ZEE, CNBC, CNN, HBO, GOD, R, FAS, SONY, CAF, NGE, PRO, BBC}

R	{AXN, DDN, ZEE, CNBC, CNN, HBO, GOD, R, FAS, SONY, CAF, NGE, PRO, BBC}	8	{AXN, DDN, ZEE, CNBC, CNN, HBO, R, GOD, FAS, SONY, CAF, NGE, PRO, BBC}

PROBLEM 16.2.–

For the ordered list L = {B, D, F, G, H, I, K, L, M, N, O, P, Q, T, U, V, W, X, Y, Z} undertake interpolation search (trace of Algorithm 16.4) for keys H and Y. Make use of the respective alphabetical sequence number for the keys, during the computation of the interpolation function.

Solution:

The table given below illustrates the trace of the algorithm during the search for keys H and Y.

Search key K	i	j	mid	$< $ $K = L[mid]$ $>$
H	1	20	$1 + (20 - 1).\dfrac{(8 - 2)}{(26 - 2)} = \lfloor 5.75 \rfloor = 5$	$H = (L[5] = H)$ **Key found**
Y	1	20	$1 + (20 - 1).\dfrac{(25 - 2)}{(26 - 2)} = \lfloor 19.20 \rfloor = 19$	$Y = (L[19] = Y)$ **Key found**

PROBLEM 16.3.–

For the ordered list L and the search keys given in illustrative problem 16.2, trace the steps of binary search during the search process.

Solution:

The binary search processes for the search keys H and Y over the list L are shown in Figure P16.3. The median of the list (*mid*) during each step of the search process and the key comparisons made are also shown. While H calls for only two key comparisons, Y calls for four key comparisons.

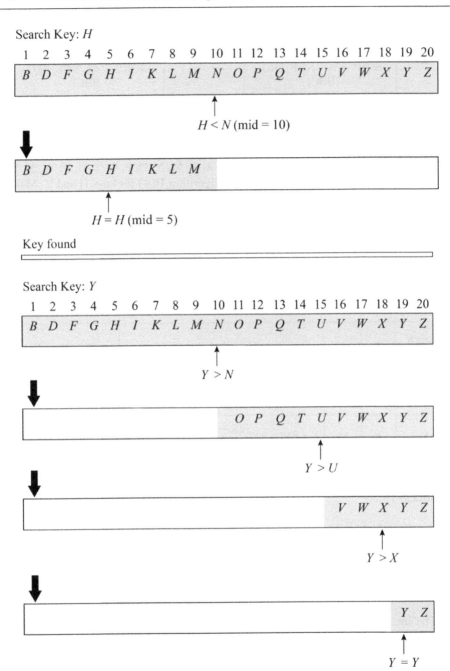

Figure P16.3. *Trace of binary search for the ordered list L and search keys given in illustrative problem 16.2*

PROBLEM 16.4.–

For the ordered list L shown in illustrative problem 16.2, trace the steps of binary search for the search key R.

Solution:

The steps of the binary search process for the search key R is shown in Figure P16.4. The median of the list during each step and the key comparisons made are shown in the figure. The search is deemed unsuccessful.

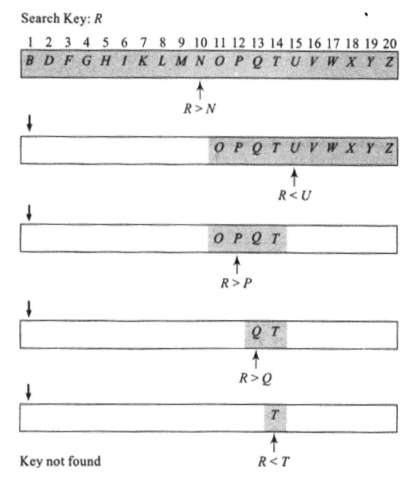

Figure P16.4. *Trace of binary search for the ordered list L in illustrative problem 16.2 and search key R*

PROBLEM 16.5.–

Given the ordered list $L = \{2, 4, 8, 9, 17, 36, 44, 55, 65, 100\}$ trace the steps of the Fibonacci search algorithm (Algorithm 16.6) for the search key 100.

Solution:

The number of data elements in the list L is $n = 10$ and n is such that $F_7 > (n+1)$ and $F_6 + m = (n+1)$. Here, F_7 and F_6 are the two consecutive Fibonacci numbers between which n lies and m is obviously 3. The trace of the Fibonacci search is shown below:

Search key K	< $K = L[p]$ >	t	p	q	r	Remarks
			5	3	2	$n = 10$ $m = 3$
100	$K > L[5] = 17$		$5 + 3 = 8$	3	2	Since $K > L[p]$, $p = p + m$
	$K > L[8] = 55$		10	1	1	
	$K = L[10] = 100$	Key found				

PROBLEM 16.6.–

For the undirected graph G shown in Example 9.1 (Figure 9.26 of Chapter 9, Volume 2) and reproduced here for convenience, undertake Breadth first search for the key 9, by refining the Breadth first traversal algorithm (Algorithm 9.1).

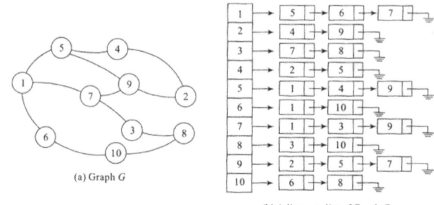

(a) Graph G

(b) Adjacency list of Graph G

Solution:

The Breadth first search procedure is derived from Algorithm 9.1 **procedure** BFT(s) (Chapter 9, Volume 2), by replacing the procedure parameters as **procedure** BFT(s, *K*) where *K* is the search key and s is the start node of the graph.

Also, the statement **print**(s) is replaced by:

if (s = *K*) **then** { **print**("key found"); **exit**();}.

Unsuccessful searches may be trapped by including the statement:

if EMPTY_QUEUE(Q) **then print**("key not found");

soon after the **while** loop in **procedure** BFT(s, *K*).

The trace of the Breadth first search procedure for the search key 9 is shown below:

Search key *K*	Current vertex	Queue *Q*	Status of the visited flag (0/1) of the vertices (1-10) of graph *G*									
	1 (start vertex)	1	1 2 3 4 5 6 7 8 9 10 [1 0 0 0 0 0 0 0 0 0]									
	1	5 6 7	1 2 3 4 5 6 7 8 9 10 [1 0 0 0 1 1 1 0 0 0]									
	5	6 7 4 9	1 2 3 4 5 6 7 8 9 10 [1 0 0 1 1 1 1 0 1 0]									
9	6	7 4 9 10	1 2 3 4 5 6 7 8 9 10 [1 0 0 1 1 1 1 0 1 1]									
	7	4 9 10 3	1 2 3 4 5 6 7 8 9 10 [1 0 1 1 1 1 1 0 1 1]									
	4	9 10 3 2	1 2 3 4 5 6 7 8 9 10 [1 1 1 1 1 1 1 0 1 1]									
	9	10 3 2	**Key found**									

During the expansion of the current vertex, the algorithm sets the visited flag of the vertices (visited) to 1 before they are enqueued into the queue Q. Column 4 of the table illustrates the status of the visited flags. Once the current vertex reaches vertex 9, the key is found and the search is deemed successful.

PROBLEM 16.7.–

For the undirected graph G shown in Example 9.1 (Figure 9.26 of Chapter 9, Volume 2) and reproduced in illustrative problem 16.6 for convenience, undertake a Depth first search for the key 9, by refining the Depth first traversal algorithm (Algorithm 9.2, Chapter 9, Volume 2). Trace the tree of recursive calls.

Solution:

The recursive Depth first search procedure can be derived from **procedure** DFT(s) (Algorithm 9.2), where s is the start node of the graph, by replacing the procedure parameters as **procedure** DFT(s, K) where K is the search key. Also, the statement **print** (s) is replaced by **if** (s = K) **then** {**print** ("key found"); **exit**();}.

The tree of recursive calls for the depth first search of key 9 is shown in Figure P16.7.

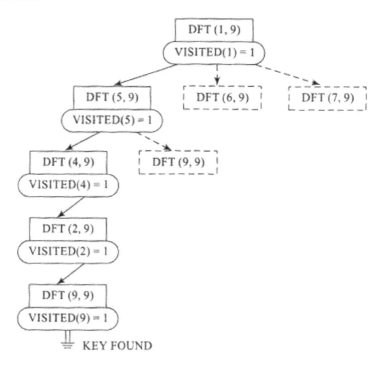

Figure P16.7. *The tree of recursive calls for the depth first search of key 9*

Each solid rectangular box indicates a call to the **procedure** DFT(s, K). In the case of Depth first search, as soon as a vertex is visited it is checked against the search key K. If the search key is found, the recursive procedure terminates with the message "key found".

The broken line rectangular box indicates a "pending" call to the **procedure** DFT(s, K). For example, during the call DFT(5, 9), vertex 5 has two adjacent unvisited nodes, for example, 4 and 9. Since Depth first search proceeds with the processing of vertex 4, vertex 9 is kept waiting.

During the call to the procedure DFT(9, 9), the search key is found in the graph.

An unsuccessful search is signaled when all the visited flags of the vertices have been set to 1 and the search key is nowhere in sight.

PROBLEM 16.8.–

For the skip list shown in Figure P16.8(a), undertake the following operations in a sequence:

i) search 345;

ii) insert 546 assuming that randomization signaled "Tails" for duplicating the node in layer S_1; and

iii) delete 461.

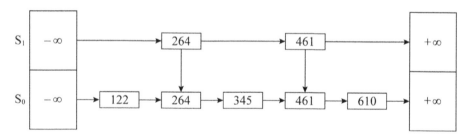

Figure P16.8(a). *An example skip list*

Solution:

i) For the skip list given, searching for 345 begins with layer S_1 and at node 264 descends to layer S_0 and traverses forward to retrieve the node 345.

ii) Figure P16.8(b) illustrates the insertion of node 546 assuming that no duplication was allowed in layer S_1. The broken lines show the sequence in which the insert operation was carried out. Sequence 1–3 in the trail shows the search undertaken to reach the position of inserting the new node and sequences 4 and 5 illustrate insertion of the new node. Since the randomization process did not permit insertion of the node in the upper layer, the insertion process terminates.

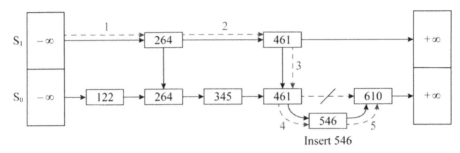

Figure P16.8(b). *Insert 546 into the skip list shown in Figure P16.8(a) assuming that randomization signaled "Tails" for duplicating the node in layer S₁*

iii) Figure P16.8(c) illustrates the deletion of node 461. Note how the tower for 461 is deleted in its entirety and the links of the respective predecessor nodes are reset to point to the respective successor nodes.

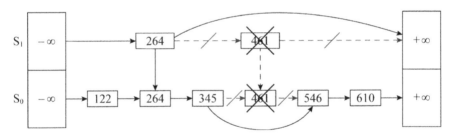

Figure P16.8(c). *Deletion of node 461 from the skip list shown in Figure P16.8(b)*

Review questions

1) Binary search is termed uniform binary search since its decision tree holds the characteristic of:

a) the indexes of the left and the right child nodes differing by the same amount from that of the parent node;

b) the list getting exactly halved in each phase of the search;

c) the height of the decision tree being $log_2 n$;

d) each parent node of the decision tree has two child nodes.

2) In the context of binary search, state whether true or false:

i) the difference in index of all the leaf nodes from their respective parent nodes is 2^0;

ii) the height of the decision tree is n

a) i) true ii) true   b) i) true ii) false

c) i) false ii) true   d) i) false ii) false

3) For a list $L = \{K_1, K_2, K_3, \ldots K_{33}\}$, $K_1 < K_2 < \ldots K_{33}$, undertaking Fibonacci search for a key K would yield a decision tree whose root node is given by:

a) K_{16} b) K_{17} c) K_1 d) K_{21}

4) Which among the following search techniques does not report a worst case time complexity of $O(n)$?

a) linear search   b) interpolation search

c) transpose sequential search   d) binary search

5) Which of the following search techniques works on unordered lists?

a) Fibonacci search   b) interpolation search

c) transpose sequential search   d) binary search

6) What are the advantages of binary search over sequential search?

7) When is a transpose sequential search said to be most successful?

8) What is the principle behind interpolation search?

9) Distinguish between internal searching and external searching.

10) What are the characteristics of the decision tree of Fibonacci search?

11) How is Breadth first search evolved from the Breadth first traversal of a graph?

12) For the following search list undertake i) linear ordered search and ii) binary search of the data list given. Tabulate the number of comparisons made for each key in the search list.

Search list: {766, 009, 999, 238}

Data list: {111 453 231 112 679 238 876 655 766 877 988 009 122 233 344 566}

13) For the given data list and search list, tabulate the number of comparisons made when i) a transpose sequential search and ii) interpolation search is undertaken on the keys belonging to the search list.

Data list: {pin, ink, pen, clip, ribbon, eraser, duster, chalk, pencil, paper, stapler, pot, scale, calculator}

Search list: {pen, clip, paper, pen, calculator, pen}

14) Undertake Fibonacci search of the key $K = 67$ in the list {11, 89, 34, 15, 90, 67, 88, 01, 36, 98, 76, 50}. Trace the decision tree for the search.

15) Perform i) Breadth first search and ii) Depth first search, on the graph given below for the key V.

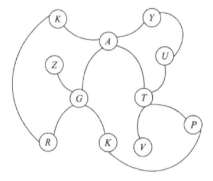

16) A skip list is a:

a) tree with ordered list of elements;

b) binary search tree with unordered list of elements;

c) a linked data structure that allows faster search with unordered elements;

d) a linked data structure that allows faster search with ordered elements.

17) Build a skip list for the following list of elements making your own assumptions on the randomization aspect.

10 40 50 70 80

18) For the skip list constructed in review question 17, undertake the following operations:

i) Delete 80

ii) Delete 10

Programming assignments

1) Implement binary search and Fibonacci search algorithms (Algorithms 16.5 and 16.6) on an ordered list. For the list L = {2, 3, 4, 5, 6, 7, 8, 9, 10, 11, 12, 13, 14, 15, 16, 17, 18, 19, 20} undertake search for the elements in the list {3, 18, 1, 25}. Compare the number of key comparisons made during the searches.

2) Execute an online dictionary (with a limited list of words) which makes use of interpolation search to search through the dictionary given a word. Refine the program to correct any misspelled word with the nearest and/or the correct word from the dictionary.

3) L is a linear list of data elements. Implement the list as:

i) a linear open addressed hash table using an appropriate hash function of your choice; and

ii) an ordered list.

Search for a list of keys on the representations i) and ii) using a) hashing and b) binary search, respectively. Compare the performance of the two methods over the list L.

4) Implement a procedure to undertake search for keys L and M in the graph shown below.

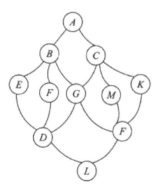

5) Implement a menu-driven program to construct a skip list and search for keys available/unavailable in the list.

Internal Sorting

17.1. Introduction

Sorting in the English language refers to separating or arranging things according to different classes. However, in computer science, ***sorting***, also referred to as ***ordering***, deals with arranging elements of a list or a set or records of a file in ascending or descending order.

In the case of sorting a list of alphabetical, numerical or alphanumerical elements, the elements are arranged in ascending or descending order based on their alphabetical or numerical sequence number. The sequence is also referred to as a ***collating sequence***. In the case of sorting a file of records, one or more fields of the records are chosen as the key based on which the records are arranged in ascending or descending order.

Examples of lists before and after sorting are shown below:

Unsorted lists	Sorted lists
{34, 12, 78, 65, 90, 11, 45}	{11, 12, 34, 45, 65, 78, 90}
{tea, coffee, cocoa, milk, malt, chocolate}	{chocolate, cocoa, coffee, malt, milk, tea}
{n12x, m34b, n24x, a78h, g56v, m12k, k34d}	{a78h, g56v, k34d, m12k, m34b, n12x, n24x}

Sorting has acquired immense significance in the discipline of computer science. Several data structures and algorithms display efficient performance when presented with sorted data sets.

Many different sorting algorithms have been invented, each having their own advantages and disadvantages. These algorithms may be classified into families such as *sorting by exchange*, *sorting by insertion*, *sorting by distribution*, *sorting by selection* and so on. However, in many cases, it is difficult to classify the algorithms as belonging to a specific family only.

A sorting technique is said to be **stable** if keys that are equal retain their relative orders of occurrence, even after sorting. In other words, if K_1 and K_2 are two keys such that $K_1 = K_2$, and $p(K_1) < p(K_2)$ where $p(K_i)$ is the position index of the keys in the unsorted list, then after sorting, $p'(K_1) < p'(K_2)$, where $p'(K_i)$ is the position index of the keys in the sorted list.

If the list of data or records to be sorted are small enough to be accommodated in the internal memory of the computer, then it is referred to as **internal sorting**. On the other hand, if the data list or records to be sorted are voluminous and are accommodated in external storage devices such as tapes, disks and drums, then the sorting undertaken is referred to as **external sorting**. External sorting methods are quite different from internal sorting methods and are discussed in Chapter 18.

In this chapter, we discuss the internal sorting techniques of **bubble sort, insertion sort, selection sort, merge sort, shell sort, quick sort, heap sort, radix sort, counting sort** and **bucket sort**.

17.2. Bubble sort

Bubble sort belongs to the family of **sorting by exchange** or **transposition**, where during the sorting process, pairs of elements that are out of order are interchanged until the whole list is ordered. Given an unordered list $L = \{K_1, K_2, K_3, \ldots K_n\}$, bubble sort orders the elements in ascending order (i.e.), $L = \{K_1, K_2, K_3, \ldots K_n\}$, $K_1 \leq K_2 \leq \ldots K_n$.

Given the unordered list $L = \{K_1, K_2, K_3, \ldots K_n\}$ of keys, bubble sort compares pairs of elements K_i and K_j, swapping them if $K_i > K_j$. At the end of the first pass of comparisons, the largest element in the list L moves to the last position in the list. In the next pass, the sublist $\{K_1, K_2, K_3, \ldots K_{n-1}\}$ is considered for sorting. Once again the pair-wise comparison of elements in the sublist results in the next largest element floating to the last position of the sublist. Thus, in $(n-1)$ passes, where n is the number of elements in the list, the list L is sorted. The sorting is called bubble sorting for the reason that with each pass the next largest element of the list floats or "bubbles" to its appropriate position in the sorted list.

Algorithm 17.1 illustrates the procedure for bubble sort.

```
procedure BUBBLE_SORT(L, n)

/* L[1:n] is an unordered list of data elements to be
sorted in ascending order */

  for i = 1 to n-1 do   /* n-1 passes*/
    for j = 1 to n-i do
      if (L[j] > L[j+1]) then swap(L[j],L[j+1]);
                          /*swap pair wise elements*/
    end          /* the next largest element "bubbles"
                                to the last position*/
  end
end BUBBLE_SORT.
```

Algorithm 17.1. *Procedure for bubble sort*

EXAMPLE 17.1.–

Let L = {92, 78, 34, 23, 56, 90, 17, 52, 67, 81, 18} be an unordered list. As the first step in the first pass of bubble sort, 92 is compared with 78. Since 92 > 78, the elements are swapped, yielding the list {**78, 92**, 34, 23, 56, 90, 17, 52, 67, 81, 18}. The swapped elements are shown in bold. Now, the pairs 92 and 34 are compared, resulting in a swap which yields the list {78, **34, 92**, 23, 56, 90, 17, 52, 67, 81, 18}. It is easy to see that at the end of pass one, the largest element of the list, which is 92, would have moved to the last position in the list. At the end of pass one, the list would be {78, 34, 23, 56, 90, 17, 52, 67, 81, 18, **92**}.

In the second pass, the list considered for sorting discounts the last element, which is 92, since 92 has found its rightful position in the sorted list. At the end of the second pass, the next largest element, which is 90, would have moved to the end of the list. The partially sorted list at this point would be {34, 23, 56, 78, 17, 52, 67, 81, 18, **90**, **92**}. The elements shown in boldface and underlined, indicate elements discounted from the sorting process.

In pass 10 the whole list would be completely sorted.

The trace of algorithm BUBBLE_SORT (Algorithm 17.1) over L is shown in Table 17.1. Here, i keeps count of the passes and j keeps track of the pair-wise element comparisons within a pass. The lower (l) and upper (u) bounds of the loop controlled by j in each pass are shown as $l..u$. Elements shown in boldface and underlined in the list L at the end of pass i, indicate those discounted from the sorting process.

(Pass) i	j	List L at the end of Pass i
1	1..10	{78, 34, 23, 56, 90, 17, 52, 67, 81, 18, 92}
2	1..9	{34, 23, 56, 78, 17, 52, 67, 81, 18, 90, **92**}
3	1..8	{23, 34, 56, 17, 52, 67, 78, 18, 81, **90, 92**}
4	1..7	{23, 34, 17, 52, 56, 67, 18, 78, **81, 90, 92**}
5	1..6	{23, 17, 34, 52, 56, 18, 67, **78, 81, 90, 92**}
6	1..5	{17, 23, 34, 52, 18, 56, **67, 78, 81, 90, 92**}
7	1..4	{17, 23, 34, 18, 52, **56, 67, 78, 81, 90, 92**}
8	1..3	{17, 23, 18, 34, **52, 56, 67, 78, 81, 90, 92**}
9	1..2	{17, 18, 23, **34, 52, 56, 67, 78, 81, 90, 92**}
10	1..1	{17, 18, **23, 34, 52, 56, 67, 78, 81, 90, 92**}

Table 17.1. *Trace of Algorithm 17.1 over the
list L = {92, 78, 34, 23, 56, 90, 17, 52, 67, 81, 18}*

17.2.1. *Stability and performance analysis*

Bubble sort is a stable sort since equal keys do not undergo swapping, as can be observed in Algorithm 17.1, and this contributes to the keys maintaining their relative orders of occurrence in the sorted list.

EXAMPLE 17.2.–

Consider the unordered list $L = \{7^1, 7^2, 7^3, 6\}$. The repeating keys have been distinguished using their orders of occurrence as superscripts. The partially sorted lists at the end of each pass of the bubble sort algorithm are shown below:

Pass 1: $\{7^1, 7^2, 6, 7^3\}$

Pass 2: $\{7^1, 6, 7^2, \underline{7^3}\}$

Pass 3: $\{6, 7^1, \underline{7^2, 7^3}\}$

Observe how the equal keys 7^1, 7^2 and 7^3 also maintain their relative orders of occurrence in the sorted list, verifying the stability of bubble sort.

The time complexity of bubble sort in terms of key comparisons is given by $\Theta(n^2)$. It is easy to see this since the procedure involves two loops with their total frequency count given by $O(n^2)$.

17.3. Insertion sort

Insertion sort as the name indicates belongs to the family of *sorting by insertion,* which is based on the principle that a new key K is *inserted* at its appropriate position in an already sorted sub-list.

Given an unordered list $L = \{K_1, K_2, K_3, ... K_n\}$, insertion sort employs the principle of constructing the list $L = \{K_1, K_2, K_3, ... K_i, K, K_j, K_{j+1}, ... K_n\}$, $K_1 \leq K_2 \leq ... K_i$ and inserting a key K at its appropriate position by comparing it with its sorted sublist of predecessors $\{K_1, K_2, K_3, ... K_i\}, K_1 \leq K_2 \leq ... K_i$ for every key K $(K = K_i, i = 2,3,.. n)$ belonging to the unordered list L.

In the first pass of insertion sort, K_2 is compared with its sorted sublist of predecessors, which is K_1. K_2 inserts itself at the appropriate position to obtain the sorted sublist $\{K_1, K_2\}$. In the second pass, K_3 compares itself with its sorted sublist of predecessors which is $\{K_1, K_2\}$, to insert itself at its appropriate position, yielding the sorted list $\{K_1, K_2, K_3\}$ and so on. In the $(n-1)^{th}$ pass, K_n compares itself with its sorted sublist of predecessors $\{K_1, K_2, ...K_{n-1}\}$, and having inserted itself at the appropriate position, yields the final sorted list $L = \{K_1, K_2, K_3, ... K_i, ... K_j, ... K_n\}$, $K_1 \leq K_2 \leq ... K_i \leq ... \leq K_j \leq ... K_n$. Since each key K finds its appropriate position in the sorted list, such a technique is referred to as the *sinking* or *sifting* technique.

Algorithm 17.2 illustrates the procedure for insertion sort. The **for** loop in the algorithm keeps count of the passes and the **while** loop implements the comparison of the key **key** with its sorted sublist of predecessors. As long as the preceding element in the sorted sublist is greater than **key**, the swapping of the element pair is done. If the preceding element in the sorted sublist is less than or equal to **key**, then **key** is left at its current position and the current pass terminates.

EXAMPLE 17.3.–

Let $L = \{16, 36, 4, 22, 100, 1, 54\}$ be an unordered list of elements. The various passes of the insertion sort procedure are shown below. The snapshots of the list before and after each pass are shown. The key chosen for insertion in each pass is shown in bold and the sorted sublist of predecessors against which the key is compared is shown in brackets.

Pass 1 (**Insert 36**)	{[16] **36**, 4, 22, 100, 1, 54}
After Pass 1	{[16 36] 4, 22, 100, 1, 54}
Pass 2 (**Insert 4**)	{[16 36] **4**, 22, 100, 1, 54}
After Pass 2	{[4 16 36] 22, 100, 1, 54}
Pass 3 (**Insert 22**)	{[4 16 36] **22**, 100, 1, 54}
After Pass 3	{[4 16 22 36] 100, 1, 54}
Pass 4 (**Insert 100**)	{[4 16 22 36] **100**, 1, 54}
After Pass 4	{[4 16 22 36 100] 1, 54}
Pass 5 (**Insert 1**)	{[4 16 22 36 100] **1**, 54}
After Pass 5	{[1 4 16 22 36 100] 54}
Pass 6 (**Insert 54**)	{[1 4 16 22 36 100] **54**}
After Pass 6	{[1 4 16 22 36 54 100]}

17.3.1. *Stability and performance analysis*

```
procedure INSERTION_SORT(L, n)
/* L[1:n] is an unordered list of data elements to be sorted
in the ascending order */

  for i = 2 to n do                      /* n-1 passes*/
    key = L[i];       /*   key is the key to be inserted
    position = 1;         and position its location in the
                                      unordered list*/

      /* compare key with its sorted  sublist of
      predecessors for insertion at the appropriate
      position*/

    while (position > 1) and (L[position-1]> key) do
       L[position] = L[position-1];
       position = position - 1;
       L[position] = key
    end while
  end
end INSERTION_SORT.
```

Algorithm 17.2. *Procedure for insertion sort*

Insertion sort is a stable sort. It is evident from the algorithm that the insertion of key K at its appropriate position in the sorted sublist affects the position index of the elements in the sublist as long as the elements in the sorted sublist are greater than K. When the elements are less than or equal to the key K, there is no displacement of elements and this contributes to retaining the original order of keys which are equal in the sorted sublists.

EXAMPLE 17.4.–

Consider the list $L = \{3^1, 1, 2^1, 3^2, 3^3, 2^2\}$ where the repeated keys have been superscripted with numbers indicative of their relative orders of occurrence. The keys for insertion are shown in bold and the sorted sublists are bracketed.

The passes of the insertion sort are shown below:

Pass 1 (**Insert 1**)	$\{[3^1]\, \mathbf{1}, 2^1, 3^2, 3^3, 2^2\}$
After Pass 1	$\{[1\ 3^1]\, 2^1, 3^2, 3^3, 2^2\}$
Pass 2 (**Insert 2**)	$\{[1\ 3^1\,]\, \mathbf{2^1}, 3^2, 3^3, 2^2\}$
After Pass 2	$\{[1\ 2^1\ 3^1]\, 3^2, 3^3, 2^2\}$
Pass 3 (**Insert 3**)	$\{[1\ 2^1\ 3^1]\, \mathbf{3^2}, 3^3, 2^2\}$
After Pass 3	$\{[1\ 2^1\ 3^1\ 3^2]\, 3^3, 2^2\}$
Pass 4 (**Insert 3**)	$\{[1\ 2^1\ 3^1\ 3^2]\, \mathbf{3^3}, 2^2\}$
After Pass 4	$\{[1\ 2^1\ 3^1\ 3^2 3^3]\, 2^2\}$
Pass 5 (**Insert 2**)	$\{[1\ 2^1\ 3^1\ 3^2 3^3\ ]\, \mathbf{2^2}\}$
After Pass 5	$\{[1\ 2^1\ 2^2\ 3^1\ 3^2 3^3\ ]\}$

The stability of insertion sort can be easily verified in this example. Observe how keys that are equal maintain their original relative orders of occurrence in the sorted list.

The worst-case performance of insertion sort occurs when the elements in the list are already sorted in descending order. It is easy to see that in such a case every key that is to be inserted has to move to the front of the list and therefore undertakes the maximum number of comparisons. Thus, if the list $L = \{K_1, K_2, K_3, \dots K_n\}$, $K_1 \geq K_2 \geq \dots K_n$ is to be insertion sorted then the number of comparisons for the insertion of key K_i would be *(i-1)*, since K_i would swap positions with each of the *(i-1)* keys occurring before it until it moves to position 1. Therefore, the total number of comparisons for inserting each of the keys is given by

$$1 + 2 + 3 + \ldots (n-1) = \frac{(n-1)(n)}{2} \approx O(n^2)$$

The best case complexity of insertion sort arises when the list is already sorted in ascending order. In such a case, the complexity in terms of comparisons is given by *O(n)*. The average case performance of insertion sort reports *O(n²)* complexity.

17.4. Selection sort

Selection sort is built on the principle of repeated *selection* of elements satisfying a specific criterion to aid the sorting process.

The steps involved in the sorting process are listed below:

i) Given an unordered list $L = \{K_1, K_2, K_3, \ldots K_j \ldots K_n\}$, select the minimum key K.

ii) Swap K with the element in the first position of the list L, which is K_1. By doing so the minimum element of the list has secured its rightful position of number one in the sorted list. This step is termed pass 1.

iii) Exclude the first element and select the minimum element K from amongst the remaining elements of the list L. Swap K with the element in the second position of the list, which is K_2. This is termed pass 2.

iv) Exclude the first two elements which have occupied their rightful positions in the sorted list L. Repeat the process of selecting the next minimum element and swapping it with the appropriate element, until the entire list L gets sorted in the ascending order. The entire sorting gets done in *(n-1)* passes.

Selection sort can also sort in descending order by selecting the *maximum element* instead of the minimum element and swapping it with the element in the *last position* of the list L.

Algorithm 17.3 illustrates the working of selection sort. The procedure FIND_MINIMUM (L, i, n) selects the minimum element from the array L[i:n] and returns the position index of the minimum element to procedure SELECTION_SORT. The **for** loop in the SELECTION_SORT procedure represents the *(n-1)* passes needed to sort the array L[1:n] in the ascending order. Function **swap** swaps the elements input into it.

```
procedure SELECTION_SORT(L, n)
/* L[1:n] is an unordered list of data elements to be sorted
in the ascending order */

   for i = 1 to n-1 do                    /* n-1 passes*/

      minimum_index = FIND_MINIMUM(L,i,n); /* find
            minimum element of the list L[i:n] and store the
            position index of the element in minimum_index*/

      swap(L[i], L[minimum_index]);
   end
end SELECTION_SORT


procedure FIND_MINIMUM(L,i,n)
/* the position index of the minimum element in the
array L[i:n] is returned*/

   min_indx = i;
   for j = i+1 to n do
      if (L[j] < L[min_indx])then  min_indx = j;
   end
   return (min_indx)
end FIND_MINIMUM
```

Algorithm 17.3. *Procedure for selection sort*

EXAMPLE 17.5.–

Let $L = \{71, 17, 86, 100, 54, 27\}$ be an unordered list of elements. Each pass of selection sort is traced below. The minimum element is shown in bold and the arrows indicate the swap of the elements concerned. The elements underlined indicate their exclusion in the passes concerned.

Pass	List *L* (During Pass)	List *L* (After Pass)
1	{71, 17, 86, 100, 54, 27}	{17, 71, 86, 100, 54, 27}
2	{17, 71, 86, 100, 54, 27}	{17, 27, 86, 100, 54, 71}
3	{17, 27, 86, 100, 54, 71}	{17, 27, 54, 100, 86, 71}

| 4 | $\{\underline{17, 27, 54}, 100, 86, 71\}$ | $\{17, 27, 54, 71, 86, 100\}$ |
| 5 | $\{\underline{17, 27, 54, 71, 86}, 100\}$ | $\{17, 27, 54, 71, 86, 100\}$ |

(Sorted list)

17.4.1. *Stability and performance analysis*

Selection sort is not stable. Example 17.6 illustrates a case.

The computationally expensive portion of the selection sort occurs when the minimum element has to be selected in each pass. The time complexity of the FIND_MINIMUM procedure is $O(n)$. The time complexity of the SELECTION_SORT procedure is, therefore, $O(n^2)$.

EXAMPLE 17.6.–

Consider the list $L = \{6^1, 6^2, 2\}$. The repeating keys have been superscripted with numbers indicative of their relative orders of occurrence. A trace of the selection sort procedure is shown below. The minimum element is shown in bold and the swapping is indicated by the curved arrow. The elements excluded from the pass are shown underlined.

Pass	List *L* (During Pass)	List *L* (After Pass)
1	$\{6^1, 6^2, 2\}$	$\{2, 6^2, 6^1\}$
2	$\{\underline{2}, 6^2, 6^1\}$	$\{2, 6^2, 6^1\}$

(Sorted list)

The selection sort on the given list L is therefore not stable.

17.5. Merge sort

Merging or *collating* is a process by which two ordered lists of elements are combined or merged into a single ordered list. *Merge sort* makes use of the principle of the merge to sort an unordered list of elements and hence the name. In fact, a variety of sorting algorithms belonging to the family of *sorting by merge* exist. Some of the well-known external sorting algorithms belong to this class.

17.5.1. *Two-way merging*

Two-way merging deals with the merging of two ordered lists.

Let $L_1 = \{a_1, a_2, \ldots a_i \ldots a_n\}$ $a_1 \leq a_2 \leq \ldots \leq a_i \leq \ldots a_n$ and

$L_2 = \{b_1, b_2, \ldots b_j \ldots b_m\}$ $b_1 \leq b_2 \leq \ldots \leq b_j \leq \ldots b_m$ be two ordered lists. Merging combines the two lists into a single list L by making use of the following cases of comparison between the keys a_i and b_j belonging to L_1 and L_2, respectively:

A1. If ($a_i < b_j$) then drop a_i into the list L

A2. If ($a_i > b_j$) then drop b_j into the list L

A3. If ($a_i = b_j$) then drop both a_i and b_j into the list L

In the case of **A1**, once a_i is dropped into the list L, the next comparison of b_j proceeds with a_{i+1}. In the case of **A2**, once b_j is dropped into the list L, the next comparison of a_i proceeds with b_{j+1}. In the case of **A3**, the next comparison proceeds with a_{i+1} and b_{j+1}. At the end of merge, list L contains $(n+m)$ ordered elements.

The series of comparisons between pairs of elements from the lists L_1 and L_2 and the dropping of the relatively smaller elements into the list L proceeds until one of the following cases happens:

B1. L_1 gets exhausted earlier to that of L_2. In such a case, the remaining elements in list L_2 are dropped into the list L in the order of their occurrence in L_2 and the merge is done.

B2. L_2 gets exhausted earlier to that of L_1. In such a case the remaining elements in list L_1 are dropped into the list L in the order of their occurrence in L_1 and the merge is done.

B3. Both L_1 and L_2 are exhausted, in which case the merge is done.

EXAMPLE 17.7.–

Consider the two ordered lists $L_1 = \{4, 6, 7, 8\}$ and $L_2 = \{3, 5, 6\}$. Let us merge the two lists to get the ordered list L. L contains 7 elements in all. Figure 17.1 illustrates the snapshots of the merge process. Observe how when elements 6 and 6 are compared, both the elements drop into the list L. Also, note how list L_2 gets exhausted earlier to L_1, resulting in all the remaining elements of list L_1 getting flushed into list L.

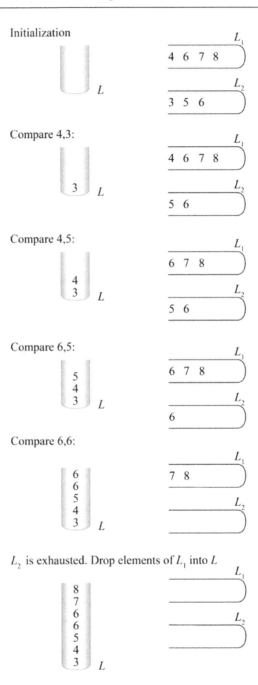

Figure 17.1. *Two-way merge*

Algorithm 17.4 illustrates the procedure for merge. Here, the two ordered lists to be merged are given as $(x_1, x_2, \ldots x_t)$ and $(x_{t+1}, x_{t+2}, \ldots x_n)$ to enable reuse of the algorithm for merge sort to be discussed in the subsequent section. The input parameters to procedure MERGE are given as (x, first, mid, last), where first is the starting index of the first list, mid is the index related to the end/beginning of the first and second list respectively and last is the ending index of the second list.

The call to merge the two lists, $(x_1, x_2, \ldots x_t)$ and $(x_{t+1}, x_{t+2}, \ldots x_n)$ would be MERGE (x, 1, t, n). While the first **while** loop in the procedure performs the pair-wise comparison of elements in the two lists, as discussed in cases **A1–A3**, the second **while** loop takes care of case **B1** and the third loop take care of case **B2**. Case **B3** is inherently taken care of in the first **while** loop.

17.5.1.1. *Performance analysis*

The first **while** loop in Algorithm 17.4 executes at most (last-first+1) times and plays a significant role in the time complexity of the algorithm. The rest of the **while** loops only move the elements of the unexhausted lists into the list x. The complexity of the first **while** loop and hence the algorithm is given by O(last-first+1).

In the case of merging two lists $(x_1, x_2, \ldots x_t)$, $(x_{t+1}, x_{t+2}, \ldots x_n)$ where the number of elements in the two lists sums to n, the time complexity of MERGE is given by $O(n)$.

17.5.2. k-way merging

The two-way merge principle could be extended to k-ordered lists in which case it is termed **k-way merging**. Here, k ordered lists

$$L_1 = \{a_{11}, a_{12}, \ldots a_{1i} \ldots a_{1n_1}\}, \quad a_{11} \leq a_{12} \leq \ldots \leq a_{1i} \leq \ldots a_{1n_1},$$

$$L_2 = \{a_{21}, a_{22}, \ldots a_{2i} \ldots a_{2n_2}\}, \quad a_{21} \leq a_{22} \leq \ldots \leq a_{2i} \leq \ldots a_{2n_2},$$

$$\ldots$$

$$L_k = \{a_{k1}, a_{k2}, \ldots a_{ki} \ldots a_{kn_k}\}, \quad a_{k1} \leq a_{k2} \leq \ldots \leq a_{ki} \leq \ldots a_{kn_k}$$

each comprising $n_1, n_2, \ldots n_k$ number of elements are merged into a single ordered list L comprising $(n_1 + n_2 + \ldots n_k)$ number of elements. At every stage of comparison, k keys a_{ij}, one from each list, are compared before the smallest of the keys are dropped into the list L. Cases **A1–A3** and **B1–B3**, discussed in section 17.5.1 with regard to two-way merge, also hold true in this case, but are extended to k lists. Illustrative problem 17.3 discusses an example k-way merge.

17.5.3. *Non-recursive merge sort procedure*

Given a list $L = \{K_1, K_2, K_3, \ldots K_n\}$ of unordered elements, merge sort sorts the list making use of procedure MERGE repeatedly over several passes.

The non-recursive version of merge sort merely treats the list L of n elements as n independent ordered lists of one element each. In pass one, the n singleton lists are pair-wise merged. At the end of pass 1, the merged lists would have a size of 2 elements each. In pass 2, the lists of size 2 are pair-wise merged to obtain ordered lists of size 4 and so on. In the ith pass, the lists of size $2^{(i-1)}$ are merged to obtain ordered lists of size $2^{(i)}$.

During the passes, if any of the lists are unable to find a pair for their respective merge operation, then they are simply carried forward to the next pass.

EXAMPLE 17.8.–

Consider the list $L = \{12, 56, 1, 34, 89, 78, 43, 10\}$ to be merge sorted using its non-recursive formulation. Figure 17.2 illustrates the pair-wise merging undertaken in each of the passes. The sublists in each pass are shown in brackets. Observe how pass 1 treats the list L as 8 ordered sublists of one element each and at the end of merge sort, pass 3 obtains a single list of size 8 which is the final sorted list.

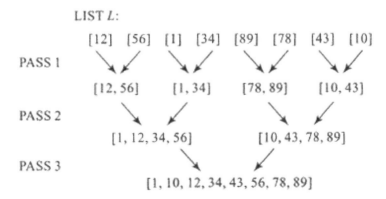

Figure 17.2. *Non-recursive merge sort of list*
$L = \{12, 56, 1, 34, 89, 78, 43, 10\}$ *(Example 17.8)*

17.5.3.1. *Performance analysis*

Merge sort proceeds by running several passes over the list that is to be sorted. In pass 1 sublists of size 1 are merged, in pass 2 sublists of size 2 are merged and in the ith pass sublists of size $2^{(i-1)}$ are merged. Thus, one could expect a total of $\lceil log_2 n \rceil$ passes over the list. With the merge operation commanding $O(n)$ time complexity, each pass of merge sort takes $O(n)$ time. The time complexity of merge sort, therefore, turns out to be $O(n.log_2 n)$.

17.5.3.2. *Stability*

Merge sort is a stable sort since the original relative orders of occurrence of repeating keys are maintained in the sorted list. Illustrative problem 17.4 demonstrates the stability of the sort over a list.

17.5.4. *Recursive merge sort procedure*

The recursive merge sort procedure is built on the design principle of ***Divide and Conquer***. Here, the original unordered list of elements is recursively divided roughly into two sublists until the sublists are small enough where a merge operation is done before they are combined to yield the final sorted list.

Algorithm 17.5 illustrates the recursive merge sort procedure. The procedure makes use of MERGE (Algorithm 17.4) for its merging operation.

EXAMPLE 17.9.–

Let us merge sort the list L = {12, 56, 1, 34, 89, 78, 43, 10} using Algorithm 17.5. The tree of recursive calls demonstrating the working of the procedure on the list L is shown in Figure 17.3. The list is recursively divided into two sublists to be merge-sorted before they are merged to obtain the final sorted list. Each rectangular node of the tree indicates a procedure call to MERGE_SORT with the parameters to the call inscribed inside the box. Beneath the parameter list, the output sublist obtained at the end of the execution of the procedure call is shown.

The invocation of MERGE_SORT (L, 1, 8) generates two other calls, which are MERGE_SORT (L, 1, 4) and MERGE_SORT (L, 5, 8) and so on, leading to the construction of the tree.

Down the tree, the procedure calls MERGE_SORT (L, 1, 1) and MERGE_SORT (L, 2, 2) in that order, are the first to terminate, releasing the lists [12] and [56] respectively. This triggers the MERGE (L, 1, 1, 2) procedure yielding the sublist [12, 56] as the output of the procedure called MERGE_SORT (L, 1, 2). Observe [12, 56] inscribed in the rectangular box 3, which corresponds to the procedure called MERGE_SORT (L, 1, 2).

Proceeding in a similar fashion, it is easy to build the tree and obtain the sorted sublists resulting from each of the calls. The number marked over each rectangular node indicates the order of execution of the recursive procedure calls to MERGE_SORT.

With MERGE_SORT (L, 1, 4) yielding the sorted sublist [1, 12, 34, 56] and MERGE_SORT (L, 5, 8) yielding [10, 43, 78, 89], the execution of the call MERGE (L, 1, 4, 8) terminates the call to MERGE_SORT (L, 1, 8) resulting in the sorted list [1, 10, 12, 34, 43, 56, 78, 89].

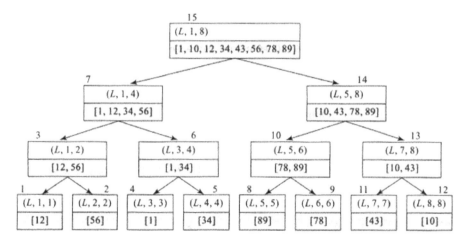

Figure 17.3. *Tree of recursive calls illustrating recursive merge sort of list   L = {12, 56, 1, 34, 89, 78, 43, 10} (Example 17.9)*

17.5.4.1. *Performance analysis*

Recursive merge sort follows a Divide and Conquer principle of algorithm design. Let *T(n)* be the time complexity of MERGE_SORT where *n* is the size of the list. The recurrence relation for the time complexity of the algorithm is given by

$$T(n) = 2.T\left(\frac{n}{2}\right) + O(n), \quad n \geq 2$$

$$= d$$

Here $T\left(\frac{n}{2}\right)$ is the time complexity for each of the two recursive calls to MERGE_SORT over a list of size $n/2$ and d is a constant. $O(n)$ is the time complexity of merge. Framing the recurrence relation as

$$T(n) = 2.T\left(\frac{n}{2}\right) + c.n, \quad n \geq 2$$
$$= d$$

where c is a constant and solving the relation yields the time complexity $T(n) = O(n.log_2 n)$ (see illustrative problem 17.5).

17.6. Shell sort

Insertion sort (section 17.3) moves items only one position at a time and therefore reports a time complexity of $O(n^2)$ on average. **Shell sort** is a substantial improvement over insertion sort in the sense that elements move in long strides rather than single steps, thereby yielding a comparatively short subfile or a comparatively well-ordered subfile that quickens the sorting process.

The shell sort procedure was proposed by Shell (1959). The general idea behind the method is to choose an **increment** h_t and divide a list of unordered keys $L = \{K_1, K_2, K_3, \ldots K_j \ldots K_n\}$ into sub-lists of keys that are h_t units apart. Each of the sub-lists is individually sorted (preferably insertion sorted) and gathered to form a list. This is known as a **pass**. Now we repeat the pass for any sequence of increments $\{h_{t-1}, h_{t-2}, \ldots h_2, h_1, h_0\}$ where h_0 must equal 1. The increments h_t are kept in the diminishing order and therefore shell sort is also referred to as **diminishing increment sort**.

```
procedure MERGE(x, first, mid, last )

/* x[first:mid] and x[mid+1:last] are ordered lists of   data
       elements  to  be  merged  into  a  single  ordered  list
   x[first:last] */

   first1 = first;
   last1 = mid;
   first2 = mid + 1;
   last2 = last;      /* set the beginning and the ending
              indexes of the two lists into the appropriate
                                         variables*/
   i = first;         /* i is the index variable for the
                          temporary output list temp*/
```

```
/* begin pair wise comparisons of elements from the two
lists*/

  while (first1 ≤ last1) and (first2 ≤ last2) do
      case
      :x[first1] < x[first2]: {temp[i]= x[first1];
                                first1 = first1 + 1;
                                i = i+1;}

      :x[first1] > x[first2]: {temp[i]= x[first2];
                                first2 = first2 + 1;
                                i = i+1;}

      :x[first1]= x[first2]:  {temp[i]= x[first1];
                                temp[i+1]=x[first2];
                                first1 = first1 + 1;
                                first2 = first2 + 1;
                                i = i+2;}
      end case
   end  while
                   /* the first list gets exhausted*/
  while (first2 ≤ last2) do
   temp[i]= x[first2];
   first2 = first2 + 1;
   i = i+1;
  end while
                   /* the second list gets exhausted*/
  while (first1 ≤ last1) do
   temp[i]= x[first1];
   first1 = first1 + 1;
   i = i+1;
  end while
                   /* copy list  temp to list x*/
  for j = first to last do
   x[j] = temp[j]
  end


end MERGE.
```

Algorithm 17.4. *Procedure for merge*

Example 17.10 illustrates shell sort on the given list L for an increment sequence $\{8, 4, 2, 1\}$.

EXAMPLE 17.10.–

Trace the shell sort procedure on the unordered list L of keys given by $L = \{24, 37, 46, 11, 85, 47, 33, 66, 22, 84, 95, 55, 14, 09, 76, 35\}$ for an increment sequence $\{h_3, h_2, h_1, h_0\} = \{8, 4, 2, 1\}$.

The steps traced are shown in Figure 17.4. Pass 1 for an increment 8, divides the unordered list L into eight sublists, each comprising two keys that are eight units apart. After each of the sublists has been individually insertion sorted, they are gathered together for the next pass.

procedure MERGE_SORT(a, first, last)

```
/* a[first:last]is the unordered list of elements to be merge
sorted. The call to the procedure to sort the list a[1:n]
would be MERGE_SORT(a, 1, n)*/
```

```
if (first < last) then
```

$\{ \quad mid = \left\lfloor \dfrac{(first+last)}{2} \right\rfloor;$ /* divide the list into two sublists*/

```
    MERGE_SORT(a, first, mid);
                /* merge sort the sublist a[first, mid]*/

    MERGE_SORT(a, mid+1, last);
              /* merge sort the sublist   a[mid+1, last]*/

    MERGE(a, first, mid, last);
                        /* merge the two sublists
                  a[first, mid] and a[mid+1, last]*/
}
end MERGE_SORT.
```

Algorithm 17.5. *Procedure for recursive merge sort*

In Pass 2, for increment 4, the list gets divided into four groups, each comprising elements which are four units apart in the list L. The individual sub-lists are again insertion sorted and gathered together for the next pass and so on until in Pass 4 the entire list gets sorted for an increment 1.

The shell sort, in fact, could work for any sequence of increments as long as h_0 equals 1. Several empirical results and theoretical investigations have been undertaken regarding the conditions to be followed by the sequence of increments.

Example 17.11 illustrates shell sort for the same list L used in Example 17.10, but for a different sequence of increments, for example, $\{7, 5, 3, 1\}$.

Unordered list L:

K_1	K_2	K_3	K_4	K_5	K_6	K_7	K_8	K_9	K_{10}	K_{11}	K_{12}	K_{13}	K_{14}	K_{15}	K_{16}
24	37	46	11	85	47	33	66	22	84	95	55	14	09	76	35

Pass 1 (increment $h_3 = 8$)

| $(K_1$ | $K_9)$ | $(K_2$ | $K_{10})$ | $(K_3$ | $K_{11})$ | $(K_4$ | $K_{12})$ | $(K_5$ | $K_{13})$ | $(K_6$ | $K_{14})$ | $(K_7$ | $K_{15})$ | $(K_8$ | $K_{16})$ |

(24 22)   (37, 84)   (46, 95)   (11, 55)   (85, 14)   (47, 09)   (33, 76)   (66, 35)

After insertion sort:
(22   24)   (37, 84)   (46, 95)   (11, 55)   (14, 85)   (09, 47)   (33, 76)   (35, 66)

List L after Pass 1:

K_1	K_2	K_3	K_4	K_5	K_6	K_7	K_8	K_9	K_{10}	K_{11}	K_{12}	K_{13}	K_{14}	K_{15}	K_{16}
22	37	46	11	14	09	33	35	24	84	95	55	85	47	76	66

Pass 2 (increment $h_2 = 4$)

| $(K_1$ | K_5 | K_9 | $K_{13})$ | $(K_2$ | K_6 | K_{10} | $K_{14})$ | $(K_3$ | K_7 | K_{11} | $K_{15})$ | $(K_4$ | K_8 | K_{12} | $K_{16})$ |

(22   14   24   85)   (37   09   84   47)   (46   33   95   76)   (11   35   55   66)

After insertion sort:
(14   22   24   85)   (09   37   47   84)   (33   46   76   95)   (11   35   55   66)

List L after Pass 2

K_1	K_2	K_3	K_4	K_5	K_6	K_7	K_8	K_9	K_{10}	K_{11}	K_{12}	K_{13}	K_{14}	K_{15}	K_{16}
14	09	33	11	22	37	46	35	24	47	76	55	85	84	95	66

Pass 3 (increment $h_1 = 2$)

| $(K_1$ | K_3 | K_5 | K_7 | K_9 | K_{11} | K_{13} | $K_{15})$ | $(K_2$ | K_4 | K_6 | K_8 | K_{10} | K_{12} | K_{14} | $K_{16})$ |

(14   33   22   46   24   76   85   95)   (09   11   37   35   47   55   84   66)

After insertion sort:
(14   22   24   33   46   76   85   95)   (09   11   35   37   47   55   66   84)

List L after Pass 3:

K_1	K_2	K_3	K_4	K_5	K_6	K_7	K_8	K_9	K_{10}	K_{11}	K_{12}	K_{13}	K_{14}	K_{15}	K_{16}
14	09	22	11	24	35	33	37	46	47	76	55	85	66	95	84

Pass 4 (increment $h_0 = 1$)

| $(K_1$ | K_2 | K_3 | K_4 | K_5 | K_6 | K_7 | K_8 | K_9 | K_{10} | K_{11} | K_{12} | K_{13} | K_{14} | K_{15} | $K_{16})$ |

(14   09   22   11   24   35   33   37   46   47   76   55   85   66   95   84)

After insertion sort:
(09   11   14   22   24   33   35   37   46   47   55   66   76   84   85   95)

Sorted List L

K_1	K_2	K_3	K_4	K_5	K_6	K_7	K_8	K_9	K_{10}	K_{11}	K_{12}	K_{13}	K_{14}	K_{15}	K_{16}
09	11	14	22	24	33	35	37	46	47	55	66	76	84	85	95

Figure 17.4. *Shell sorting of L = {24, 37, 46, 11, 85, 47, 33, 66, 22, 84, 95, 55, 14, 09, 76, 35} for the increment sequence {8, 4, 2, 1}*

Example 17.11.–

Trace the shell sort procedure on the unordered list L of keys given by $L = \{24,$ 37, 46, 11, 85, 47, 33, 66, 22, 84, 95, 55, 14, 09, 76, 35\} for an increment sequence $\{h_3, h_2, h_1, h_0\} = \{7, 5, 3, 1\}$.

Figure 17.5 illustrates the steps involved in the sorting process. In Pass 1, the increment of 7 divides the sublist L into seven groups of a varying number of elements. The sub-lists are insertion sorted and gathered for the next pass. In Pass 2, for an increment of 5, the list L gets divided into five groups of a varying number of elements. As before, they are insertion sorted and so on until in Pass 4 the entire list gets sorted for an increment of 1.

Algorithm 17.6 describes the skeletal shell sort procedure. The array $L[1:n]$ represents the unordered list of keys, $L = \{K_1, K_2, K_3, \ldots K_j \ldots K_n\}$. H is the sequence of increments $\{h_t, h_{t-1}, h_{t-2}, \ldots . h_2, h_1, h_0\}$.

Unordered list L:

K_1	K_2	K_3	K_4	K_5	K_6	K_7	K_8	K_9	K_{10}	K_{11}	K_{12}	K_{13}	K_{14}	K_{15}	K_{16}
24	37	46	11	85	47	33	66	22	84	95	55	14	09	76	35

Pass 1 (increment $h_3 = 7$)

(K_1 K_8 K_{15})   (K_2 K_9 K_{16})   (K_3 K_{10})   (K_4 K_{11})   (K_5 K_{12})   (K_6 K_{13})   (K_7 K_{14})

(24   66   76)   (37   22   35)   (46   84)   (11   95)   (85   55)   (47   14)   (33   09)

After insertion sort:

(24   66   76)   (22   35   37)   (46   84)   (11   95)   (55   85)   (14   47)   (09   33)

List L after Pass 1:

K_1	K_2	K_3	K_4	K_5	K_6	K_7	K_8	K_9	K_{10}	K_{11}	K_{12}	K_{13}	K_{14}	K_{15}	K_{16}
24	22	46	11	55	14	09	66	35	84	95	85	47	33	76	37

Pass 2 (increment $h_2 = 5$)

(K_1 K_6 K_{11} K_{16})   (K_2 K_7 K_{12})   (K_3 K_8 K_{13})   (K_4 K_9 K_{14})   (K_5 K_{10} K_{15})

(24   14   95   37)   (22   09   85)   (46   66   47)   (11   35   33)   (55   84   76)

After insertion sort:

(14   24   37   95)   (09   22   85)   (46   47   66)   (11   33   35)   (55   76   84)

List L after Pass 2:

K_1	K_2	K_3	K_4	K_5	K_6	K_7	K_8	K_9	K_{10}	K_{11}	K_{12}	K_{13}	K_{14}	K_{15}	K_{16}
14	09	46	11	55	24	22	47	33	76	37	85	66	35	84	95

Pass 3(increment $h_1 = 3$)

(K₁	K₄	K₇	K₁₀	K₁₃	K₁₆)	(K₂	K₅	K₈	K₁₁	K₁₄)	(K₃	K₆	K₉	K₁₂	K₁₅)
(14	11	22	76	66	95)	(09	55	47	37	35)	(46	24	33	85	84)

After insertion sort:

(11	14	22	66	76	95)	(09	35	37	47	55)	(24	33	46	84	85)

List L after Pass 3:

K₁	K₂	K₃	K₄	K₅	K₆	K₇	K₈	K₉	K₁₀	K₁₁	K₁₂	K₁₃	K₁₄	K₁₅	K₁₆
11	09	24	14	35	33	22	37	46	66	47	84	76	55	85	95

Pass 4 (increment $h_0 = 1$)

(K₁	K₂	K₃	K₄	K₅	K₆	K₇	K₈	K₉	K₁₀	K₁₁	K₁₂	K₁₃	K₁₄	K₁₅	K₁₆)
(11	09	24	14	35	33	22	37	46	66	47	84	76	55	85	95)

After insertion sort:

(09	11	14	22	24	33	35	37	46	47	55	66	76	84	85	95)

Sorted List L

K₁	K₂	K₃	K₄	K₅	K₆	K₇	K₈	K₉	K₁₀	K₁₁	K₁₂	K₁₃	K₁₄	K₁₅	K₁₆
09	11	14	22	24	33	35	37	46	47	55	66	76	84	85	95

Figure 17.5. *Shell sorting of L = {24, 37, 46, 11, 85, 47, 33, 66, 22, 84, 95, 55, 14, 09, 76, 35} for the increment sequence {7, 5, 3, 1}*

```
procedure SHELL_SORT(L, n, H )
/* L[1:n] is the unordered list of keys to    be shell
sorted.
```
$L = \{K_1, K_2, K_3, \ldots K_j \ldots K_n\}$ and $H = \{h_t, h_{t-1}, h_{t-2}, \ldots . h_2, h_1, h_0\}$ is the
```
sequence of increments */

    for each hⱼ ∈ H do
        Insertion sort the sublist of elements in
        L[1:n]which are hⱼ units apart, such that
```
$L[i] \leq L[i + h_j]$, for $1 \leq i \leq n - h_j$
```
    end
print (L)

end SHELL_SORT.
```

Algorithm 17.6. *Procedure for shell sort*

17.6.1. *Analysis of shell sort*

The analysis of shell sort is dependent on a given choice of increments. Since there is no best possible sequence of increments that have been formulated, especially for large values of n (the size of the list L), the time complexity of shell sort is not completely resolved. In fact, it has led to some interesting mathematical problems! An interested reader is referred to Knuth (2002) for discussions on these results.

17.7. Quick sort

The **quick sort** procedure formulated by Hoare (1962) belongs to the family of **sorting by exchange** or **transposition**, where elements that are out of order are exchanged amongst themselves to obtain the sorted list.

The procedure works on the principle of **partitioning** the unordered list into two sublists at every stage of the sorting process based on what is called a **pivot element**. The two sublists occur to the left and right of the pivot element. The pivot element determines its appropriate position in the sorted list and is therefore freed of its participation in the subsequent stages of the sorting process. Again, each of the sublists is partitioned against their respective pivot elements until no more partitioning can be called for. At this stage, all the elements would have determined their appropriate positions in the sorted list and a quick sort is done.

17.7.1. *Partitioning*

Consider an unordered list $L = \{K_1, K_2, K_3, \ldots K_n\}$. How does partitioning occur? Let us choose K_1 to be the pivot element. Now, K_1 compares itself with each of the keys on a left to right encounter looking for the first key K_i, $K_i \geq K$. Again, K compares itself with each of the keys on a right to left encounter looking for the first key K_j, $K_j \leq K$. If K_i and K_j are such that $i < j$, then K_i and K_j are exchanged. Figure 17.6(a) illustrates the process of exchange.

Now, K moves ahead from position index i on a left to right encounter looking for a key K_s, $K_s \geq K$. Again, as before, K moves on a right to left encounter beginning from position index j looking for a key K_t, $K_t \leq K$. As before, if $s < t$, then K_s and K_t are exchanged and the process repeats (Figure 17.6(b)). If $s > t$, then K exchanges itself with K_t, the key which is the smaller of K_s and K_t. At this stage, a **partition** is said to occur. The pivot element K, which has now exchanged position with K_t, is the median around which the list partitions itself or splits itself into two.

Figure 17.6(c) illustrates partition. Now, what do we observe about the partitioned sublists and the pivot element?

i) The sublist occurring to the left of the pivot element K (now at position t) has all its elements less than or equal to K and the sublist occurring to the right of the pivot element K has all its elements greater than or equal to K.

ii) The pivot element has settled down in its appropriate position which would turn out to be its rank in the sorted list.

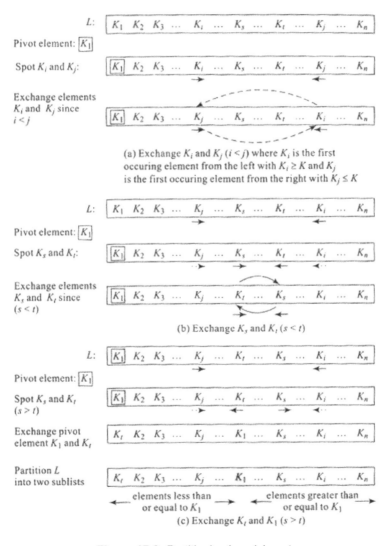

(a) Exchange K_i and K_j $(i < j)$ where K_i is the first occuring element from the left with $K_i \geq K$ and K_j is the first occuring element from the right with $K_j \leq K$

(b) Exchange K_s and K_t $(s < t)$

(c) Exchange K_t and K_1 $(s > t)$

Figure 17.6. *Partitioning in quick sort*

EXAMPLE 17.12.–

Let $L = \{34, 26, 1, 45, 18, 78, 12, 89, 27\}$ be an unordered list of elements. We now demonstrate the process of partitioning, on the above list.

Let us choose 34 as the pivot element. Figure 17.7 illustrates the snapshots of partitioning the list. Here, 34 moves left to right looking for the first element that is greater than or equal to it and spots 45. Again, moving from right to left looking for the first element less than or equal to 34, it spots 27. Since the position index of 45 is less than that of 27 (arrows face each other), they are exchanged.

Proceeding from the points where the moves were last stopped, 34 encounters 78 during its left to right move and encounters 12 during its right to left move. As before, the arrows face each other resulting in an exchange of 78 and 12. In the next lap of the move, we notice the elements 78 and 12 are spotted again but this time note that the arrows have crossed each other. This implies that the position index of 78 is greater than that of 12 calling for a partition. 34 exchanges position with 12 and the list is partitioned into two as shown.

It may be seen that all elements less than or equal to 34 have accumulated to its left and those greater than or equal to 34 have accumulated to its right. Again, the pivot element 34 has settled down at position index 6, which is its rank in the sorted list.

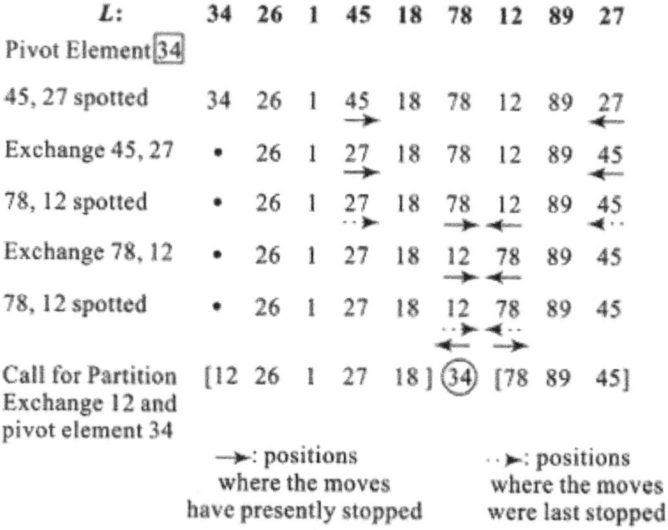

Figure 17.7 *Partitioning a list (Example 17.12)*

17.7.2. *Quick sort procedure*

Once the method behind partitioning is known, quick sort is nothing but repeated partitioning until every pivot element settles down to its appropriate position, thereby sorting the list.

Algorithm 17.8 illustrates the quick sort procedure. The algorithm employs the Divide and Conquer principle by exploiting procedure PARTITION (Algorithm 17.7) to partition the list into two sublists and recursively call procedure QUICK_SORT to sort the two sublists.

```
procedure PARTITION(L, first, last, loc )
/* L[first:last] is the list to be partitioned. loc is
the position where the pivot element finally settles
down*/


  left = first;
  right = last+1;
  pivot_elt = L[first]; /* set the pivot element to
                        the first element in list L */

  while (left < right) do
     repeat
       left = left+1;  /* pivot element moves left to
                                        right*/
     until L[left]≥ pivot_elt;

     repeat
        right = right -1;  /* pivot element moves right
                                         to left*/
     until L[right]≤ pivot_elt;

     if (left < right) then swap(L[left], L[right]);
                       /*arrows face each other*/
  end while
  loc = right
  swap(L[first], L[right]);  /* arrows have crossed
                        each other - exchange pivot
                    element L[first]  with L[right]*/
end PARTITION
```

Algorithm 17.7. *Procedure for partition*

Procedure PARTITION partitions the list L[first:last] at the position loc where the pivot element settles down.

EXAMPLE 17.13.–

Let us quick sort the list L = {5, 1, 26, 15, 76, 34, 15}. The various phases of the sorting process are shown in Figure 17.8. When the partitioned sublists contain only one element then no sorting is done. Also, in phase 4 of Figure 17.8, observe how the pivot element 34 exchanges with itself. The final sorted list is {1, 5, 15, 15, 26, 34, 76}.

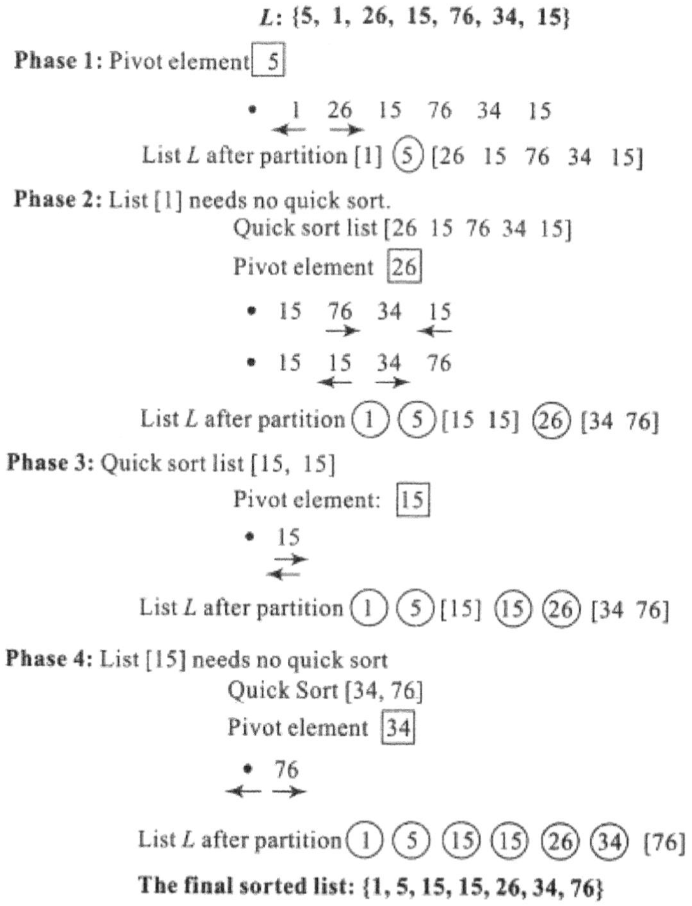

L: {5, 1, 26, 15, 76, 34, 15}

Phase 1: Pivot element 5

• 1   26   15   76   34   15

List L after partition [1] ⑤ [26 15 76 34 15]

Phase 2: List [1] needs no quick sort.
Quick sort list [26 15 76 34 15]

Pivot element 26

• 15   76   34   15

• 15   15   34   76

List L after partition ① ⑤ [15 15] ㉖ [34 76]

Phase 3: Quick sort list [15, 15]
Pivot element: 15

• 15

List L after partition ① ⑤ [15] ⑮ ㉖ [34 76]

Phase 4: List [15] needs no quick sort
Quick Sort [34, 76]
Pivot element 34

• 76

List L after partition ① ⑤ ⑮ ⑮ ㉖ ㉞ [76]

The final sorted list: {1, 5, 15, 15, 26, 34, 76}

Figure 17.8. *Snapshots of the quick sort process (Example 17.13)*

```
procedure QUICK_SORT(L, first, last )
/* L[first:last] is the unordered list of elements to be quick
sorted. The call to the procedure to sort the list L[1:n]
would be QUICK_SORT(L, 1, n)*/

   if (first < last) then
   {PARTITION(L, first, last, loc) ;    /* partition
                    the list into two sublists at loc*/
    QUICK_SORT(L, first, loc-1 );    /* quick sort
                    the sublist L[first,loc-1]*/
    QUICK_SORT(L, loc+1, last );    /* quick sort
                    the sublist L[loc+1, last]*/

   }
end QUICK_SORT.
```

Algorithm 17.8. *Procedure for quick sort*

17.7.3. *Stability and performance analysis*

Quick sort is not a stable sort. During the partitioning process, keys which are equal are subject to exchange and hence undergo changes in their relative orders of occurrence in the sorted list.

EXAMPLE 17.14.–

Let us quick sort the list $L = \{5^1, 5^2, 5^3\}$, where the superscripts indicate the relative orders of their occurrence in the list. Figure 17.9 illustrates the sorting process. It can be easily seen that quick sort is not stable.

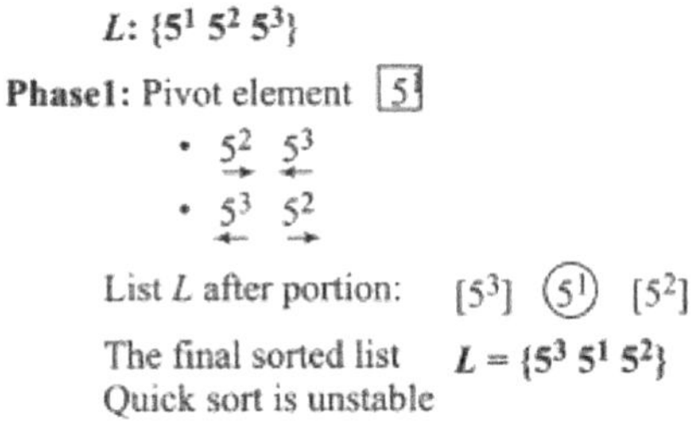

$$L: \{5^1\ 5^2\ 5^3\}$$

Phase1: Pivot element $\boxed{5^1}$

• 5^2 5^3

• 5^3 5^2

List L after portion: $[5^3]$ (5^1) $[5^2]$

The final sorted list $L = \{5^3\ 5^1\ 5^2\}$
Quick sort is unstable

Figure 17.9. *Stability of quick sort*

Quick sort reports a worst-case performance when the list is already sorted in its ascending order (see illustrative problem 17.6). The worst-case time complexity of the algorithm is given by $O(n^2)$. However, quick sort reports a good average case complexity of $O(n \, logn)$.

17.8. Heap sort

Heap sort is a sorting procedure belonging to the family of *sorting by selection*. This class of sorting algorithms is based on the principle of repeated selection of either the smallest or the largest key from the remaining elements of the unordered list and their inclusion in an output list. At every pass of the sort, the smallest or the largest key is selected by a well-devised method and added to the output list, and when all the elements have been selected, the output list yields the sorted list.

Heap sort is built on a data structure called *heap* and hence the name heap sort. The heap data structure aids the selection of the largest (or smallest) key from the remaining elements of the list. Heap sort proceeds in two phases as follows:

i) construction of a heap where the unordered list of elements to be sorted are converted into a heap;

ii) repeated selection and inclusion of the root node key of the heap into the output list after reconstructing the remaining tree into a heap.

17.8.1. *Heap*

A heap is a complete binary tree in which each parent node u labeled by a key or element $e(u)$ and its respective child nodes v, w labeled $e(v)$, $e(w)$ respectively are such that $e(u) \geq e(v)$ and $e(u) \geq e(w)$. Since the parent node keys are greater than or equal to their respective child node keys at each level, the key at the root node would turn out to be the largest amongst all the keys represented as a heap.

It is also possible to define the heap such that the root holds the smallest key for which every parent node key should be less than or equal to that of its child nodes. However, by convention, a heap sticks to the principle of the root holding the largest element. In the case of the former, it is referred to as a *minheap* and in the case of the latter, it is known as a *maxheap*. A binary tree that displays this property is also referred to as a *binary heap*.

EXAMPLE 17.15.–

The binary tree shown in Figure 17.10(a) is a heap, while that shown in Figure 17.10(b) is not.

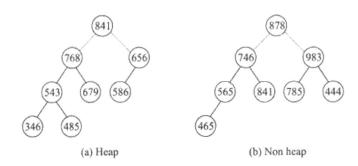

(a) Heap   (b) Non heap

Figure 17.10. *An example of heap and non-heap*

It may be observed in Figure 17.10(a) how each parent node key is greater than or equal to that of its child node keys. As a result, the root represents the largest key in the heap. In contrast, the non-heap shown in Figure 17.10(b) violates the above characteristics.

17.8.2. *Construction of heap*

Given an unordered list of elements, it is essential that a heap is first constructed before heap sort works on it to yield the sorted list. Let $L = \{K_1, K_2, K_3, \ldots K_n\}$ be the unordered list. The construction of the heap proceeds by inserting keys from L one by one into an existing heap. K_1 is inserted into the initially empty heap as its root. K_2 is inserted as the left child of K_1. If the property of heap is violated then K_1 and K_2 swap positions to construct a heap out of themselves. Next K_3 is inserted as the right child of node K_1. If K_3 violates the property of heap, it swaps position with its parent K_1 and so on.

In general, a key K_i is inserted into the heap as the child of node $\left\lfloor \frac{i}{2} \right\rfloor$ following the principle of a complete binary tree (the parent of child i is given by $\left\lfloor \frac{i}{2} \right\rfloor$ and the right and left child of i is given by $2i$ and $(2i+1)$ respectively). If the property of the heap is violated then it calls for a swap between K_i and $K_{\left\lfloor \frac{i}{2} \right\rfloor}$, which in turn may trigger further adjustments between $K_{\left\lfloor \frac{i}{2} \right\rfloor}$ and its parent and so on. In short, a major adjustment across the tree may have to be carried out to reconstruct the heap.

Though a heap is a binary tree, the principle of the complete binary tree that it follows favors its representation as an array (see section 8.5.1 of Chapter 8, Volume 2). The algorithms pertaining to heap and heap sort employ arrays for their implementation of heaps.

EXAMPLE 17.16.–

Let us construct a heap out of $L = \{D, B, G, E, A, H, C, F\}$. Figure 17.11 illustrates the step-by-step process of insertion and heap reconstruction before the final heap is obtained. The adjustments made between the keys of the node during the heap reconstruction are shown with dotted lines.

As mentioned earlier, for the implementation of the algorithm for the construction of a heap, it is convenient to make use of an array representation. Thus, if the list $L = \{D, B, G, E, A, H, C, F\}$ shown in Example 17.16 is represented as an array then the same after construction of the heap would be as shown in Figure 17.12.

List L: $\begin{Bmatrix} D & B & G & E & A & H & C & F \\ 1 & 2 & 3 & 4 & 5 & 6 & 7 & 8 \end{Bmatrix}$

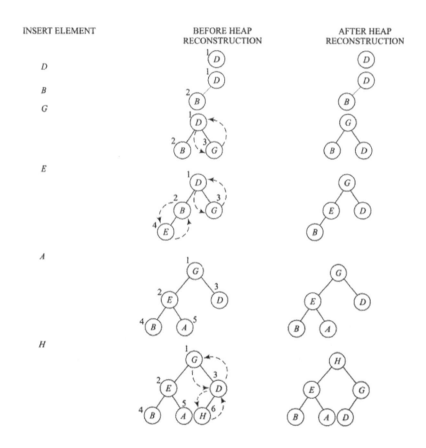

C

F

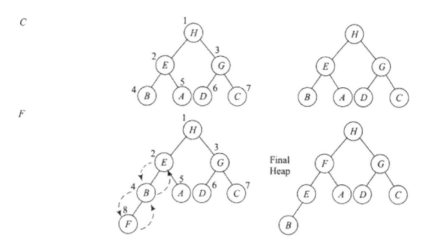

Figure 17.11. *Construction of heap (Example 17.16)*

Algorithm 17.9 illustrates the procedure for inserting a key K ($L[\texttt{child\_index}]$) into an existing heap $L[1:\texttt{child\_index-1}]$.

List L
as an array $L[1:8]$
before heap construction

List L
as an array $L[1:8]$
after heap construction

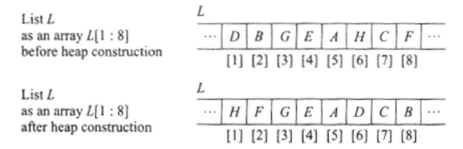

Figure 17.12. *Array representation of a heap for the list L = {D, B, G, E, A, H, C, F}*

To build a heap out of a list *L[1:n]*, each element beginning from *L[2]* to *L[n]* will have to be inserted one by one into the constructed heap. Algorithm 17.10 illustrates the procedure of constructing a heap out of *L[1:n]*. Illustrative problem 17.8 illustrates the trace of the algorithm for the construction of a heap given a list of elements.

```
procedure INSERT_HEAP(L, child_index )
/* L[1:child_index-1] is an existing heap into which
L[child_index] is to be included*/

   heap = false;
   parent_index  = ⌊child_index/2⌋;   /* identify parent*/
   while (not heap) and (child_index >1) do
       if (L[parent_index] < L[child_index])
       then  /* heap property violated- swap
                         parent and child*/
         { swap(L[parent_index], L[child_index]);
           child_index = parent_index;
           parent_index  = ⌊child_index/2⌋;
         }
       else
          {heap = true;}
   end while
end INSERT_HEAP.
```

Algorithm 17.9. *Procedure for inserting a key into a heap*


```
procedure CONSTRUCT_HEAP(L, n)
/* L[1:n] is a list to be constructed into a heap*/

   for child_index = 2 to n do
       INSERT_HEAP(L, child_index);   /* insert
                elements one by one into the heap*/

   end

end CONSTRUCT_HEAP.
```

Algorithm 17.10. *Procedure for construction of heap*

17.8.3. *Heap sort procedure*

To sort an unordered list $L = \{K_1, K_2, K_3, \ldots K_n\}$, heap sort procedure first constructs a heap out of L. The root which holds the largest element of L swaps places with the *largest numbered* node of the tree. The largest numbered node is now disabled from further participation in the heap reconstruction process. This is akin to the highest key of the list getting included in the output list.

Now, the remaining tree with (n-1) active nodes is again reconstructed to form a heap. The root node now holds the next largest element of the list. The swapping of the root node with the next largest numbered node in the tree which is disabled thereafter, yields a tree with (n-2) active nodes and so on. This process of heap reconstruction and outputting the root node to the output list continues until the tree is left with no active nodes. At this stage, heap sort is done and the output list contains the elements in the sorted order.

EXAMPLE 17.17.–

Let us heap sort the list $L = \{D, B, G, E, A, H, C, F\}$ made use of in Example 17.16. The first phase of heap sort is to construct a heap out of the list. The heap constructed for the list L is shown in Fig.17.11.

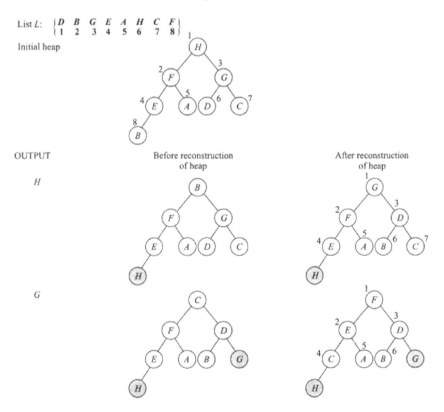

F

E

D

C

B

A

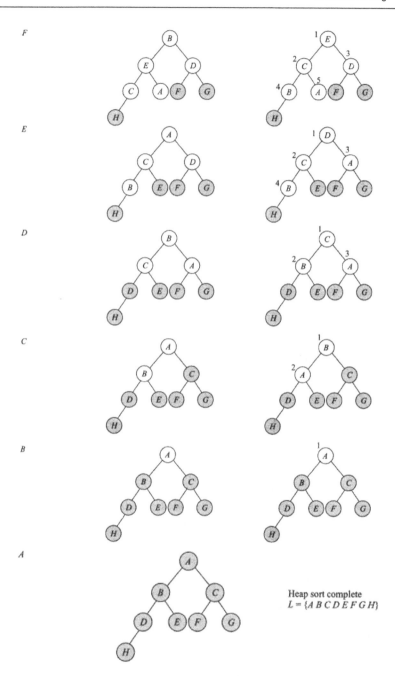

Heap sort complete
L = {A B C D E F G H}

Figure 17.13. *Heap sorting of the list*
L = {D, B, G, E, A, H, C, F} (Example 17.17)

```
procedure HEAP_SORT(L, n)
/* L[1:n] is the unordered list to be sorted. The output list
is returned in L itself*/

 CONSTRUCT_HEAP(L, n);   /* construct the initial heap
                                     out of L[1:n] */
 BUILD_TREE(L, n);       /* output root node and
                                     reconstruct heap*/
end HEAP_SORT.

procedure BUILD_TREE(L,n)

  for end_node_index = n to 2 step -1 do

    swap( L[1], L[end_node_index]); /* swap root node
             with the largest numbered node (end node)*/
    RECONSTRUCT_HEAP(L,end_node_index);
             /*procedure for reconstructing a heap*/
  end
end BUILD_TREE.

procedure RECONSTRUCT_HEAP(L, end_node_index )

  heap = false;
  parent_index  = 1;
  child_index = parent_index * 2;

  while(not heap)and (child_index < end_node_index)
                                                   do
      right_child_index = child_index + 1;
       if (right_child_index < end_node_index)
               /* choose which of the child nodes are
               greater than or equal to the parent*/
      then
           if (L[right_child_index]>L[child_index])
           then   child_index = right_child_index;

           if (L[child_index]> L[parent_index])
           then
             {swap(L[child_index],L[parent_index]);
              parent_index = child_index;
              child_index = parent_index * 2;
              }
      else heap = true;

   end while
end RECONSTRUCT_HEAP.
```

Algorithm 17.11. *Procedure for heap sort*

In the second stage, the root node key is exchanged with the largest numbered node of the tree and the heap reconstruction of the remaining tree continues until the entire list is sorted. Figure 17.13 illustrates the second stage of heap sort. The disabled nodes of the tree are shown shaded in grey. After reconstruction of the heap, the nodes are numbered to indicate the largest numbered node that is to be swapped with the root of the heap. The sorted list is obtained as $L = \{A, B, C, D, E, F, G, H\}$.

Algorithm 17.11 illustrates the heap sort procedure. The procedure CONSTRUCT_HEAP builds the initial heap out of the list L given as input. RECONSTRUCT_HEAP reconstructs the heap after the root node and the largest numbered node has been swapped. Procedure HEAP_SORT accepts the list $L[1:n]$ as input and returns the output sorted list in L itself.

17.8.4. Stability and performance analysis

Heap sort is an unstable sort (see illustrative problem 17.9). The time complexity of heap sort is $O(n \ log_2 n)$.

17.9. Radix sort

Radix sort belongs to the family of sorting by distribution where keys are repeatedly distributed into groups or classes based on the digits or characters forming the key until the entire list at the end of a distribution phase gets sorted. For a long time, this sorting procedure was used to sort punched cards. Radix sort is also known as **bin sort, bucket sort** or **digital sort.**

17.9.1. Radix sort method

Given a list L of n number of keys, where each key K is made up of l digits, $K = k_1 k_2 k_3 \ldots k_l$, radix sort distributes the keys based on the digits forming the key. If the distribution proceeds from the **least significant digit (LSD)** onwards and progresses left digit after digit, then it is termed **LSD first sort.** We illustrate LSD first sort in this section.

Let us consider the case of LSD first sort of the list L of n keys each comprising l digits (i.e.) $K = k_1 k_2 k_3 \ldots k_l$, where each k_i is such that $0 \le k_i < r$. Here, r is termed as the *radix* of the key representation and hence the name radix sort. Thus, if L were to deal with decimal keys then the radix would be 10. If the keys were octal the radix would be 8 and if they were hexadecimal it would be 16 and so on.

In order to understand the distribution passes of the LSD first sort procedure, we assume that r bins corresponding to the radix of the keys are present. In the first pass of the sort, all the keys of the list L, based on the value of their last digit, which is k_l, are thrown into their respective bins. At the end of the distribution, the keys are collected in order from each of the bins. At this stage, the keys are said to have been sorted based on their LSD.

In the second pass, we undertake a similar distribution of the keys, throwing them into the bins based on their next digit, k_{l-1}. Collecting them in order from the bins yields the keys sorted according to their last but one digit. The distribution continues for l passes, at the end of which the entire list L is obtained sorted.

EXAMPLE 17.18.–

Consider a list L = {387, 690, 234, 435, 567, 123, 441}. Here, the number of elements $n = 7$, the number of digits $l = 3$ and radix $r = 10$. This means that radix sort would require 10 bins and would complete the sorting in 3 passes.

Figure 17.14 illustrates the passes of radix sort over the list. It is assumed that each key is thrown into the bin face down. At the end of each pass, when the keys are collected from each bin in order, the list of keys in each bin is turned upside down to be appended to the output list.

During the implementation of the radix sort procedure in the computer, it is convenient to make use of linked lists for the representation of the bins. The linked list implementation of the sort for the list shown in Example 17.18, is illustrated in Figure 17.15. Here, the bins are implemented as an array of head nodes (shaded in grey). Each of the headed linked lists representing the bins could be implemented as a linked queue with two pointers front and rear, each pointing to the first and last node of the singly linked list, respectively. At the end of each pass, the elements from each list could be appended to the output list by undertaking deletions in each of the linear queues representing the bins until they are empty.

Algorithm 17.12 illustrates the skeletal procedure for the LSD first radix sort.

$L = \{387, 690, 234, 435, 567, 123, 441\}$

Pass 1

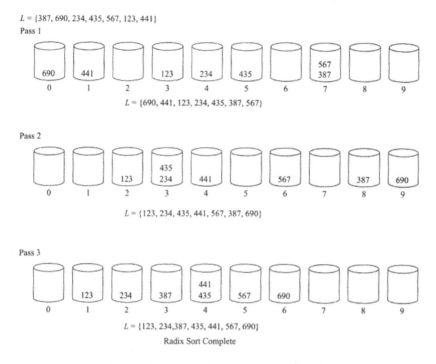

$L = \{690, 441, 123, 234, 435, 387, 567\}$

Pass 2

$L = \{123, 234, 435, 441, 567, 387, 690\}$

Pass 3

$L = \{123, 234, 387, 435, 441, 567, 690\}$

Radix Sort Complete

Figure 17.14. *Radix sort (Example 17.18)*

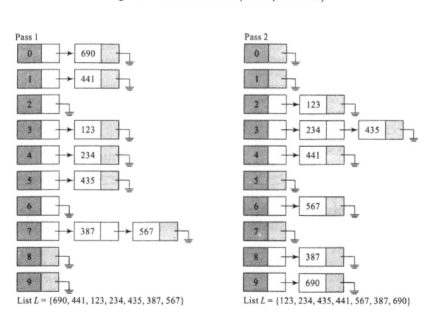

Pass 1

List $L = \{690, 441, 123, 234, 435, 387, 567\}$

Pass 2

List $L = \{123, 234, 435, 441, 567, 387, 690\}$

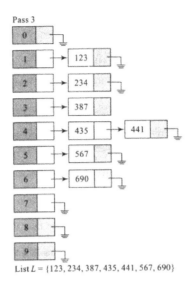

List $L = \{123, 234, 387, 435, 441, 567, 690\}$

Figure 17.15. *Linked list implementation of radix sort (Example 17.18)*

```
procedure RADIX_SORT(L, n, r, d )
/* radix sort sorts a list L of n keys, each comprising
d digits with radix r*/

    Initialize each of the Q[0:r-1] linked queues
    representing the bins to be empty;

    for i = d to 1 step -1     /* for each of the d
                                  passes over the list*/
        Sort the list L of n keys K = k₁k₂k₃...k_d based
        on the digit i, inserting each of the keys K
        into the linked queue Q[k_i],  0 ≤ k_i < r;

            /* distribute the keys into Q[0:(r-1)]
            based on the radix value of the digits*/

        Delete the keys from the queues  Q[0:r-1] in
        order, and append  the elements to the output
        list L;
    end

    return(L);

end RADIX_SORT.
```

Algorithm 17.12. *Procedure for radix sort*

17.9.2. *Most significant digit first sort*

Radix sort can also be undertaken by considering the ***most significant digits*** of the key first. The distribution proceeds from the most significant digit (**MSD**) of the key onwards and progresses right digit after digit. In such a case, the sort is termed *MSD first sort.*

MSD first sort is similar to what happens in a post office during the sorting of letters. Using the pin code, the letters are first sorted into zones, for a zone into its appropriate states, for a state into its districts, and so on until they are easy enough for efficient delivery to the respective neighborhoods. Similarly, MSD first sort distributes the keys to the appropriate bins based on the MSD. If the sub pile in each bin is small enough then it is prudent to use a non-radix sort method to sort each of the sub-piles and gather them together. On the other hand, if the sub pile in each bin is not small enough, then each of the sub-piles is once again radix sorted based on the second digit and so on until the entire list of keys gets sorted.

17.9.3. *Performance analysis*

The performance of the radix sort algorithm is given by $O(d.(n+r))$, where d is the number of passes made over the list of keys of size n and radix r. Each pass reports a time complexity of $O(n+r)$ and therefore for d passes the time complexity is given by $O(d.(n+r))$.

17.10. Counting sort

Counting sort is a linear sorting algorithm that was developed by Harold Seward in 1954. The sorting method works on keys whose values are small integers and lie between a specific range. Unlike most other sorting algorithms, counting sort does not work on comparisons of keys.

Given an unordered set of keys $D = \{K_1, K_2, K_3, \dots K_n\}$, it is essential that the keys K_i are all small integers and lie between a specific range a to b, where a and b are integers and $b = a + r$, for a small positive r. The keys need not be distinct and the list may comprise repetitive occurrences of keys. Counting sort works as follows.

In the first stage, it finds the frequency count or the number of occurrences of each distinct key K_i. Obviously K_i would be distinct elements lying between a and b. Therefore counting sort creates a one-dimensional array COUNT whose indexes are the integers lying between a and b and whose values are their respective frequency counts. The COUNT array now indicates the number of occurrences of each distinct key K_i in the original data set.

In the second stage, counting sort undertakes simple arithmetic over the COUNT array and stores the output in a new one-dimensioned array POSITION whose indexes just like those of COUNT vary from a to b. For each index value, POSITION stores the sum of previous counts available in COUNT. Thus, array POSITION indicates the exact position of the distinct key K_i in the sorted array, represented by its index value.

In the third stage, counting sort opens an output array OUTPUT[$1{:}n$] to hold the sorted keys. Each key K_j from the set D of unordered keys is pulled out, and its position p is determined by retrieving $p = $ POSITION$[K_j]$. However, it proceeds to verify if there are repetitive occurrences of key K_j from the COUNT array and retrieves the value $v = $ COUNT$[K_j]$. Now, counting sort computes the revised position as $p\text{-}(v\text{-}1)$ and stores key K_j in OUTPUT[$p\text{-}(v\text{-}1)$]. COUNT$[K_j]$ is decremented by 1. It can be observed that counting sort not only determines the exact position of the key K_j in the sorted output, but also undertakes the arithmetic of $p\text{-}(v\text{-}1)$ so that in the case of repetitive keys the relative order of the elements in the original list are maintained after sorting. This is termed **stability** and therefore counting sort is a *stable sort* algorithm, as it ensures the relative order of keys with equal values even after the keys are sorted.

EXAMPLE 17.19.–

Let $D = \{2, 3, 3, 0, 0, 4, 5, 5, 5, 1\}$ be an unordered set of keys in the range 0 to 5. To sort the data, Counting sort works as follows.

In the first stage, the frequency count of the distinct elements in the range 0–5 belonging to D is computed. Figure 17.16(a) illustrates the creation of the one-dimensioned array COUNTER[0:5] that stores the frequency counts of the distinct elements. It can be observed that the frequency count of element 5 is 3 and therefore COUNT[5] stores the value of 3. The frequency count of $\{1, 2, 4\}$ is $\{1, 1, 1\}$ and therefore the respective indexes of COUNT store the value 1 in each of the respective locations.

In the second stage, the one-dimensioned array POSITION[0:5] stores the sum of the previous counts available in COUNT, as shown in Figure 17.16(b). To begin with, POSITION[0] is set to the value of COUNT[0]. For POSITION[1], COUNT[0]+COUNT[1] is stored and for POSITION[3], COUNT[0]+COUNT[1] +COUNT[3] is stored, and so on. A short cut to undertake this computation would be to compute POSITION[$i\text{-}1$] + COUNT[i] and store this value in POSITION[i],

$i \geq 1$. The diagonal arrows in the figure indicate this computation and the vertical arrows the storage of the values in the respective locations of POSITION. Observe that POSITION represents the exact position of the element indicated by its index value. Thus, POSITION[4]=7 indicates that element 4 in D after sorting would occupy the 7th position in the list and so on.

In the third stage, the sorted output is stored in OUTPUT[1:10], as shown in Figure 17.16(c). To undertake this, counting sort pulls out each element in D in the order of its appearance in D and finds out its position in the sorted list by accessing the corresponding index of POSITION and COUNT arrays. Thus, when 2, which is the first element in D, is pulled out, POSITION[2]=4 and COUNT[2]=1. This means that 2 is a distinct element and occupies position 4 in the sorted list. Therefore, OUTPUT[4]=2 is set and COUNT[2] is decremented by 1. In the case of the first occurring 3 in D, indicated as $3^{(1)}$, POSITION[3]=6 and COUNT[3]=2, therefore, to tackle the repetitive occurrence of 3 and ensure stability in sorting, $3^{(1)}$ will be accommodated in OUTPUT[6-(2-1)], (i.e.) OUTPUT[5]=3. COUNT[3] is decremented by 1. In the case of the second occurring 3 in D indicated as $3^{(2)}$, following a similar argument, POSITION[3]=6 and COUNT[3]=1, therefore OUTPUT[6-(1-1)] =OUTPUT[6]=$3^{(2)}$ and COUNT[3] is set to 0. Figure 17.16(c) illustrates the aforementioned entries in OUTPUT [1:10]. The rest of the entries are similarly made in OUTPUT[1:10], which finally represents the sorted output of D.

Algorithm 17.13 illustrates the counting sort algorithm. For simplicity of implementation and understanding, the range (a, b) within which the unordered set of keys lie is assumed to be within $(0, k)$.

```
procedure COUNTING_SORT(L, k)
/*L[1:n] is an unordered list of keys lying within the
range    [a, b]= [0, k]   */

/* initialize array COUNT */
  for i = 0 to k do
    COUNT[i] =0
  end

/*  store  frequency  count  of  each  key  against
corresponding index of  array COUNT */
  for j = 1 to n do
     COUNT[L[j]] = COUNT[L[j]] + 1;
  end

/* create array POSITION which will indicate the actual
position of the distinct keys in the sorted output */
```

```
POSITION[0]  =  COUNT[0];
for i = 1 to k do
   POSITION[i]= POSITION[i-1]+COUNT[i]
end
```

/* create array OUTPUT that holds the sorted list of
elements in L[1:n] */

```
for j = 1 to n do
   p = POSITION[L[j]];
   v = COUNT[L[j]];
   OUTPUT[p-(v-1)] = L[j];
   COUNT[L[j]] = COUNT[L[j]]-1;
end
```

end COUNTING_SORT

Algorithm 17.13. *Procedure for counting sort*

$D = \{2, 3, 3, 0, 0, 4, 5, 5, 5, 1\}$ Range: $(a,b) = (0,5)$

COUNT:	0	1	2	3	4	5	INDEX
Counting sort
Stage 1:

	2	1	1	2	1	3	VALUE

(a)

Stage 2:   COUNT:

0	1	2	3	4	5	INDEX
2	1	1	2	1	3	VALUE

POSITION:

2	3	4	6	7	10	VALUE
0	1	2	3	4	5	INDEX

(b)

Stage 3:

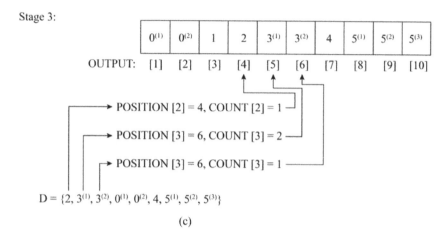

Figure 17.16. *Illustration of counting sort*

17.10.1. *Performance analysis*

Counting sort is a non-comparison sorting method and has a time complexity of $O(n+k)$, where n is the number of input elements and k is the range of non-negative integers within which the input elements lie. The algorithm can be implemented using a straightforward application of array data structures and therefore, the space complexity of the algorithm is also given by $O(n+k)$. Counting sort is a stable sort algorithm.

17.11. Bucket sort

Bucket sort is a *comparison sort* algorithm that works best when employed over a list of keys that are *uniformly distributed over a range*. Given a list of keys spread over a range, a definite number of *buckets* or bins are opened, which will collect keys belonging to a specific sub-range, in an ordered sequence. Each key from the unordered list, based on a formula evolved using the keys in the list and the number of buckets, is dropped into the appropriate bucket. Thus, in the first stage, all the keys in the unordered list are *scattered* over the buckets. In the next stage, all the keys in the non-empty buckets are *sorted* using any known algorithm, although it would be prudent to use *insertion sort* for the purpose. In the final stage, all the sorted keys from each bucket are *gathered* in a sequential fashion from each of the buckets to yield the output sorted list.

Considering the three stages of scattering, sorting, and gathering that bucket sort calls for, an *array of lists* would be a convenient data structure to handle all three efficiently. Figure 17.17 illustrates the array of lists data structure for bucket sort. The size of the array would be k, the number of buckets decided upon, and each array location would hold a pointer to a *singly linked list* that will represent the keys dropped into the bucket. As and when the keys get dropped into their respective buckets, they are inserted into the singly linked list. If *insertion sort* (discussed in section 17.3) were to be employed, then each of the singly-linked lists gets maintained as a sorted list every time an insertion happens, and therefore the final gathering of keys from the buckets in a sequence, to release the sorted output is easy and efficient. Algorithm 17.14 illustrates the pseudocode for bucket sort, implemented using an array of lists.

EXAMPLE 17.20.–

Let $L[1:8] = \{50, 30, 25, 5, 10, 35, 20, 40\}$ be a list of unordered keys distributed uniformly within the range $[0:50]$. Tracing Algorithm 17.14 for a number of buckets $k = 5$ yields an array of lists shown in Figure 17.18. With max = *maximum* $(L[1:8]) = 50$, the bucket positions calculated for $L[1:8]$ is given by $\{5, 3, 3, 1, 1, 4, 2, 4\}$. For example, for key $L[8] = 40$, position $= \lceil L[8]/\text{max}*k \rceil$ yields $\lceil 40/50*5 \rceil = 4$. Similarly, the rest of the bucket positions for the other keys can be computed. Inserting the respective keys in the corresponding singly linked lists following the principle of insertion sort yields the array of lists shown in the figure. Gathering all the keys in the buckets in an ordered sequence yields the sorted list $\{5, 10, 20, 25, 30, 35, 40, 50\}$.

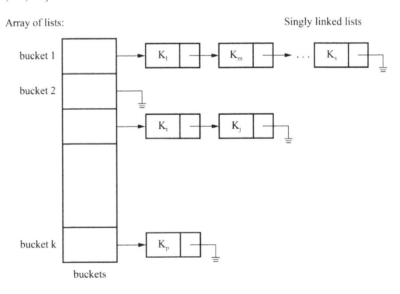

Figure 17.17. *Array of lists data structure to implement bucket sort*

L [1 : 8] = {50, 30, 25, 5, 10, 35, 20, 40}
Position = {5, 3, 3, 1, 1, 4, 2, 4}

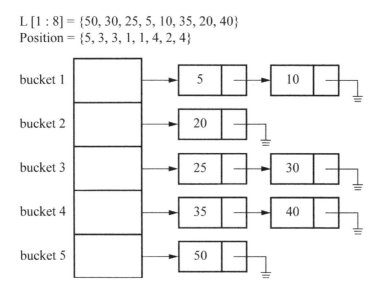

Figure 17.18. *Illustration of bucket sort*

procedure BUCKET_SORT(L, n, k)

```
/* L[1:n] is a unordered list of n keys uniformly
distributed within a range and k is the number of
buckets*/

/* Let buckets[1:k] represent the array of singly linked
lists */

   initialize buckets[1:k] to empty lists;

   max = maximum(L); /* max is the maximum key in L */

   for  i = 1 to n do
        position = ⌈L[i]/max*k⌉;

        insert  L[i]  into  the  singly  linked  list
        represented  by  buckets[position]  in  its
        appropriate position, following the principle of
        insertion sort;
   end
```

```
gather all the keys in each of the sorted singly
linked lists in an ordered sequence to output the
sorted list of keys;
```

end BUCKET_SORT

Algorithm 17.14. *Procedure for bucket sort*

17.11.1. *Performance analysis*

The performance of bucket sort depends on the distribution of keys, the number of buckets, the sorting algorithm undertaken for sorting the list of keys in each bucket and the gathering of keys together to produce the sorted list.

The worst-case scenario is when all the keys get dropped into the same bucket and therefore insertion sort can report an average case complexity of $O(n^2)$ to order the keys in the bucket. In such a case, bucket sort would report a complexity of $O(n^2)$, which is worse than a typical comparison sort algorithm that reports an average performance of $O(n.\ log\ n)$. Here, n is the size of the list.

However, on average, bucket sort reports a time complexity of $O(n+k)$, if the input keys are uniformly distributed over a range. Here, n is the size of the list and k is the number of buckets.

Summary

– Sorting deals with the problem of arranging elements in a list according to the ascending or descending order.

– Internal sort refers to sorting of lists or files that can be accommodated in the internal memory of the computer. On the other hand, external sorting deals with sorting of files or lists that are too huge to be accommodated in the internal memory of the computer and hence need to be stored in external storage devices such as disks or drums.

– The internal sorting methods of bubble sort, insertion sort, selection sort, merge sort, quick sort, shell sort, heap sort and radix sort are discussed.

– Bubble sort belongs to the family of sorting by exchange or transposition. In each pass, the elements are compared pair wise until the largest key amongst the participating elements bubbles to the end of the list.

– Insertion sort belongs to the family of sorting by insertion. The sorting method is based on the principle that a new key K is inserted at its appropriate position in an already sorted sub list.

– Selection sort is built on the principle of selecting the minimum element of the list and exchanging it with the element in the first position of the list, and so on until the whole list gets sorted.

– Merge sort belonging to the family of sorting by merge makes use of the principle of merge to sort an unordered list. The sorted sublists of the original lists are merged to obtain the final sorted list.

– Shell sort divides the list into sub lists of elements making use of a sequence of increments and insertion sorts each sub list, before gathering them for the subsequent pass. The passes are repeated for each of the increments until the entire list gets sorted.

– Quick sort belongs to the family of sorting by exchange. The procedure works on the principle of partitioning the unordered list into two sublists at every stage of the sorting process based on the pivot element and recursively quick sorting the sublists.

– Heap sort belongs to the family of sorting by selection. It is based on the principle of repeated selection of either the smallest or the largest key from the remaining elements of the unordered list constructed as a heap, for inclusion in the output list.

– Radix sort belongs to the family of sorting by distribution and is classified as LSD first sort and MSD first sort. The sorting of the keys is undertaken digit wise in d passes, where d is the number of digits in the keys over a radix r.

– Counting sort is a non-comparison sort and a stable sort that works on keys which lie within a small specific range.

– Bucket sort is a comparison sort that works best over keys that are uniformly distributed over a range.

17.12. Illustrative problems

PROBLEM 17.1.–

Trace bubble sort algorithm on the list $L = \{$K, Q, A, N, C, A, P, T, V, B$\}$. Verify the stability of bubble sort over L.

Solution:

The partially sorted lists at the end of the respective passes of the sorting procedure are shown below. Repeated elements in the list have been superscripted with indexes.

Unsorted list	$\{K, Q, A^1, N, C, A^2, P, T, V, B\}$
Pass 1	$\{K, A^1, N, C, A^2, P, Q, T, B, V\}$
Pass 2	$\{A^1, K, C, A^2, N, P, Q, B, T, \underline{V}\}$
Pass 3	$\{A^1, C, A^2, K, N, P, B, Q, \underline{T, V}\}$
Pass 4	$\{A^1, A^2, C, K, N, B, P, \underline{Q, T, V}\}$
Pass 5	$\{A^1, A^2, C, K, B, N, \underline{P, Q, T, V}\}$
Pass 6	$\{A^1, A^2, C, B, K, \underline{N, P, Q, T, V}\}$
Pass 7	$\{A^1, A^2, B, C, \underline{K, N, P, Q, T, V}\}$
Pass 8	$\{A^1, A^2, B, \underline{C, K, N, P, Q, T, V}\}$
Pass 9	$\{A^1, A^2, \underline{B, C, K, N, P, Q, T, V}\}$

Since the relative order of positions of equal keys remains unaffected even after the sort, bubble sort is stable over L.

PROBLEM 17.2.–

Trace the passes of insertion sort on the following lists:

i) $\{H, K, M, N, P\}$ ii) $\{P, N, M, K, H\}$

Compare their performance in terms of the comparisons made.

Solution:

The lists at the end of each pass of insertion sort are shown in Table P17.2. It may be observed that while list (i) is already in ascending order, list (ii) is in descending order. The sorted sublists are shown in brackets. The number of comparisons made in each of the passes is shown in bold. While list (i) needs to make a total of four comparisons, list (ii) needs to make a total of 10 comparisons to sort themselves using insertion sort.

Pass	Insertion sort of {H, K, M, N, P}	Number of comparisons	Insertion sort of {P, N, M, K, H}	Number of comparisons
1	{[H K] M N P}	**1**	{[N P] M K H}	**1**
2	{[H K M] N P}	**1**	{[M N P] K H}	**2**
3	{[H K M N] P}	**1**	{[K M N P] H}	**3**
4	{[H K M N P]}	**1**	{[H K M N P]}	**4**

Table P17.2. *Trace of insertion sort on the lists {H, K, M, N, P} and {P, N, M, K, H}*

PROBLEM 17.3.–

Undertake a 3-way merge for the lists shown below:

$L_1 = \{F, J, L\}, \quad L_2 = \{F, H, M, N, P\}, \quad L_3 = \{G, M\}$

Solution:

The snapshots of the 3-way merge of the lists into the list L are shown in Figure P17.3. At every stage, three elements, one from each of the lists, are compared and the smallest of them are dropped into the list. At the end of step 5, L_1 gets exhausted and at the end of step 6, L_3 also gets exhausted. In the last step, the remaining elements in list L_2 are merely flushed into list L.

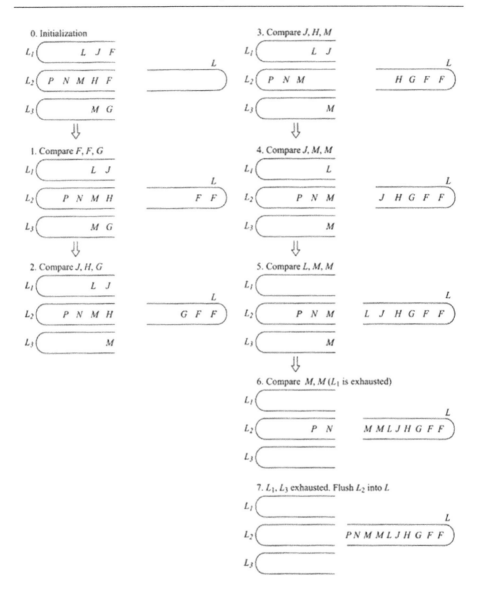

Figure P17.3. *Snapshots of the 3-way merge of the lists shown in illustrative problem 17.3*

PROBLEM 17.4.–

Undertake non-recursive merge sort for the list $L = \{78, 78, 78, 1\}$ and check for the stability of the sort.

Solution:

We undertake the non-recursive formulation of merge sort procedure for the list $L = \{78^1, 78^2, 78^3, 1\}$. The repeated keys in the list L are superscripted to track their orders of occurrence in the list. Figure P17.4 shows the passes over the list L. The final sorted list verifies that merge sort is stable.

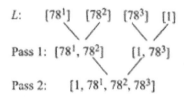

Figure P17.4. *Non-recursive merge sort for the list $L = \{78, 78, 78, 1\}$*

PROBLEM 17.5.–

Solve the recurrence relation for the time complexity of merge sort given in section 17.5.4, assuming the size of the list $n = 2^k$.

Solution:

The recurrence relation is given by

$$T(n) = 2.T\left(\frac{n}{2}\right) + c.n, \quad n \geq 2$$

$$= d$$

Solving the relation results in the following steps:

$$T(n) = 2.T\left(\frac{n}{2}\right) + c.n \qquad (i)$$

$$= 2\left(2.T\left(\frac{n}{4}\right) + c.\frac{n}{2}\right) + c.n$$

$$= 2^2.T\left(\frac{n}{4}\right) + 2.c.n \qquad (ii)$$

$$= 2^3.T\left(\frac{n}{8}\right) + 3.c.n \qquad (iii)$$

In step (k), $T(n)$ is obtained as,

$$T(n) = 2^k.T\left(\frac{n}{2^k}\right) + k.c.n$$
$$= n.T(1) + log_2 n . c.n \quad (\because n = 2^k, k = log_2 n)$$
$$= n.d + c.n.log_2 n$$
$$= O(n.log_2 n)$$

PROBLEM 17.6.–

Quick sort the list $L = \{A, B, N, M, P, R\}$. What are your observations? How can the observations help you in determining the worst-case complexity of quick sort?

Solution:

The quick sort process is demonstrated in Figure P17.6.

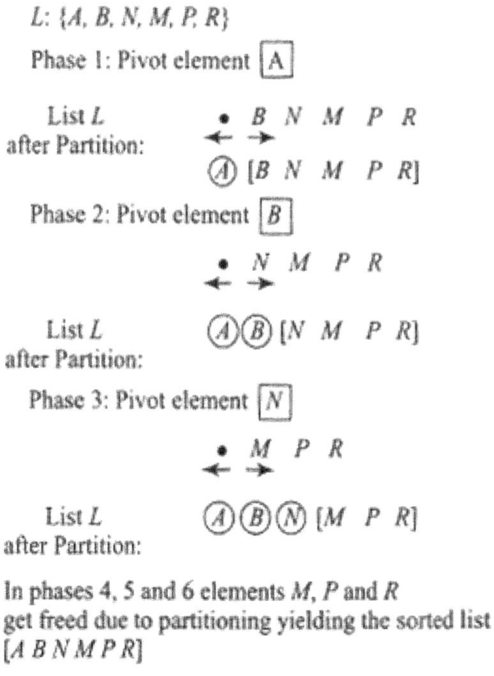

Figure P17.6. *Demonstration of quick sort over the list L= {A, B, N, M, P, R}*

Since the list is already in ascending order, during each phase of the sort, the elements in the order given get thrown out one by one during the subsequent partitions. In other words, with each partition the size of the list decrements by 1. The quick sort procedure is therefore recursively called, for lists of sizes n, $(n-1)$, $(n-2)$....3 2 1. Hence, the worst-case time complexity is given by,

$$O(\ (n)\ +(n-1)+(n-2)+.....3+2+1) = O(n^2).$$

PROBLEM 17.7.–

Discuss a procedure to obtain the rank of an element K in an array $LIST[1:n]$. How can procedure PARTITION (Algorithm 17.7) be effectively used for the same problem? What are the time complexities of the methods discussed?

Solution:

A direct method to obtain the rank of an element in an array $LIST[1:n]$ is to sort the list and search for the element K in the sorted list. The time complexity of the procedure in such a case would be $O(n\ log_2 n)$, since the best sorting algorithm reports a time complexity of $O(n\ log_2 n)$.

In the case of employing procedure PARTITION for the problem, K is first compared with the pivot element (P) that gets dropped off the list during the first partition. If $K=P$ then the problem is done. The index of P in the list $LIST$ would be the rank of the element K. On the other hand, if $(K < P)$ or $(K > P)$, then it would only call for searching for the rank of K in any one of the sublists occurring to the left or right of P by repeatedly invoking the procedure PARTITION. Hence, in this case, the time complexity would be $O(n)$ in the worst case.

PROBLEM 17.8.–

Trace procedure CONSTRUCT_HEAP (Algorithm 17.10) over the list $L[1:5] =$ $\{12, 45, 21, 67, 34\}$.

Solution:

Table P17.8 illustrates the trace of the procedure CONSTRUCT_HEAP, which invokes procedure INSERT_HEAP repeatedly for the elements belonging to $L[2:5] = \{45, 21, 67, 34\}$. At the end of the execution, procedure CONSTRUCT_HEAP yields the list $L[1:5] = \{67, 45, 21, 12, 34\}$, which is the heap.

Call to INSERT_HEAP	child_index	parent_index	L[1:5]	Remarks
			{12, 45, 21, 67, 34}	Initialization
INSERT_HEAP (L, 2)	2	1	{45, 12, 21, 67, 34}	L[1]<L[2] swap(L[1], L[2]) done.
	1	0	{45, 12, 21, 67, 34}	
INSERT_HEAP (L, 3)	3	1	{45, 12, 21, 67, 34}	L[1]>L[3] No swap.
INSERT_HEAP (L, 4)	4	2	{45, 67, 21, 12, 34}	L[2]<L[4] swap(L[2], L[4]) done.
	2	1	{67, 45, 21, 12, 34}	L[1]<L[2] swap(L[1], L[2]) done.
	1	0	{67, 45, 21, 12, 34}	
INSERT_HEAP (L, 5)	5	2	{67, 45, 21, 12, 34}	L[2]>L[5] No swap.

Table P17.8. *Trace of* `procedure CONSTRUCT_HEAP` *(Algorithm 17.10) over the list L[1:5]={12, 45, 21, 67, 34}*

PROBLEM 17.9.–

Test for the stability of heap sort on the list $L = \{7^1, 7^2, 7^3\}$.

Solution:

Figure P17.9 demonstrates the heap sort process on L. The final sorted list $L = \{7^3, 7^2, 7^1\}$. This verifies that heap sort is unstable.

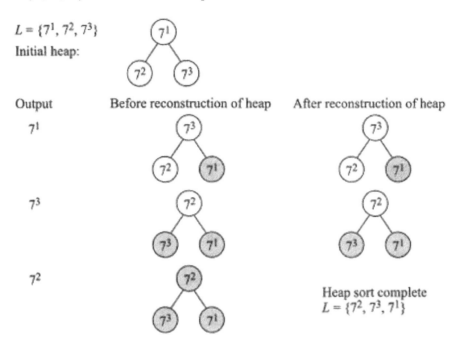

$L = \{7^1, 7^2, 7^3\}$

Initial heap:

Output

7^1

7^3

7^2

Before reconstruction of heap

After reconstruction of heap

Heap sort complete
$L = \{7^2, 7^3, 7^1\}$

Figure P17.9. *Demonstration of heap sort on the list L = {7, 7, 7}*

PROBLEM 17.10.–

Radix sort the list $L = \{001, 101, 010, 000, 111, 110, 011, 100\}$.

Solution:

The list L commands the following parameters: $n = 8$, $d = 3$ and $r = 2$. The radix sort process is shown in Figure P17.10.

$L = \{001, 101, 010, 000, 111, 110, 011, 100\}$

Phase 1:

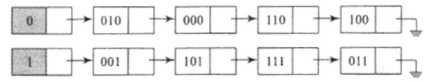

List $L = \{010, 000, 110, 100, 001, 101, 111, 011\}$

Phase 2:

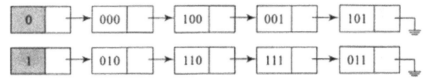

$L = \{000, 100, 001, 101, 010, 110, 111, 011\}$

Phase 3:

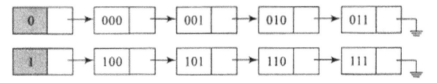

List $L = \{000, 001, 010, 011, 100, 101, 110, 111\}$

The final radix sorted list

$L = \{000, 001, 010, 011, 100, 101, 110, 111\}$

Figure P17.10. *Demonstration of radix sort on the list L= {001, 101, 010, 000, 111, 110, 011, 100}*

PROBLEM 17.11.–

Selection sort the list $L = \{H, V, A, T, L, M, K \}$.

Solution:

The sorting steps are shown below. The minimum element in each pass is shown in bold. The arrows indicate the swap of the minimum element with that in the first position of the sublist considered for the pass. The elements underlined are indicative of the exclusion of elements from the pass.

Pass	List L (During Pass)	List L (After Pass)
1	{H, V, **A**, T, P, M, K}	{A, V, H, T, P, M, K}
2	{<u>A</u>, V, **H**, T, P, M, K}	{A, H, V, T, P, M, K}
3	{<u>A, H,</u> V, T, P, M, **K**}	{A, H, K, T, P, M, V}
4	{<u>A, H, K,</u> T, P, **M**, V}	{A, H, K, M, P, T, V}
5	{<u>A, H, K, M,</u> **P**, T, V}	{A, H, K, M, P, T, V}
6	{<u>A, H, K, M, P,</u> **T**, V}	{A, H, K, M, P, T, V}

Sorted list: {A, H, K, M, P, T, V}

PROBLEM 17.12.–

Test whether shell sort is stable on the list $L = \{7, 5^1, 5^2, 5^3, 5^4, 5^5, 5^6, 5^7, 5^8, 5^9\}$ for a sequence of increments {4, 2, 1}. The repeated occurrences of element 5 have been superscripted with their orders of occurrence.

Solution:

The trace of shell sort on the list L is shown in Figure P17.12. It is unstable.

Unordered list L:

K_1	K_2	K_3	K_4	K_5	K_6	K_7	K_8	K_9	K_{10}
7	5^1	5^2	5^3	5^4	5^5	5^6	5^7	5^8	5^9

Pass 1 (increment $h_2 = 4$)

$(K_1 \quad K_5 \quad K_9) \quad (K_2 \quad K_6 \quad K_{10}) \quad (K_3 \quad K_7) \quad (K_4 \quad K_8)$
$(7 \quad 5^4 \quad 5^8) \qquad (5^1 \quad 5^5 \quad 5^9) \qquad (5^2 \quad 5^6) \qquad (5^3 \quad 5^7)$

After insertion sort:
$(5^4 \quad 5^8 \quad 7) \quad (5^1 \quad 5^5 \quad 5^9) \quad (5^2 \quad 5^6) \quad (5^3 \quad 5^7)$

List L after Pass 2

K_1	K_2	K_3	K_4	K_5	K_6	K_7	K_8	K_9	K_{10}
5^4	5^1	5^2	5^3	5^8	5^5	5^6	5^7	7	5^9

Pass 2 (increment $h_1 = 2$)

$(K_1 \quad K_3 \quad K_5 \quad K_7 \quad K_9) \quad (K_2 \quad K_4 \quad K_6 \quad K_8 \quad K_{10})$
$(5^4 \quad 5^2 \quad 5^8 \quad 5^6 \quad 7) \quad (5^1 \quad 5^3 \quad 5^5 \quad 5^7 \quad 5^9)$

After insertion sort:
$(5^4 \quad 5^2 \quad 5^8 \quad 5^6 \quad 7) \quad (5^1 \quad 5^3 \quad 5^5 \quad 5^7 \quad 5^9)$

List L after Pass 3:

K_1	K_2	K_3	K_4	K_5	K_6	K_7	K_8	K_9	K_{10}
5^4	5^1	5^2	5^3	5^8	5^5	5^6	5^7	7	5^9

Pass 3 (increment $h_0 = 1$)

K_1	K_2	K_3	K_4	K_5	K_6	K_7	K_8	K_9	K_{10}
5^4	5^1	5^2	5^3	5^8	5^5	5^6	5^7	7	5^9

After insertion sort:
$5^4 \quad 5^1 \quad 5^2 \quad 5^3 \quad 5^8 \quad 5^5 \quad 5^6 \quad 5^7 \quad 5^9 \quad 7$

Sorted List L $5^4 \quad 5^1 \quad 5^2 \quad 5^3 \quad 5^8 \quad 5^5 \quad 5^6 \quad 5^7 \quad 5^9 \quad 7$

Figure P17.12. *Testing the stability of shell sort on the list L given in illustrative problem 17.12*

PROBLEM 17.13.–

Trace counting sort on the following list L of unordered keys which lie within the range [10, 18].

$L[1:10]$:   16 11 18 13 11 12 15 15 18 16

Solution:

Figure P17.13 illustrates the three stages in the counting sort procedure, adopting the same labels for the arrays involved in Algorithm 17.13. COUNT [10:18] holds the frequency counts of the keys in $L[1:10]$, POSITION [10:18] the positions of the distinct keys in $L[1:10]$ and OUTPUT [1:10] the sorted list of keys. The arrays COUNT and POSITION have been indexed between the range [10:18] for ease of implementation.

$L = [1:10] = \{16\ 11\ 18\ 13\ 11\ 12\ 15\ 15\ 18\ 16\}$

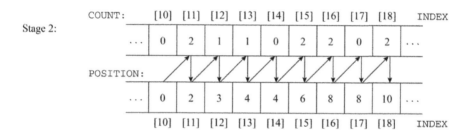

Figure P17.13. *Trace of counting sort on the list L given in illustrative problem 17.13*

PROBLEM 17.14.−

Trace bucket sort for a list $L[1:9] = \{0.56, 0.87, 0.21, 0.43, 0.77, 0.62, 0.33, 0.28, 0.99\}$ of floating point numbers which lie within the range [0-1], for a number of buckets $k = 10$.

Solution:

The list $L[1:9]$ comprises floating point numbers, which need to be scattered across the ten buckets which are labeled as 1, 2, 3, ...10. Therefore, it is essential to evolve a formula that will determine the bucket in which the respective keys need to be dropped. A simple and elegant formula would be to compute position $= \lceil L[i]*k \rceil$ (Algorithm 17.14), which yields the bucket labels as {6, 9, 3, 5, 8, 7, 4, 3, 10} for the list L.

Figure P17.14 illustrates the array of lists for bucket sorting $L[1:9]$ for the number of buckets $k = 10$. Gathering the sorted lists in an ordered sequence yields the final sorted list {0.21, 0.28, 0.33, 0.43, 0.56, 0.62, 0.77, 0.87, 0.99}.

$L[1:9] = \{0.56, 0.87, 0.21, 0.43, 0.77, 0.62, 0.33, 0.28, 0.99\}$

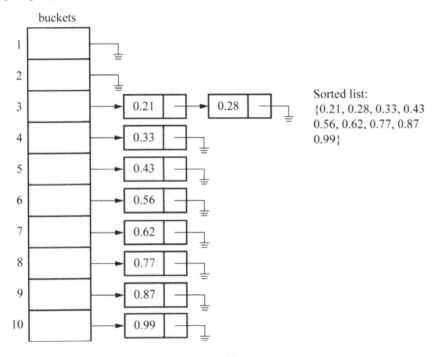

Figure P17.14. *Trace of bucket sort over the list L shown in illustrative problem 17.14*

PROBLEM 17.15.–

Convert a binary search tree into a min-heap. Demonstrate the method on the following binary search tree.

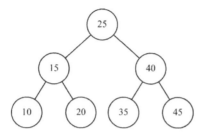

Solution:

A binary search tree has every left child value to be less than its parent node value and every right child value to be greater than its parent node value, in each subtree. A min-heap, on the other hand, has every parent node value in each of its subtrees to be smaller than the values of its child nodes, eventually leading to the root holding the smallest value in the entire tree.

The conversion of a binary search tree to a min-heap can be achieved by the following:

i) Undertake inorder traversal of the binary search tree, which yields the node values in the sorted order and stores them in an array DATA[1: n], where n is the number of nodes in the binary search tree.

ii) Undertake a preorder traversal of the binary search tree and every time a node is processed (the action sequence is PLR- Process node, move Left, move Right), replace the value of the node by DATA[1: n] in a linear sequence. At the end of the preorder traversal, the binary search tree transforms itself into a min-heap.

For the given binary search tree after inorder traversal is undertaken, DATA [1:7] = [10, 15, 20, 25, 35, 40, 45]. Now, performing preorder traversal and replacing the node traversed with DATA[1:7] in the sequential order, yields the min-heap shown below.

Solution

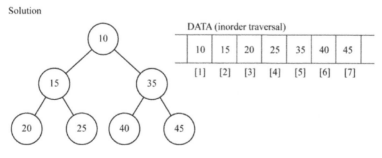

DATA (inorder traversal)

10	15	20	25	35	40	45
[1]	[2]	[3]	[4]	[5]	[6]	[7]

Review questions

1) Which of the following is unstable sort?

a) quick sort   b) insertion sort

c) bubble sort   d) merge sort

2) The worst-case time complexity of quick sort is

a) $O(n)$ b) $O(n^2)$ c) $O(n.logn)$ d) $O(n^3)$

3) Which among the following belongs to the family of sorting by selection?

a) merge sort   b) quick sort   c) heap sort   d) shell sort

4) Which of the following actions does not occur during the two-way merge of two lists L_1 and L_2 into the output list L?

a) If both L_1 and L_2 get exhausted, then the merge is done.

b) If L_1 gets exhausted before L_2, then simply output the remaining elements of L_2 into L and the merge is done.

c) If L_2 gets exhausted before L_1, then simply output the remaining elements of L_1 into L and the merge is done.

d) If one of the two lists (L_1 or L_2) gets exhausted, with the other still containing elements, then the merge is done.

5) For a list $L = \{7, 3, 9, 1, 8\}$ the output list at the end of Pass 1 of bubble sort would yield

a) {3, 7, 1, 9, 8}   b) {3, 7, 1,8,9}   c) {3, 1, 7, 9, 8}   d) {1, 3, 7, 8, 9}

6) Distinguish between internal sorting and external sorting.

7) When is a sorting process said to be stable?

8) Why is bubble sort stable?

9) What is k-way merging?

10) What is the time complexity of selection sort?

11) Distinguish between a heap and a binary search tree. Give an example.

12) What is the principle behind shell sort?

13) When is radix sort termed LSD first sort?

14) What is the principle behind the quick sort procedure?

15) What is the time complexity of merge sort?

16) Can bubble sort ever perform better than quick sort? If so, list a case.

17) Trace i) bubble sort, ii) insertion sort and iii) selection sort on the list

   L = {H, V, A, X, G, Y, S}

18) Demonstrate 3-way merging on the lists:

   L_1 = {123, 678, 345, 225, 890, 345, 111}, L_2 = {345, 123, 654, 789, 912, 144, 267, 909, 111, 324} and L_3 = {567, 222, 111, 900, 545, 897}

19) Trace quick sort on the list L = {11, 34, 67, 78, 78, 78, 99}. What are your observations?

20) Trace radix sort on the following list:

   L = {5678, 2341, 90, 3219, 7676, 8704, 4561, 5000}

21) Undertake heap sort for the list L shown in review question 17.

22) Which is a better data structure to retrieve (find) an element in a list, heap or binary search tree? Why?

23) Is counting sort a stable sort? If so, how? Illustrate with an example.

24) Which of the following are comparison sort algorithms?

   a) counting sort

   b) bubble sort

   c) insertion sort

25) Trace counting sort for the list L = {1, 5, 6, 5, 1, 7, 6, 2, 4, 6}.

26) Undertake bucket sort over a list L of equal length strings. Choose an appropriate number of buckets (k) and evolve a formula that will assign an appropriate bucket for each of the strings. Trace the array of lists for the defined L and k.

27) Compare and contrast bucket sort with radix sort and counting sort.

Programming assignments

1) Implement i) bubble sort and ii) insertion sort in a language of your choice. Test for the performance of the two algorithms on input files with elements already

sorted in i) descending order and ii) ascending order. Record the number of comparisons. What are your observations?

2) Implement quick sort algorithm. Enhance the algorithm to test for its stability.

3) Implement the non-recursive version of merge sort. Enhance the implementation to test for its stability.

4) Implement the LSD first and MSD first version of radix sort for alphabetical keys.

5) Implement heap sort with the assumption that the smallest element of the list floats to the root during the construction of heap.

6) Implement shell sort for a given sequence of increments. Display the output list at the end of each pass.

7) Implement counting sort over a list of keys that lie within the range (a, b), where a and b are small positive integers input by the user.

8) Implement bucket sort with an array of lists data structure to sort i) a list of strings, ii) a list of floating point numbers and iii) a list of integers, which are uniformly distributed over a range, for an appropriate choice of the number of buckets.

18

External Sorting

18.1. Introduction

Internal sorting deals with the ordering of records (or keys) of a file (or list) in ascending or descending order when the whole file or list is compact enough to be accommodated in the internal memory of the computer. Chapter 17 detailed internal sorting techniques such as Bubble Sort, Insertion Sort, Selection sort, Merge Sort, Shell sort, Quick Sort, Heap Sort, Radix Sort, Counting Sort and Bucket Sort.

However, in many applications and problems, it is quite common to encounter huge files comprising millions of records, which need to be sorted for their effective use in the application concerned. The application domains of e-governance, digital library, search engines, online telephone directory and electoral system, to list a few, deal with voluminous files of records.

The majority of the internal sorting techniques that we learned are virtually incapable of sorting large files since they require the whole file in the internal memory of the computer, which is impossible. Hence, the need for external sorting methods which are exclusive strategies to sort huge files.

18.1.1. *The principle behind external sorting*

Due to their large volume, the files are stored in external storage devices such as tapes, disks or drums. The external sorting strategies, therefore, need to take into consideration the kind of medium on which the files reside, since these influence their work strategy.

The files residing on these external storage devices are read 'piece meal' since only this many records, that can be accommodated in the internal memory of the computer, can be read at a time. These batches of records are sorted by making use of any efficient internal sorting method. Each of the sorted batches of records is referred to as *runs*. The file is now viewed as a collection of runs. The runs, as and when they are generated, are written out onto the external storage devices. The variety in the external sorting methods for a particular storage device is brought about only by the ways in which these runs are gathered and processed before the final sorted file is obtained. However, the majority of the popular external sorting methods make use of *merge sort* for gathering and processing the runs.

A common principle behind most popular external sorting methods is outlined below:

i) Internally sort batches of records from the source file to generate runs. Write out the runs as and when they are generated, onto the external storage device(s).

ii) Merge the runs generated in the earlier phase, to obtain larger but fewer runs, and write them out onto the external storage devices.

iii) Repeat the run generation and merge, until in the final phase only one run gets generated, on which the sorting of the file is done.

Since external storage devices play an imminent role in external sorting, we discuss sorting methods as applicable to two popular storage devices, for example, *magnetic tapes* and *magnetic disks*, the latter commonly referred to as *hard disks*. The reason for the choice is that these devices are representative of two different genres and display different characteristics. While magnetic tapes are undoubtedly obsolete these days, it is worthwhile to go through the external sorting methods applicable to these devices, considering the numerous research efforts and innovations that went into them, during their 'heydays'!

Section 18.2 briefly discusses the external storage devices of magnetic tapes and disks. The external sorting method of balanced merge applicable to files stored on both tapes and disks is elaborately discussed. A crisp description of polyphase merge and cascade merge sort procedures is presented finally.

18.2. External storage devices

In this section, we briefly explain the characteristics of magnetic tapes and magnetic disks.

18.2.1. *Magnetic tapes*

Magnetic tape is a *sequential device* whose principle is similar to that of an audio tape/cassette device. It consists of a reel of magnetic tape, approximately ½" wide, and wound around a *spool*. Data is stored on the tape using the principle of magnetization. Each tape has about seven or nine *tracks* running lengthwise. A spot on the tape represents a 0 or 1 bit depending on the direction of magnetization. A combination of bits on the tracks, at any point along the length of the tape, represents a character. The number of bits per inch that can be written on the tape is known as *tape density* and is expressed as *bpi* (bits per inch). Magnetic tapes with densities of 800 bpi and 1600 bpi were in common use during the earlier days.

The magnetic tape device consists of two *spindles*. While one spindle holds the *source reel*, the other holds the *take-up reel*. During a forward read/write operation, the tape moves from the source reel to the take-up reel. Figure 18.1 illustrates a schematic diagram of the magnetic tape drive.

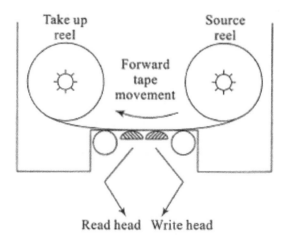

Figure 18.1. *Schematic diagram of a magnetic tape drive*

The data to be stored on a tape is written onto it in *blocks*. These blocks may be of fixed or variable size. A gap of ¾" is left between the blocks and is referred to as *Inter Block Gap* (IBG). The IBG is long enough to permit the tape to accelerate from rest to reach its normal speed before it begins to read the next block. Figure 18.2 shows the IBG of a tape.

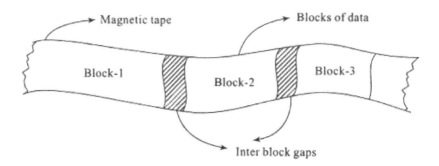

Figure 18.2. *Inter block gap of a tape*

Magnetic tape is a sequential device since having read a block of data, if one desires to read another block that is several feet down the tape, then it is essential to *fast forward* the tape until the correct block is reached. Again, if we desire to read blocks of data that occur towards the beginning of the tape, then it is essential that the tape is *rewound* and the reading starts from the beginning onward. In these aspects, the characteristic of tapes is similar to that of audio cassettes.

18.2.2. Magnetic disks

Magnetic disks are still in vogue and are commonly referred to as *hard disks*, these days. Hard disks are random access storage devices. This means that hard disks store data in such a manner that they permit both sequential access as well as random or direct access to data.

A *disk pack* is mountable on a *disk drive* and comprises platters that are similar to phonograph records. The number of platters in a disk pack varies according to its capacity. Figure 18.3 shows a schematic diagram of a disk pack comprising 6 platters.

Recording of data is done on all *surfaces* of the platters except the outer surfaces of the first and last platter. Thus, for a 6-platter disk pack, of the 12 surfaces available, data recording is done only on 10 of the surfaces. Each surface is accessed by a *read/write head*. The *access assembly* comprises an assembly of *access arms* ending in the read/write head. The access assembly moves in and out together with the access arms so that all the read/write heads at any point of time are stationed at the same position on the surface. During a read/write operation, the read/write head is held stationary over the appropriate position on the surface, while the disk rotates at high speed to enable the read/write operation. Disk speeds ranging from 3000 rpm to 7200 rpm are common these days.

Each surface of the platter, like a phonograph record, is made up of concentric circles of *tracks* of decreasing radii, on which the data is recorded. Modern versions of the hard disk contain tens of thousands of tracks per surface. The tracks are numbered from 0 beginning from the outer edge of the platter. The collection of tracks of the same radii, occurring on all the surfaces of the disk pack, is referred to as a *cylinder* (Figure 18.3). Thus, a disk pack is virtually viewed as a collection of cylinders of decreasing radii. Each track is divided into *sectors,* which is the smallest addressable segment of a track. Typically, a sector can hold 512 bytes of data approximately. The early disk packs had all tracks holding the same number of sectors. The modern versions have however rid themselves of this feature to increase the storage capacity of the disk.

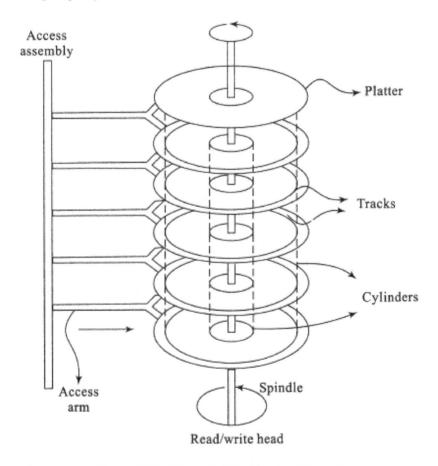

Figure 18.3. *Schematic diagram of a disk pack*

To access information on a disk, it is essential to first specify the cylinder number, followed by the track number and the sector number. A multilevel index-based ISAM file organization (section 14.7) is adopted for obtaining the physical locations of records stored on the disk. The *cylinder index* records the highest key in each cylinder and the cylinder number. The *surface index* or the *track index* stores the highest key in each track and the track number. Finally, the *sector index* records the highest key in each sector and the sector number. In practice, each of the index entries also contains other spatial information to help locate the records efficiently. Thus, the cylinder, track and sector indexes form a hierarchy of indexes that help identify the physical location of the record.

The read/write head moves across the cylinders to position itself on the right cylinder. The time taken to position the read/write head on the correct cylinder is known as *seek time*. Once the read/write head has positioned itself on the correct track of the cylinder, it has to wait for the right sector in the track to appear under the corresponding read/write head. The time taken for the right sector to appear under the read/write head is known as *latency time* or *rotational delay*. Once the sector is reached, the corresponding data is read or written onto the disk. The time taken for the transfer of data to and from the disk is known as *data transmission time*.

18.3. Sorting with tapes: balanced merge

Balanced merge sort makes use of an internal sorting technique to generate the runs and employs merging to gather the runs for the next phase of the sorting. The repeated run generation and merging continue until a single run generated in the final phase delivers the sorted file.

In this section, we discuss the balanced merge when the file resides on a tape. Besides the input tape, the sorting method has to make use of a few more work tapes to hold the runs that are generated from time to time and to perform the merging of the runs as well. Example 18.1 illustrates a balanced merge sort on tapes. The sorting method makes use of a two-way merge to gather the runs.

EXAMPLE 18.1.–

Let us suppose we had to sort a file of 50,000 records (R_1, R_2, R_3, ...$R_{50,000}$) which is available on a tape (Tape T_0) using a balanced two-way merge sort. Assume that the internal memory can hold only 10,000 records. Also let us suppose that there are four work tapes (T_1, T_2, T_3 and T_4) available to assist in the sorting process. R_{ij} indicates the jth run in the ith phase of the sorting.

↑ indicates the read/write head position on the tape. The steps in the sorting process are listed below:

Step 1: Rewind all tapes and mount tapes T_0, T_1 and T_2 onto the tape drive.

Step 2: *Phase 1*: Read blocks of 10,000 records each from tape T_0 and internally sort them to generate runs.

Let R_{11} $(R_1....R_{10,000})$, R_{12} $(R_{10,001}....R_{20,000})$, R_{13} $(R_{20,001}....R_{30,000})$, R_{14} $(R_{30,001}....R_{40,000})$ and R_{15} $(R_{40,001}....R_{50,000})$ be the five runs that are to be generated.

Distribute the runs alternately onto tapes T_1 and T_2. The distribution of runs on the tapes T_1 and T_2 are as shown below:

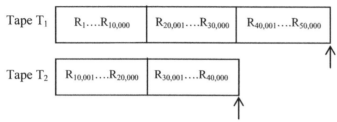

Step 3: Dismount tape T_0 and rewind tapes T_1 and T_2. Mount tapes T_1, T_2, T_3 and T_4 onto the drives. Here T_1 and T_2 are the input tapes and T_3 and T_4 are the output tapes.

Step 4: *Phase 2*: Merge runs on tapes T_1 and T_2 using a two-way merge to obtain longer runs R_{21} $(R_1....R_{20,000})$, R_{22} $(R_{20,001}....R_{40,000})$ and R_{23} $(R_{40,001}....R_{50,000})$. The distribution of runs on the output tapes T_3 and T_4 is shown below. Note that run R_{23} is simply copied onto tape T_3 and is just a dummy run.

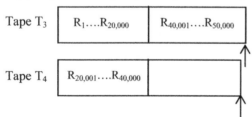

Step 5: Rewind all tapes T_1, T_2, T_3 and T_4. Mount T_3 and T_4 as the input tapes and T_1 and T_2 as the output tapes.

Step 6: *Phase 3*: Merge runs on tapes T_3 and T_4 using a two-way merge to obtain runs R_{31} $(R_1....R_{40,000})$ and R_{32} $(R_{40,001}....R_{50,000})$. The distribution of runs on the output tapes T_1 and T_2 are shown below. Note that run R_{32} is simply copied onto tape T_2 and is just a dummy run.

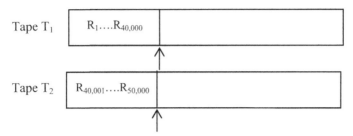

Step 7: Rewind all tapes T_1, T_2, T_3 and T_4. Mount T_1 and T_2 as the input tapes and T_3 as the output tape.

Step 8: *Phase 4:* Merge runs on tapes T_1 and T_2 using a two-way merge to obtain the final run R_{41} (R_1....$R_{50,000}$). The final run is written onto tape T_3.

18.3.1. *Buffer handling*

While merging runs in the balanced merge sort procedure, it needs to be observed that due to the limited capacity of the internal memory of the computer, it is not always possible to completely accommodate the runs and the merged list in it. In fact, the problem gets severe as the phases in the sort procedure progress, since the runs get longer and longer.

To tackle this problem, in the case of a two-way merge let us say, we trifurcate the internal memory into blocks known as **buffers**. Two of these blocks will be used as **input buffers** and the third as the **output buffer**. During the merge of two runs R_1 and R_2, for example, as many records as can be accommodated in the two input buffers are read from the runs R_1 and R_2 respectively. The merged records are sent to the output buffer. Once the output buffer is full, the records are written onto the disk. If during the merging process, any of the input buffers gets empty, it is once again filled with the rest of the records from the runs.

EXAMPLE 18.2.–

Let us consider the merge of two runs R_1 and R_2 each of which holds 500 records. The output run would contain 1000 records after merging. Let us suppose the internal memory of the computer can hold only 750 records. To undertake merging we divide the internal memory into two input buffers and an output buffer, each of which can hold 250 records. The merge process is shown below:

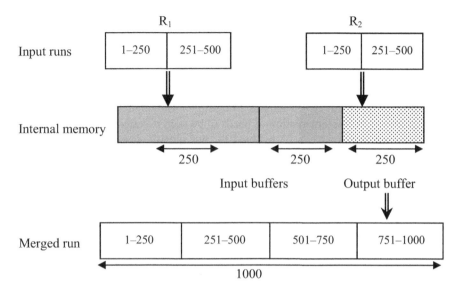

The input buffers read in 250 records each, from the two runs R_1 and R_2 respectively. The merging which yields 500 records is emptied by the output buffer into the disk as two blocks of 250 records each. The final merged run which contains 1000 records is, in fact, a collection of 4 blocks of merged records each containing 250 records.

Example 18.2 presented a naïve view of buffer handling. In reality, issues such as proper choice of buffer lengths, efficient utilization of program buffers to enable maximum overlapping of input/output and CPU processing times need to be attended to.

18.3.2. *Balanced P-way merging on tapes*

In the case of a balanced two-way merge, if M runs were produced in the internal sorting phase and if $2^{k-1} < M \le 2^k$ then the sort procedure makes $k = \lceil log_2 M \rceil$ merging passes over the data records.

Now balanced merging can easily be generalized to the inclusion of T tapes, $T \ge 3$. We divide the tapes, T, into two groups, with P tapes on the one side and

(T-P) tapes on the other, where $1 \le P < T$. The initial runs generated after internal sorting are evenly distributed onto the P tapes in the first group. A P-way merge is undertaken and the resulting runs are evenly distributed onto the next group containing (T-P) tapes. This is followed by a (T-P) merge of the runs available on the (T-P) tapes, with the output runs getting evenly distributed onto the P tapes of the first group and so on. However, it has been proved that $P = \left\lceil \frac{T}{2} \right\rceil$ is the best choice.

Illustrative problem 18.4 discusses an example. Though balanced merging can be quite simple in its implementation, it needs to be seen if better merging patterns that save time and resources can be evolved for the specific cases in hand. Illustrative problems 18.5 and 18.6 discuss specific cases.

18.4. Sorting with disks: balanced merge

Tapes being sequential access devices, the balanced merge sort methods had to employ sizable resources for the efficient distribution of runs besides spending time for mounting, dismounting and rewinding tapes. In the case of disks which are random access storage devices, we are spared of this burden. The seek time and latency time to access blocks of data from a disk are comparatively negligible, to the time taken to access blocks of data on tapes.

The balanced merge sort procedure for disk files, though similar in principle to that of tape files, is a lot simpler. The runs generated by the internal sorting methods are repeatedly merged until a single run emerges with the entire file sorted in the final pass. Example 18.3 demonstrates a balanced merge sort on a disk file.

EXAMPLE 18.3.–

Let us suppose a file comprising 4500 records (R_1, R_2, R_3,….R_{4500}) is available on a disk. The internal memory of the computer can accommodate only 750 records. Another disk is available as a scratch pad. The input disk is not to be written on. Making use of buffer handling, we presume that during internal sorting as well as merging, blocks of data comprising 250 records each are read/written. Rij indicates the jth run generated in the ith pass. The steps involved in undertaking a balanced two-way merge for sorting the file are shown below:

Step 1: Read three blocks of data (total 750 records) at a time from the file residing on the disk. Internally sort the blocks in the internal memory of the computer to generate six runs, which are, R01, R02, R03, R04, R05 and R06. Write the runs onto the scratch disk.

Step 2: Trifurcate the internal memory into two input buffers and a single output buffer each capable of holding 250 records.

Step 3: Read runs from the disk and merge them pair-wise, appropriately making use of buffer handling during the merging process and writing the output runs onto the scratch disk.

Step 4: Repeat step 3 until a single run emerges, holding the entire sorted file. The merging passes are schematically shown in Figure 18.4.

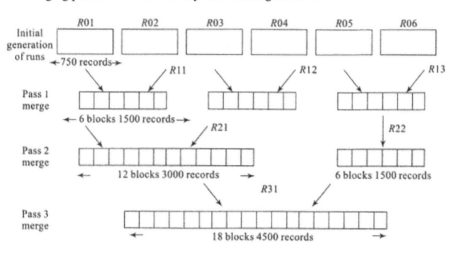

Figure 18.4. *Balanced merge sort on disks: merging the runs (Example 18.3)*

18.4.1. *Balanced k-way merging on disks*

As discussed in Section 18.3.2, balanced two-way merge sort can be generalized to k-way merging. For a two-way merge, as can be deduced from Figure 18.4, the number of passes over data is given by $\lceil log_2 M \rceil$ where M is the number of runs in the first level of the merge tree. A higher order merge can serve to reduce the number of passes over data. Thus, in the case of a k-way merge, $k \geq 2$, the number of passes is given by $\lceil log_k M \rceil$, where M is the number of runs. Figure 18.5 shows the merge tree for $k = 4$, for an initial generation of 16 runs in a specific case.

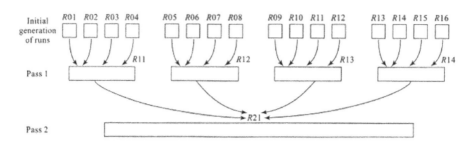

Figure 18.5. *Balanced k-way merge*
sort: merging the runs for k = 4

Though the k-way merge can significantly reduce input/output due to the reduction in the number of passes, it is not without its ill effects. Let us suppose R_1, R_2, R_3, ...R_k are the k runs generated initially with size r_i, $1 \leq i \leq k$. During a k-way merge, the next record which is to be output is the one with the smallest key. A direct method to find the smallest key would call for $(k\text{-}1)$ comparisons. The computing time to merge the k runs would be given by $O((k-1).\sum_{i=1}^{k} r_i)$. Since $\lceil log_2 M \rceil$ passes are being made, the total number of key comparisons is given by $n(k-1) log_2 M$, where n is the total number of records in the source file. We have $n(k-1) log_2 M = n(k-1)\frac{log_2 M}{log_2 k}$. In other words for a k-way merge sort, the number of key comparisons increases by a factor of $\frac{(k-1)}{log_2 k}$. Thus, for large k $(k \geq 6)$ the CPU time needed to perform the k-way merge will overweigh the reduction achieved in input/output time due to the reduction in the number of passes. A significant reduction in the number of comparisons to find the smallest key can be achieved by using what is known as a ***selection tree***.

18.4.2. Selection tree

A ***selection tree*** is a complete binary tree that serves to obtain the smallest key from among a set of keys. Each internal node represents the smaller of its two children and external nodes represent the keys from which the selection of the smallest key needs to be made. The root node represents the smallest key that was selected.

Figure 18.6(a) represents a selection tree for an eight-way merge. The eight lists to be merged are L_1 (5, 7, 8), L_2 (6, 9, 9), L_3 (2, 4, 5), L_4 (1, 7, 8), L_5 (3, 6, 9), L_6 (5, 5, 6), L_7 (3, 4, 9), L_8 (6, 8, 9). The external nodes represent the first set of

8 keys that were selected from the lists. Progressing from the bottom up, each of the internal nodes represents the smaller key of its two children until at the root node the smallest key gets automatically represented. The construction of the selection tree can be compared to a tournament being played with each of the internal nodes recording the winners of the individual matches. The final winner is registered by the root node. A selection tree, therefore, is also referred to as a ***tree of winners***.

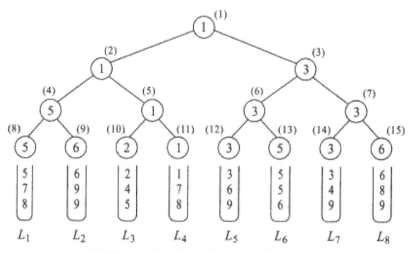

(a) The smallest key (key 1) is the winner

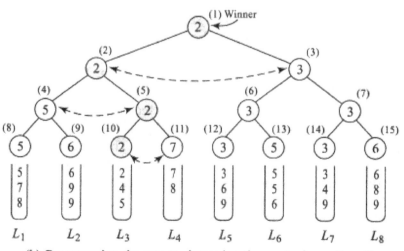

(b) Restructuring the tree to determine the next winner (key 2)

Figure 18.6. *Selection tree for an eight-way merge*

In this case, the smallest key, for example, 1 is dropped into the output list. Now the next key from L_4 for example, 7 enters the external node. It is now essential to restructure the tree to determine the next winner. Observe how it is now sufficient to restructure only that portion of the tree occurring along the path from the node numbered 11 to the root node. The revised key values of the internal nodes are shown in Figure 18.6(b). Note how in this case, the keys compared and revised along the path are (2,7), (5,2) and (2,3). The root node now represents 2 which is the next smallest key.

In practice, the external nodes of the selection tree are represented by the records and the internal nodes are only pointers to the records which are winners. For ease of understanding the internal nodes in Figure 18.6 were represented using the keys themselves, though in reality, they are only pointers to the winning records.

Despite its merits, a selection tree can result in increased overheads associated with maintaining the tree. This happens especially when the restructuring of the tree takes place to determine the next winner. It can be seen that when the next key walks into the tree, tournaments have to be played between sibling nodes who earlier, were losers.

Note how in the case of 7 entering the tree, the tournaments played were between (2,7), (5,2) and (2,3), where 2, 5 and 3 were losers in the earlier case. It would therefore be prudent if the internal nodes could represent the losers rather than the winners. A tournament tree in which each internal node retains a pointer to the loser is called a *tree of losers*.

Figure 18.7(a) illustrates the tree of losers for the selection tree discussed in Figure 18.6. Node 0 is a special node that shows the winner. As said earlier, each of the internal nodes is shown carrying the key when in reality they represent only pointers to the loser records. To determine the smallest key, as before, a tournament is played between pairs of external nodes. Though the winners are 'remembered', it is the losers that the internal nodes are made to point to. Thus, nodes numbered ((4), (5), (6) and (7)) record pointers to the losing external nodes, which are the ones with the key values of 6, 2, 5 and 6, respectively. Now node numbered (2) conducts a tournament between the two winners of the earlier game, which are key values 5 and 1 and records the pointer to the loser which is 5. In a similar way, node numbered (3) records the pointer to the loser node with key value 3. Progressing in this way the tree of losers is constructed and node 0 outputs the winning key value which is the smallest.

Once the smallest key, which is 1 has been output and the next key 7 enters the tree, the restructuring is easier now since the sibling nodes with which the tournaments are to be played are losers and these are directly pointed to by the internal nodes. The restructured tree is shown in Figure 18.7(b).

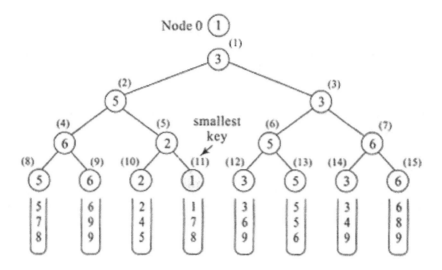

(a) The smallest key (key 1) is output

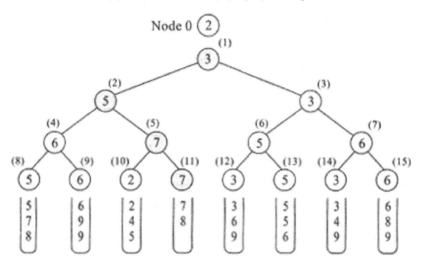

(b) Restructured tree after the smallest key is output

Figure 18.7. *Tree of losers for the eight-way merge*

18.5. Polyphase merge sort

Balanced k-way merge sort on tapes calls for an even distribution of runs on the tapes and to enable efficient merging requires $2k$ tapes to avoid wasteful passes over data. Thus, while k tapes act as input devices holding the runs generated, the other k tapes act as output devices to receive the merged runs. The k tape groups swap roles in the successive passes until a single run emerges in one of the tapes, signaling the end of sort.

It is possible to avoid wasteful redistribution of runs on the tapes while using less than $2k$ tapes by a wisely thought-out run redistribution strategy. *Polyphase merge* is one such external sorting method that makes use of an intelligent redistribution of runs during merging, so much that a k-way merge requires only $(k+1)$ tapes!

The central principle of the method is to ensure that in each pass (except the last of course!) during the merge, the runs are to be cleverly distributed so that one tape is always rendered empty while the other k tapes hold the input runs that are to be merged! The empty tape for the current pass acts as the output tape for the next pass and so on. Ultimately, as in balanced merge sort, the final pass delivers only one run in one of the tapes.

At this point of time, we introduce a useful notation mentioned in the literature to enable a crisp presentation of run distribution. Runs that are initially generated by internal sorting are thought to be of length 1 (unit of measure). Thus, if there are t runs that are initially generated then the notation would describe it as 1^t. For example, if there were 34 runs that were initially generated then it would be represented as 1^{34}. Similarly, if after a merge there were 14 runs of size 2, it would be represented as 2^{14}. In general, t runs of size s would be represented as s^t.

Example 18.4 illustrates polyphase merge on 3 tapes.

EXAMPLE 18.4.–

Let us suppose that a source file was initially sorted to generate 34 runs of size 1 (1^{34}). We demonstrate a polyphase merge on three tapes (T_1, T_2 and T_3) undertaking a two-way merge during each phase. Table 18.1 shows the redistribution of runs on the tapes in each phase.

Note how in phase 8, polyphase merge successfully completes its sorting by creating the final run of sorted records. Also, observe how in each phase one of the tapes is rendered empty while the other two are non-empty. Now, what is the trick behind this procedure?

Phase	Tape T_1	Tape T_2	Tape T_3	Remarks
1	1^{13}	1^{21}	-	Initial distribution of runs
2	-	1^8	2^{13}	Merge to T_3
3	3^8	-	2^5	Merge to T_1
4	3^3	5^5	-	Merge to T_2
5	-	5^2	8^3	Merge to T_3
6	13^2	-	8^1	Merge to T_1
7	13^1	21^1	-	Merge to T_2
8	-	-	34^1	Merge to T_3

Table 18.1. *Polyphase merge on three tapes: redistribution of runs*

Let us suppose that 'intuitively' we decided to distribute 13 runs of size 1 and 21 runs of size 1 onto tapes T_1 and T_2 respectively. In phase 2, because it is a two-way merge and polyphase merge expects one tape to fall vacant in every phase, we use up all the 13 runs of size 1 in tape T_1 for a merge operation with an equivalent number of runs in tape T_2. This yields 13 runs of double the size (2^{13}) which is written onto the empty tape T_3. So that leaves 8 runs of size 1 on tape T_2 that could not be used up and renders tape T_1 empty. Again, in phase 3, 1^8 runs in tape T_2 are merged with an equivalent amount of runs in tape T_3 to obtain 3^8 which is written onto tape T_1. This leaves a balance of 2^5 runs on tape T_3 and renders tape T_2 empty. The phases continue until in phase 8 a single run 34^1 gets written onto tape T_3.

To determine how the initial distribution of 1^{13} and 1^{21} was conceived, we work backward from the last phase. Let us suppose there were n phases for a 3-tape case. In the nth phase, we should arrive at exactly one run on a tape T_1 (let us say) with tapes T_2 and T_3 totally empty. This implies that in phase $(n-1)$ there should have been two runs of size 1 on tapes T_2 and T_3, which should have been merged as a single run on T_3 in the nth phase. Continuing in this fashion we obtain the initial distribution of runs to be 1^{13} and 1^{21} on the two tapes respectively. Table 18.2 lists the run distribution for a 3-tape polyphase merge.

It can be easily seen that the number of runs needed for an n-phase merge is given by $F_n + F_{n-1}$ where F_i is the ith Fibonacci number. Hence, this method of redistribution of runs is known as the **Fibonacci merge**. The method can be clearly generalized to k-way merging on $(k+1)$ tapes using generalized Fibonacci numbers.

Phase	Tape T_1	Tape T_2	Tape T_3
n	0	0	1
n-1	1	1	0
n-2	2	0	1
n-3	0	2	3
n-4	3	5	0
n-5	8	0	5
n-6	0	8	13
n-7	13	21	0
n-8	34	0	21

Table 18.2. *Run distribution for a 3-tape polyphase merge*

18.6. Cascade merge sort

Cascade merge is another intelligent merge pattern that was discovered before the polyphase merge. The merge pattern makes use of a perfectly devised initial distribution of runs on the tapes. While the polyphase merge sort employs a uniform merge pattern during the run generation, the cascade merge sort makes use of a 'cascading' merge pattern in each of its passes. Thus, for t tapes, while polyphase merge uniformly employs a *(t-1)* merge for the run generation, cascade sort employs *(t-1)* merge, *(t-2)* merge and so on, in the same pass for its run generation.

Example 18.5 demonstrates cascade merge on 6 tapes for an initial generation of 55 runs of length 1. We make use of the run distribution notation introduced in section 18.5.

EXAMPLE 18.5.–

There are six tapes (T_1, T_2, T_3, T_4, T_5 and T_6) using which 55 runs of length 1 (1^{55}) are to be cascade merge sorted, to generate the final run (55^1).

Table 18.3 illustrates the run distribution of cascade merge.

Pass	T_1	T_2	T_3	T_4	T_5	T_6
Initial distribution	1^{15}	1^{14}	1^{12}	1^9	1^5	-
1	-	1^1	2^2	3^3	4^4	5^5
2	15^1	14^1	12^1	9^1	5^1	-
3	-	-	-	-	-	55^1

Table 18.3. *Run distribution on six tapes by cascade merge*

As before, let us assume that the initial distribution of $(1^{15}, 1^{14}, 1^{12}, 1^9, 1^5)$ runs on the tapes (T_1, T_2, T_3, T_4, T_5), was devised through some 'intuitive' means.

In pass 1, we undertake a series of merges. A five-way merge on (T_1, T_2, T_3, T_4, T_5) yields the run 5^5 that is put onto tape T_6. A four-way merge on (T_1, T_2, T_3, T_4) yields 4^4 which is put onto tape T_5. A three-way merge on (T_1, T_2, T_3) yields 3^3 which are distributed onto tape T_4. A two-way merge on (T_1, T_2) yields 2^2 which is put onto tape T_3. Lastly, a 1-way merge (which is mere copying of the balance run) on T_1 yields 1^1 which is copied onto tape T_2. Of course, one could do away with the 1-way merge which is mere copying of the run and retain the run in the very tape itself. In pass 1, tape T_1 falls empty.

In pass 2, we repeat the cascading merge wherein the five-way merge on (T_2, T_3, T_4, T_5, T_6) yields the run 15^1, a four-way merge on (T_3, T_4, T_5, T_6) yields 14^1 and so on until at the end of pass 2, the distribution of runs on the tapes is as shown in the table. This is the penultimate pass and observes how the distribution records one run each on the tapes. In the final pass, as it always is, the five-way merge releases a single run of size 55 which is the final sorted file.

Phase	T_1	T_2	T_3	T_4	T_5
n	1	0	0	0	0
$n-1$	1	1	1	1	1
$n-2$	5	4	3	2	1
$n-3$	15	14	12	9	5
$n-4$	55	50	41	29	15
$n-5$	190	175	146	105	55
$n-6$	671	616	511	365	190

Table 18.4. *Run distribution on five tapes by cascade merge*

Now, how does one arrive at the perfect initial distribution? As was done for polyphase merge, this could be arrived at by working backward from the goal state of $(1, 0, 0, 0, 0)$ obtained during the nth pass. Table 18.4 illustrates the run distribution by cascade merge on five tapes.

For an in-depth analysis of merge patterns and other external sorting schemes, a motivated reader is referred to Volume III of the classic book "The ART of Computer Programming" (Knuth 1998).

Summary

– External sorting deals with sorting of files or lists that are too huge to be accommodated in the internal memory of the computer and hence need to be stored in external storage devices such as disks or drums.

– The principle behind external sorting is to first make use of any efficient internal sorting technique to generate runs. These runs are then merged in passes to obtain a single run at which stage the file is deemed sorted. The merge patterns called for by the strategies, are influenced by external storage medium on which the runs reside, viz., disks or tapes.

– Magnetic tapes are sequential devices built on the principle of audio tape devices. Data is stored in blocks occurring sequentially. Magnetic disks are random access storage devices. Data stored in a disk is addressed by its cylinder, track and sector numbers.

– Balanced merge sort is a technique that can be adopted on files residing on both disks and tapes. In its general form, a k-way merging could be undertaken during the runs. For the efficient management of merging runs, buffer handling and selection tree mechanisms are employed.

– Balanced k-way merge sort on tapes calls for the use of $2k$ tapes for an efficient management of runs. Polyphase merge sort is a clever strategy that makes use of only $(k+1)$ tapes to perform the k –way merge. The distribution of runs on the tapes follows a Fibonacci number sequence.

– Cascade merge sort is yet another smart strategy which unlike polyphase merge sort does not employ a uniform merge pattern. Each pass makes use of a 'cascading' sequence of merge patterns.

18.7. Illustrative problems

PROBLEM 18.1.–

The specification for a typical disk storage system is shown in Table P18.1. An employee file consisting of 100,000 records is stored on the disk. The employee record structure and the size of the fields in bytes (shown in brackets) are given below:

Employee number	Employee name	Designation	Address	Basic pay	Allowances	Deductions	Total salary
(6)	(20)	(10)	(30)	(6)	(20)	(20)	(6)

Number of platters	6
Number of cylinders	800
Number of tracks (surfaces)/cylinder	10
Number of sectors/track	50
Number of bytes/sector	512
Maximum seek time	50 ms
Average seek time	25 ms
Maximum Latency time	16.66 ms
Average latency time	8.33 ms
Time to read/write a sector	0.33 ms

Table P18.1. *Specifications of a typical disk storage system*

a) What is the storage space (in terms of bytes) needed to store the employee file in the disk?

b) What is the storage space (in terms of cylinders) needed to store the employee file in the disk?

Solution:

a) The size of the employee record = 118 bytes

Number of employee records that can be held in a sector = 512/118 = 4 records

Number of sectors needed to hold the whole employee file = 100,000/4 = 25,000 sectors

$\therefore$ The total number of bytes needed to store the file in the disk =

$25,000 \times 512 = 12,800,000$ bytes = 12.2 megabytes

b) Number of tracks needed to hold the whole employee file given that there are 50 sectors/track = 25,000 / 50 = 500 tracks

∴ Number of cylinders needed to store the whole file given that there are 10 tracks/cylinder = 500/10 = 50 cylinders

PROBLEM 18.2.–

For the employee file discussed in illustrative problem 18.1, making use of Table P18.1, answer the questions given below:

Records from the employee file are to be read and, by making use of the basic pay, allowances and deductions, the total salary is to be computed for each employee. Assume that it takes 200 μs of CPU time to perform the computation for a single record. The updated records are to be written onto the disk.

a) What is the time taken to process a sector of records?

b) Having processed a sector of records, what is the time taken to process all records in the very next sector?

c) What is the time taken to process the records, in all sectors of a track, assuming that the sectors are continuously read?

d) What is the time taken to process all records in a cylinder?

Solution:

a) The time taken to process a sector full of records =

(1) Time taken to access the cylinder + (2) Time taken to access the sector + (3) time taken to read the records + (4) time taken to compute the net salary for the records + (5) time taken to access the sector to write back the records + (6) time taken to write the updated records onto the sector.

For (1) and (2), since the question pertains to an arbitrary sector, we choose to use the average seek time of 25 ms and the average latency time of 8.33 ms, respectively. For (3) and (6), the time taken is 0.33 ms each. For (4), it is 0.8 ms (200 μs × 4 records).

The computation of (5) which is in fact the time taken for the sector to appear under the read/write head to perform the write operation, is a trifle involved. It is computed as, (the maximum latency time (time taken for the track to make a full revolution) – time taken to read the sector – time taken to process the records by the CPU).

This is given by (16.66 - 0.33 - 0.8) = 15.53 ms.

∴ the time taken to process all records in a sector =

25 + 8.33 + 0.33 + 0.8 + 15.53 + 0.33 = 50.32 ms

b) While the time taken to process records in the first sector (question a) of illustrative problem 18.2 includes the time taken to access the cylinder and the sector, to process the very next sector, there is no need to include the cylinder and sector access time since the reading is continuously done.

∴ the time taken to process the records in the very next sector =

(3) time taken to read the records + (4) time taken to compute the net salary for the records + (5) time taken to access the sector to write back the records + (6) time taken to write the updated records onto the sector.

= 0.33 + 0.8 + 15.53 + 0.33 = 16.99 ms

c) The time taken to process all records on a track =

(7) time taken to process records in the first sector of the track +

(8) time taken to process records in the next sector of the track × 49 sectors.

Here (7) and (8) have been obtained in questions (a) and (b) of illustrative problem 18.2 respectively and therefore the result is given as,

50.32 + 16.99 × 49 = 882.83 ms

d) The time taken to continuously process all records in a cylinder, calls for processing all records track after track. Once the records in the first occurring track have been processed, the rest of the tracks in the cylinder are instantaneously accessed.

∴ the time taken to process all records in a cylinder =

(9) time taken to process all records in the first track + (10) time taken to process all records in the next track of the cylinder × 9 tracks

While (9) is found in question (c) of illustrative problem 18.2, to compute (10) we simply need to use the time computed in (8) for all the 50 sectors in the next track.

Therefore, the result is given as 882.83 + 16.99 × 50 × 9 = 8.528 s

PROBLEM 18.3.–

Illustrative problem 18.2(d) computed the time taken to process all records of the employee file residing in a cylinder. Assume that the time taken for the read/write head to move from one cylinder to another is 10 ms.

a) What is the time taken to process all records in the next cylinder?

b) What is the time taken to process the entire employee file of records on the disk?

Solution:

a) Having processed a cylinder of records, the time taken to move to the next cylinder is 10 ms. The time taken to process all records in the next cylinder is a straightforward computation given by:

(8) Time taken to process all records on the next sector $\times$ 50 sectors $\times$ 10 tracks.

Here, (8) is obtained in question (b) of illustrative problem 18.2.

∴ the total time taken to process all records in the next cylinder, moving from the current cylinder = $10 + (16.99 \times 50 \times 10) = 8.505$ s

b) The entire employee file resides on 50 cylinders (question (b) of illustrative problem 18.1).

Therefore, the time taken to process the entire file =

(11) Time taken to process records in the first cylinder + (12) time taken to process records in the next cylinder $\times$ 49.

(11) is obtained in question (d) of illustrative problem 18.2 and (12) is obtained in question (a) of illustrative problem 18.3.

∴ the time taken to process the entire employee file = $8.528 + 8.505 \times 49 = 7.088$ min

PROBLEM 18.4.–

Given a file of 50,000 records with an internal memory capacity of 10,000 records, trace the steps of a Balanced P-way merge sort for $T = 6$ tapes (T_1, T_2, T_3, T_4, T_5, T_6) and $P = 3$.

Solution:

An internal sort of the file yields five runs of 10,000 records each. Since $P = 3$, we need to undertake a three-way merge. We, therefore, divide the six tapes into two groups of three tapes each. The two groups alternate as the input and output tapes during the merge passes.

The initial distribution of runs on the tapes T_1, T_2 and T_3 after internal sorting, are as follows:

Tape T_1: R_1 .... $R_{10,000}$ $R_{30,001}$ .... $R_{40,000}$

Tape T_2: $R_{10,001}$ .... $R_{20,000}$ $R_{40,001}$....$R_{50,000}$

Tape T_3: $R_{20,001}$ .... $R_{30,000}$

Rewind the tapes T_1, T_2 and T_3. In the next pass, the three-way merge of runs in tapes T_1, T_2 and T_3 yield output runs on T_4, T_5 and T_6 as follows:

Tape T_4: R_1....$R_{30,000}$

Tape T_5: $R_{30,001}$....$R_{50,000}$

Tape T_6: Empty

Rewind tapes T_4 and T_5. In the last pass a three-way merge of runs in tapes T_4 and T_5 yields the final run on tape T_1 as follows:

Tape T_1: R_1 .... $R_{50,000}$

PROBLEM 18.5.–

For a file comprising 50,000 records with an internal memory capacity of 10,000 records, the initial distribution of runs on two tapes T_1 and T_2 are as shown below:

Tape T_1: R_1 ....$R_{10,000}$ $R_{20,001}$....$R_{30,000}$ $R_{40,001}$....$R_{50,000}$

Tape T_2: $R_{10,001}$....$R_{20,000}$ $R_{30,001}$ ......$R_{40,000}$

Two standby tapes for example, T_3 and T_4 are available. The following two merge patterns were undertaken. Which of these is efficient and why?

Merge pattern A	Merge pattern B
Pass 1 (two-way merge):	**Pass 1 (two-way merge):**
Tape T_3: R_1.... $R_{20,000}$ $R_{40,001}$....$R_{50,000}$ Tape T_4: $R_{20,001}$....$R_{40,000}$	Tape T_3: R_1....$R_{20,000}$ Tape T_4: $R_{20,001}$....$R_{40,000}$

Rewind tapes T_1, T_2, T_3 and T_4.	Tape T_1: R_1....$R_{10,000}$ $R_{20,001}$....$R_{30,000}$ ↑ $R_{40,001}$....$R_{50,000}$ Rewind tapes T_2, T_3 and T_4 only. Tape T_1 retains the run $R_{40,001}$....$R_{50,000}$. The ↑ indicates the position of the read/write head from which point onward T_1 would be read for the next pass.
Pass 2 (two-way merge): Tape T_1: R_1....$R_{40,000}$ Tape T_2: $R_{40,001}$....$R_{50,000}$ Rewind tapes T_1, T_2 and T_3.	**Pass 2 (three-way merge of tapes** T1, T_3 **and** T_4**)** Tape T_2: R_1....$R_{50,000}$
Pass 3 (two-way merge): Tape T_3: R_1....$R_{50,000}$	

Solution:

Merge pattern B is efficient since the total number of records that were read to obtain the final run on tape T_2 was 40,000 + 50,000 = 90,000 records. This took place in 2 passes.

On the other hand, **Merge pattern A** read 50,000 + 50,000 + 50,000 = 150,000 records in three passes over the data, to obtain the final run on tape T_3.

PROBLEM 18.6.–

There are five runs distributed on three tapes (T_1, T2, T_3) as shown below. A standby tape (T_4) is available. The internal memory capacity is 10,000 records. Undertake a balanced P-way merge devising a smart merge pattern for some *P*.

Tape T_1: R_1 ....$R_{10,000}$ $R_{30,001}$ ......$R_{40,000}$

Tape T_2: $R_{10,001}....R_{20,000}$ $R_{40,001}....R_{50,000}$

Tape T_3: $R_{20,001}....R_{30,000}$

Solution:

We first undertake a three-way merge on the tapes T_1, T_2 and T_3 for the first three runs on the tapes. T_4 is used as the output tape. The configuration at the end of pass 1 is as shown below:

Tape T_4: $R_1....R_{30,000}$

Tape T_1: R_1 $....R_{10,000}$ $R_{30,001} ......R_{40,000}$

Tape T_2: $R_{10,001}....R_{20,000}$ $R_{40,001}....R_{50,000}$

Tapes T_3 and T_4 are alone rewound.

In the final pass, a three-way merge is undertaken on tapes T_4, T_1 and T_2. The output is delivered on tape T_3 as shown below:

Tape T_3: $R_1....R_{50,000}$

The merge pattern for the specific case is efficient since only $30,000 + 50,000 = 80,000$ records were read in the two passes put together for the final sort of the file.

PROBLEM 18.7.–

Let us suppose a source file was initially sorted to generate 55 runs of size 1 (1^{55}). Trace polyphase merge on three tapes (T_1, T_2, T_3) undertaking a two-way merge during each phase.

Solution:

Table P18.7 shows the redistribution of runs on the tapes in each phase. Observe how the initial distribution of runs is taken after the Fibonacci number sequence. The polyphase merged file is available on tape T_1 in the final phase.

Phase	Tape T_1	Tape T_2	Tape T_3	Remarks
1	1^{21}	1^{34}	-	Initial distribution of runs
2	-	1^{13}	2^{21}	Merge to T_3

3	3^{13}	-	2^8	Merge to T_1
4	3^5	5^8	-	Merge to T_2
5	-	5^3	8^5	Merge to T_3
6	13^3	-	8^2	Merge to T_1
7	13^1	21^2	-	Merge to T_2
8	-	21^1	34^1	Merge to T_3
9	55^1	-	-	Merge to T_1

Table P18.7. *Polyphase merge on three tapes: redistribution of runs*

PROBLEM 18.8.–

There are six tapes (T_1, T_2, T_3, T_4, T_5, T_6) using which 190 runs of length 1 (1^{190}) are to be cascade merge sorted, to generate the final run (190^1). Trace the steps of the sorting process.

Solution:

Table P18.8 illustrates the run distribution of cascade merge.

Pass	T_1	T_2	T_3	T_4	T_5	T_6
Initial distribution	1^{55}	1^{50}	1^{41}	1^{29}	1^{15}	-
1	-	1^5	2^9	3^{12}	4^{14}	5^{15}
2	15^5	14^4	12^3	9^2	5^1	-
3	-	15^1	29^1	41^1	50^1	55^1
4	190^1					

Table P18.8. *Run distribution on 6 tapes by cascade merge*

PROBLEM 18.9.–

Demonstrate a balanced three-way merge on the following "sample" list of keys available on a disk, with the internal memory capable of holding six keys:

12 1 65 7 34 15 90 22 63 56 18 3 9 22 12 88 41

Solution:

The internal sort of the list yields three runs as follows:

R1: 1 7 12 15 34 65

R2: 3 18 22 56 63 90

R3: 9 12 22 41 88

We divide the internal memory into three input buffers and an output buffer to undertake the three-way merge. While the input buffers can hold one key each, we shall allow the output buffer to hold a maximum of three keys. Thus, the input data will be read in blocks of one key each. During the merge, the output buffer releases blocks containing three keys each, which are written onto the run. The merging passes are shown below:

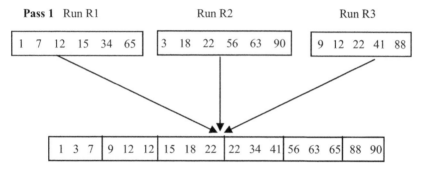

Pass 1   Run R1   Run R2   Run R3

At the end of Pass 1, the entire list is sorted.

Review questions

1) i) Cascade merge sort adopts uniform merge patterns in its passes.

ii) The distribution of runs in the last pass of cascade merge sort is given by a pattern such as (1, 0, 0, ...0).

a) (i) true (ii) true   b) (i) true (ii) false

c) (i) false (ii) false   d) (i) false (ii) true

2) Polyphase merge sort for a k-way merge on tapes requires ------------ tapes.

a) $2k$ b) $(k-2)$ c) $(k+1)$ d) k

3) The time taken for the right sector to appear under the read/write head is known as:

a) seek time   b) latency time   c) transmission time   d) data read time

4) In the case of a balanced two-way merge, if M runs were produced in the internal sorting phase and if $2^{k-1} < M \leq 2^k$ then the sort procedure makes --------- merging passes over the data records.

a) M b) $\lceil log_2 M \rceil$ c) $\lceil log_M 2 \rceil$ d) M^2

5) Match the following:

W. Magnetic tape   A. tree of winners

X. Magnetic disks   B. Fibonacci merge

Y. Polyphase merge   C. Inter Block Gap

Z. k-way merge   D. platters

a) (W A) (X B) (Y D) (Z C)   b) (W C) (X D) (Y B) (Z A)

c) (W C) (X D) (Y A) (Z B)   d) (W A) (X B) (Y C) (Z D)

6) What is the general principle behind external sorting?

7) How is a selection tree useful in a k-way merge?

8) What are the advantages of Polyphase merge sort over balanced k-way merge sort?

9) What is the principle behind the distribution of runs in a cascade merge sort?

10) How is data organized in a magnetic disk?

11) An inventory record contains the following fields: ITEM NUMBER (8 bytes), NAME (20 bytes), DESCRIPTION (20 bytes), TOTAL STOCK (10 bytes), PRICE(10 bytes), TOTAL PRICE (14 bytes).

A record comprising the data on Item number, name, description and total stock is to be read and based on the current price which is input, the total price is to be computed and updated in the fields. There are 25, 000 records to be processed. Assuming the disk characteristics given in Table P18.1:

i) How much storage space is required to store the entire file in the disk (in terms of bytes/KB/MB)?

ii) How much storage space is required to store the entire file in the disk in terms of cylinders?

iii) What is the time required to read, process and write back a given sector of records into the disk, assuming that it takes 100 μs to process a record?

iv) What is the time required to read, process and write back an entire track of records if they were read sequentially sector after sector?

v) What is the time required to read, process and write back an entire cylinder of records?

vi) What is the time required to read, process and write back the records in the next (immediate) cylinder?

vii) What is the time required to read, process and write back the entire file onto the disk?

12) A file comprising 500,000 records is to be sorted. The internal memory has the capacity to hold only 50,000 records. Trace the steps of a Balanced k-way merge for (i) $k = 2$ and (ii) $k = 4$, when (a) the file is available on a tape and (ii) the file is available on a disk. Assume the availability of any number of tapes and a scratch disk for undertaking the appropriate sorting process.

Programming assignments

1) Implement a function to construct a tree of winners to obtain the smallest key from a list of keys representing its external nodes.

2) Implement a function to construct a tree of losers to obtain the smallest key from a list of keys representing its external nodes.

3) Making use of the function(s) developed in programming assignment 1 (and programming assignment 2), implement k-way merge algorithms for any given value of k.

4) Implement a balanced k-way merge sort for disk-based files. Simulate the program for various sizes of files, internal memory capacity and choice of k. Graphically display the distribution of runs.

19

Divide and Conquer

In this chapter, the **Divide and Conquer strategy** is detailed and demonstrated over the problems of *finding the max/min element* in a list, *merge sort* and *matrix multiplication*.

19.1. Introduction

Divide and Conquer is a popular algorithm design strategy that has been widely used over a variety of problem classes. As the name indicates, the strategy solves a problem by *dividing* it repeatedly into smaller sub-problems, until the smaller sub-problems can be individually and easily solved. The strategy then backtracks, combining the solutions of the smaller sub-problems phase by phase on its return, until the solution to the original problem is automatically constructed, thereby *conquering* the problem. Needless to say, Divide and Conquer has been a time-tested political strategy too!

The fact that the strategy repeatedly moves onward to "divide" the problem and backtracks to "conquer" its solution, is suggestive of the application of *recursion*. Thus, Divide and Conquer-based solutions to problems are ideally implemented as recursive procedures or programs (see section 2.7 of Chapter 2, Volume 1, for a discussion on recursion and analysis of recursive procedures).

19.2. Principle and abstraction

Figure 19.1(a) illustrates the principle of Divide and Conquer, where a problem whose data set size is n, is repeatedly divided into smaller sub-problems each of which are solved independently, before the principle backtracks to combine the solutions of the sub-problems, to finally arrive at the solution to the original problem.

Figure 19.1(b) illustrates the abstraction of the Divide and Conquer method. The function SMALL(r,t) determines if the size of the sub-problem whose data set size is given by (r,t), is small enough to be solved independently and directly using the function B(r,t). Note that the **if** condition functions as the *base case* of the recursive procedure. DIVIDE(r,t) divides the problem into two sub-problems of smaller sizes and the function COMBINE() combines the solutions of the two sub-problems. The repeated division of the problem is handled recursively, by calling DIVIDEandCONQUER() over the sub-problems.

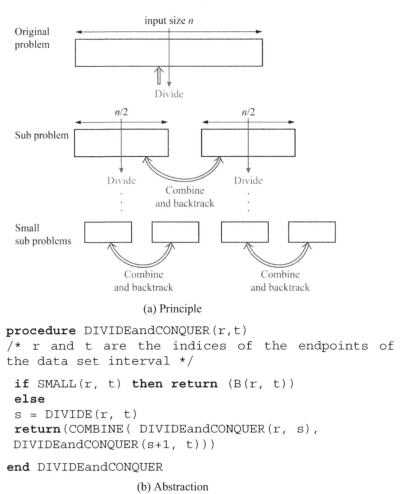

(a) Principle

```
procedure DIVIDEandCONQUER(r,t)
/* r and t are the indices of the endpoints of
the data set interval */

if SMALL(r, t) then return (B(r, t))
else
s = DIVIDE(r, t)
return(COMBINE( DIVIDEandCONQUER(r, s),
DIVIDEandCONQUER(s+1, t)))

end DIVIDEandCONQUER
```

(b) Abstraction

Figure 19.1. *The principle and abstraction of the Divide and Conquer method. a) principle and b) abstraction. For a color version of this figure, see www.iste.co.uk/pai/algorithms3.zip*

The application of the Divide and Conquer method for the solution of problems is detailed in the ensuing sections.

19.3. Finding maximum and minimum

Finding the maximum and minimum elements in a list, termed the ***max-min*** problem for ease of reference, is a simple problem. While there are different methods available to solve this problem, we use this problem only to demonstrate how Divide and Conquer works to obtain its solution.

Procedure MAXMIN() (Algorithm 19.1) illustrates the pseudo-code for the Divide and Conquer-based solution to the max-min problem. The procedure begins with the original dataset D and recursively divides the dataset D into two subsets D_1 and D_2, that comprise half the elements of D. To undertake this, the recursive procedure is called twice, one as MAXMIN(D_1) and the other as MAXMIN(D_2).

```
procedure MAXMIN(D)
   if SIZE(S) = 2 then
      {Let D = {a, b};
       return (MAX(a, b), MIN(a, b))}
   else
      if SIZE(S) = 1 then
         {Let D = {a};
          return(a, a)}
      else
               Divide data set D into two subsets, D₁, D₂
               each comprising half the elements of D;

               /* find max-min elements of D₁*/
               (MAX1, MIN1) = MAXMIN(D₁)
               /* find max-min elements of D₂*/
               (MAX2, MIN2) = MAXMIN(D₂)

               /*return the final max and min element of
               D*/
               return(max(MAX1,MAX2), min(MIN1, MIN2))

end MAXMIN
```

Algorithm 19.1. *Pseudo-code for the Divide and Conquer-based solution to the Max-Min problem*

The base cases of the recursive procedure are invoked when the divided dataset comprises just two elements {a, b} at which point, the max and min elements are computed by a mere comparison of the elements, or when the divided dataset comprises a single element {a} at which point, both the max and min elements are set to {a} and returned to their respective calling procedures. When recursion terminates, (MAX1, MIN1) and (MAX2, MIN2) store the max and min elements of D_1 and D_2, respectively.

One last comparison between the max elements and the min elements returns the final maximum and minimum element of the given dataset, at which point recursion terminates successfully.

Illustrative problem 19.1 demonstrates the working of **procedure** MAXMIN() over a problem instance.

19.3.1. *Time complexity analysis*

Since **procedure** MAXMIN() is a recursive procedure, to obtain the time complexity of the procedure, the recurrence relation needs to be framed first. Since there are two recursive calls in the procedure, for an input size n, the time complexity $T(n)$ expressed in terms of the *element comparisons* made over the data set is given by the following recurrence relation:

$$T(n) = 2.T\left(\frac{n}{2}\right) + 2, \quad n > 2$$
$$= 0, \text{ if } n = 1 \qquad\qquad\qquad\qquad [19.1]$$
$$= 1, \text{ if } n = 2$$

The base case $(n = 1)$, does not entail any element comparisons, hence $T(n) = 0$, whereas, the base case $(n = 2)$ entails only one comparison between a and b to determine the max and min elements and therefore $T(n) = 1$. For $(n > 2)$, the two recursive calls incur a time complexity of $2.T\left(\frac{n}{2}\right)$ with two more comparisons undertaken last, to determine the final maximum and minimum element of the data set.

Solving equation [19.1] assuming that $n = 2^k$ for some k, yields,

$$T(n) = 2.T(n/2) + 2 ....(step\ 1)$$
$$= 2(2T(n/4) + 2) + 2$$
$$= 2^2 T(n/2^2) + 2.(1+2) ......(step\ 2)$$
$$= 2^2 (2.T(n/2^3) + 2) + 2.(1+2)$$
$$= 2^3 T(n/2^3) + 2.(1+2+2^2) ....(step\ 3)$$

In the ith step,

$$T(n) = 2^i T(n/2^i) + 2.(1 + 2 + 2^2 + ... + 2^{i-1}).......(step\ i)$$

Since $n = 2^k$, in the step when $i = (k-1)$,

$$T(n) = 2^{k-1} T(n/2^{k-1}) + 2.(1 + 2 + 2^2 + ... + 2^{k-2}).......(step\ k-1)$$

$$= \frac{n}{2}.T(2) + 2.(2^{k-1} - 1)$$

$$= \frac{n}{2}.1 + 2.(\frac{n}{2} - 1)$$

$$= 3.\frac{n}{2} - 2$$

$$\cong O(n)$$

Thus, the time complexity of the Divide and Conquer-based max/min element finding problem is $O(n)$.

19.4. Merge sort

The merge sort algorithm which makes use of the principle of *merge* to order a data set was discussed in section 17.5. Algorithm 17.5 illustrates the recursive merge sort algorithm (**procedure** MERGE_SORT). The merge sort algorithm employs a Divide and Conquer approach to sort the elements.

Thus, the original list is divided into two sub-lists and the recursive MERGE_SORT procedure is invoked over the two sub-lists after which the two sorted sub-lists are merged one last time using **procedure** MERGE (Algorithm 17.4 in section 17.5), yielding the sorted list.

19.4.1. *Time complexity analysis*

The recurrence relation for the time complexity of **procedure** MERGE_SORT is given by,

$$T(n) = 2.T\left(\frac{n}{2}\right) + c.n, \quad n \geq 2$$

$$= d$$

where c and d are constants. Illustrative problem 17.5, shows the solution of the recurrence relation, yielding a time complexity of $O(n.log_2 n)$.

19.5. Matrix multiplication

The multiplication of two square matrices A, B of order n, is given by,

$$(C)_{n\times n} = \begin{bmatrix} a_{11} & a_{12} & \cdots & a_{1n} \\ a_{21} & a_{22} & \cdots & a_{2n} \\ \vdots & \vdots & \vdots & \vdots \\ a_{n1} & a_{n2} & \cdots & a_{nn} \end{bmatrix} \cdot \begin{bmatrix} b_{11} & b_{12} & \cdots & b_{1n} \\ b_{21} & b_{22} & \cdots & b_{2n} \\ \vdots & \vdots & \vdots & \vdots \\ b_{n1} & b_{n2} & \cdots & b_{nn} \end{bmatrix},$$

where $C_{ij} = \sum\limits_{k=1}^{n} \left(a_{ik} . b_{kj} \right)$

Known as the "high school" method, this way of multiplying two square matrices involves three **for** loops, two to keep the indices i, j of C_{ij} running and the third running over index k, to sum up the product ($a_{ik}. b_{kj}$). With all the three loops ranging from 1 to n, where n is the size of the square matrices, the time complexity of the *iterative* algorithm is bound to be $O(n^3)$.

Now, what if a Divide and Conquer-based approach was adopted to undertake this "high school" method of computing the product of two square matrices? Would it result in a better time complexity? Let us explore.

19.5.1. *Divide and Conquer-based approach to "high school" method of matrix multiplication*

A Divide and Conquer-based approach could involve dividing the square matrices A and B into four quadrants $A_{11}, A_{12,} A_{21}, A_{22}$ and $B_{11}, B_{12}, B_{21}, B_{22}$ respectively, as shown in Figure 19.2 and *recursively* undertaking the division of each of the quadrants into four other "miniature" quadrants and so on, until each of the quadrants is just left with a 2×2 matrix. At this stage, the *base case* of the recursive procedure merely does the usual "high school" method of matrix multiplication and returns the results, which eventually results in the recursive procedure returning the product of the two matrices as $(C)_{n \times n}$.

$$\left[\begin{array}{c|c} C_{11} & C_{12} \\ \hline C_{21} & C_{22} \end{array} \right] = \left[\begin{array}{c|c} A_{11} & A_{12} \\ \hline A_{21} & A_{22} \end{array} \right] \cdot \left[\begin{array}{c|c} B_{11} & B_{12} \\ \hline B_{21} & B_{22} \end{array} \right]$$

Figure 19.2. *Division of square matrices into four quadrants of size $\left\lceil \frac{n}{2} \right\rceil \times \left\lceil \frac{n}{2} \right\rceil$*

The governing recurrence relations of the Divide and Conquer-based algorithm are as follows:

$$C_{11} = A_{11}.B_{11} + A_{12}.B_{21}$$
$$C_{12} = A_{11}.B_{12} + A_{12}.B_{22}$$
$$C_{21} = A_{21}.B_{11} + A_{22}.B_{21}$$
$$C_{22} = A_{21}.B_{12} + A_{22}.B_{22}, \quad n > 2$$

and   [19.2]

$$c_{11} = a_{11}.b_{11} + a_{12}.b_{21}$$
$$c_{12} = a_{11}.b_{12} + a_{12}.b_{22}$$
$$c_{21} = a_{21}.b_{11} + a_{22}.b_{21}$$
$$c_{22} = a_{21}.b_{12} + a_{22}.b_{22}, \quad n = 2$$

where A_{ij}, B_{ij} and C_{ij} denote sub-matrices of order $\lceil \frac{n}{2} \rceil \times \lceil \frac{n}{2} \rceil$ and a_{ij}, b_{ij} and c_{ij} denote matrix elements. $A_{ij}.B_{jk}$ in general denotes the recursive matrix multiplication of the sub-matrices of $\lceil \frac{n}{2} \rceil \times \lceil \frac{n}{2} \rceil$ until the base case is triggered at $n = 2$, at which stage the matrix multiplication of two matrices of order 2×2 is undertaken as illustrated in equation [19.2].

19.5.1.1. *Time complexity analysis*

The time complexity of the Divide and Conquer-based "high school" method of matrix multiplication in terms of the *basic operations*, i.e. the matrix additions and multiplications that were carried out during recursion, are obtained as follows.

Let $T(n)$ denote the time complexity of multiplying two square matrices of order n. The recursive algorithm calls for *eight matrix multiplications* and *four matrix additions* of sub-matrices of order $\lceil \frac{n}{2} \rceil \times \lceil \frac{n}{2} \rceil$, during each call. When $n = 2$, it reduces to *eight element multiplications* and *four element additions*. The recurrence relation is therefore given by,

$$T(n) = \begin{cases} 8.T\left(\dfrac{n}{2}\right) + c.n^2, & n > 2 \\ b, & n = 2 \end{cases}$$ [19.3]

Since the addition of two square matrices of order n has a time complexity of $O(n^2)$, $c.n^2$ in equation [19.3] denotes the upper bound for the four matrix additions called for, by the recursive algorithm.

Solving equation [19.3] assuming that $n = 2^k$ for some k, yields,

$$T(n) = 8.T(n/2) + c.n^2 \ldots\ldots(step\ 1)$$
$$= 8(8T(n/4) + c.(n/2)^2) + c.n^2.$$
$$= 8^2 T(n/2^2) + c.n^2.(1+2)\ldots(step\ 2)$$
$$= 8^3 T(n/2^3) + c.n^2.(1+2+2^2)\ldots\ldots(step\ 3)$$

In the ith step,

$$T(n) = 8^i T(n/2^i) + c.n^2.(1+2+2^2 + \ldots + 2^{i-1})\ldots\ldots(step\ i)$$

Since $n = 2^k$, in the step when $i = (k\text{-}1)$,

$$T(n) = 8^{k-1} T(n/2^{k-1}) + c.n^2.(1+2+2^2 + \ldots + 2^{k-2})\ldots\ldots(step\ k-1)$$
$$= \frac{n^3}{8}.T(2) + c.n^2.(2^{k-1} - 1)$$
$$= \frac{n^3}{8}.b + c.n^2.(\frac{n}{2} - 1)$$
$$= d.n^3 - c.n^2$$
$$\cong O(n^3)$$

Thus, despite the Divide and Conquer-based approach, the "high school" method of matrix multiplication does not yield a performance better than its traditional method of element multiplications and additions, which also yielded $O(n^3)$ time complexity.

19.5.2. *Strassen's matrix multiplication algorithm*

Strassen's matrix multiplication algorithm devised by Volker Strassen is a faster matrix multiplication method when compared to the traditional method. It works best over large matrices, though not as much as other competing methods.

Adopting a Divide and Conquer-based approach, the algorithm recursively divides the matrices A and B into four quadrants as shown in Figure 19.2, and proceeds to compute the intermediary matrices P, Q, R, S, T, U and V, to obtain the final matrix C.

$$P = (A_{11} + A_{22}).(B_{11} + B_{22})$$
$$Q = (A_{21} + A_{22}).B_{11}$$
$$R = A_{11}.(B_{12} - B_{22})$$
$$S = A_{22}.(B_{211} - B_{11})$$
$$T = (A_{11} + A_{12}).B_{22}$$
$$U = (A_{21} - A_{11}).(B_{11} + B_{12})$$
$$V = (A_{12} - A_{22}).(B_{21} + B_{22})$$

and

$$C_{11} = P + S - T + V$$
$$C_{12} = R + T$$
$$C_{21} = Q + S$$
$$C_{22} = P + R - Q + U$$

[19.4]

Strassen's method recursively works on equation [19.4] until the base case of $n = 2$ is reached. At this stage, as discussed with regard to equation [19.2], the computations become element additions, subtractions and multiplications.

An observation of equation [19.4] reveals that the algorithm uses *seven matrix multiplications* and *18 matrix additions/subtractions*. Thus, the method seems to have saved on one matrix multiplication when compared to the traditional method but in the process has jacked up the matrix additions/subtractions to a whopping eighteen! Will it ensure good performance? Let's explore its time complexity.

19.5.2.1. *Time complexity analysis*

Following a similar description of *T(n)* in equation [19.3], the recurrence relation for Strassen's method is as follows:

$$T(n) = \begin{cases} 7.T\left(\dfrac{n}{2}\right) + c.n^2, & n > 2 \\ b, & n = 2 \end{cases}$$

[19.5]

$c.n^2$ in the equation denotes the upper bound for the eighteen matrix additions/subtractions called for, by the recursive algorithm.

Solving equation [19.5] using the usual steps and assuming that $n = 2^k$ for some k, yields,

$$T(n) = 7.T(n/2) + c.n^2 \quad\ldots\ldots\ldots(step\ 1)$$
$$= 7(7T(n/4) + c.(n/2)^2) + c.n^2.$$
$$= 7^2 T(n/2^2) + c.n^2.(1 + (7/4))\ldots\ldots(step\ 2)$$
$$= 7^3 T(n/2^3) + c.n^2.(1 + (7/4) + (7/4)^2)\ldots\ldots(step\ 3)$$

In the ith step,

$$T(n) = 7^i T(n/2^i) + c.n^2.(1 + (7/4) + (7/4)^2 + \ldots + (7/4)^{i-1})\ldots\ldots(step\ i)$$

Since $n = 2^k$, in the step when $i = (k-1)$,

$$T(n) = (7/4)^{k-1} T(n/2^{k-1}) + c.n^2.(1 + (7/4) + (7/4)^2 + \ldots + (7/4)^{k-2})\ldots\ldots(step\ k-1)$$
$$= \frac{7^{\log_2^n}}{7}.T(2) + c.n^2.\frac{((7/4)^{k-1} - 1)}{(7/4) - 1}$$
$$= \frac{7^{\log_2^n}}{7}.b + c.n^2.(4/3).\left((4/7).\frac{n^{\log_2^7}}{n^2} - 1 \right)$$
$$\leq d.n^{\log_2^7}$$
$$\cong O(n^{2.81})$$

Thus, the Divide and Conquer-based on Strassen's method for matrix multiplication reports a time complexity of $O(n^{2.81})$, which is a better performance especially for large matrices, when compared to the time complexity of $O(n^3)$ reported by the "high school" method.

Summary

– Divide and Conquer is an efficient method for algorithm design and works by dividing the problem into sub-problems and solving them when they are small enough, only to combine their results to yield the final solution to the problem.

– Divide and Conquer is a recursive method.

– Max-Min element finding, Merge Sort and Matrix Multiplication are examples of Divide and Conquer-based algorithms.

19.6. Illustrative problems

PROBLEM 19.1.–

Demonstrate **procedure** MAXMIN() detailed in section 19.3, which is a Divide and Conquer-based approach to finding the maximum and minimum elements in a list, on the following problem instance L, using a tree of recursive calls:

$$L = [\,36, 11, 75, 88, 55\,]$$

Solution:

Figure P19.1 illustrates the tree of recursive calls. Each box in the tree represents a recursive call to **procedure** MAXMIN(). The MAX, MIN variables in the left end of the box are indicative of the state of the variables during the initiation of the call and the same on the right end of the box are indicative of the values returned to them after the termination of the recursive call.

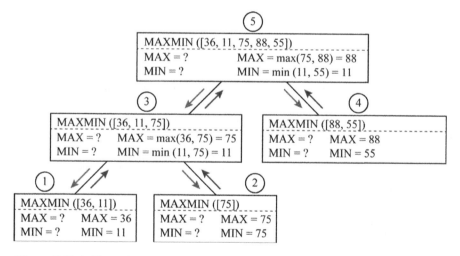

Figure P19.1. *Tree of recursive calls for the* **procedure** *MAXMIN when executed over the problem instance L = {36, 11, 75, 88, 55}. For a color version of this figure, see www.iste.co.uk/pai/algorithms3.zip*

The first call MAXMIN([36, 11, 75, 88, 55]) initiates two recursive calls to MAXMIN([36, 11, 75]) and MAXMIN([88, 55]) and so on and so forth as described by the nodes in the tree. The numeric labels above the boxes indicate the order in which the recursive calls terminate due to the respective base cases that were executed during the call. Thus, MAXMIN([36, 1]), labeled 1, is the first recursive call to terminate since it satisfies the base case condition of $(n = 2)$ and hence MAX $= 36$ and MIN $= 11$ are returned.

Similarly, the box labeled 2 terminates next since the recursive call MAXMIN([75]) satisfies the base case condition of $(n = 1)$ and hence returns MAX $=$ MIN $= 75$. Progressing in this fashion when the first call MAXMIN([36, 11, 75, 88, 55]) terminates, the maximum and minimum elements of 88 and 11 are returned to the variables MAX and MIN. In all, it can be seen that five recursive calls were executed before the final max and min elements were returned as output.

PROBLEM 19.2.–

The quick sort algorithm was discussed in section 17.7. Observe Algorithm 17.8 (**procedure** QUICK_SORT) and Algorithm 17.7 (**procedure** PARTITION) which describe the quick sort procedure. Justify the use of the Divide and Conquer approach in the algorithms.

Solution:

procedure PARTITION serves to divide the original list into two sub-lists, so that all the elements to the left of the pivot element are less than or equal to it and those to the right are greater than or equal to it, during each recursive call. The two recursive calls to **procedure** QUICK_SORT sort the two sublists recursively until the base case of each sub-list containing only one element is reached. At this stage, the **if** condition first < last in **procedure** QUICK_SORT becomes false and therefore the corresponding recursive call terminates. Eventually, when the first call to **procedure** QUICK_SORT terminates, the sorted list is output.

PROBLEM 19.3.–

Construct a Divide and Conquer-based algorithm for the following problem and analyze the same in the worst case.

Input: An ordered array L with n elements and item X that is to be searched in the array L.

Output: Index j where $L[j]=X$, if X is found or else $j = 0$, if X not found.

Solution:

Adopting the binary search algorithm, Algorithm 16.5, discussed in section 16.5, yields a classic solution to the problem. The binary search algorithm is a Divide and Conquer-based method, which divides the ordered array into two at its median, and recursively searches for X in the left or the right segment of the array, based on whether X is less than the median or greater than the median, respectively. If X is found, then it would be a median element $L[j]=X$, and therefore j is output. If X is unfound, then the search ends and therefore $j = 0$ is returned.

The worst-case time complexity analysis of the binary search algorithm is made simple by the fact that the binary search process traces out a **decision tree** with specific characteristics with regard to its parent and child nodes as portrayed in Figure 16.1 of section 16.5.1. Thus, the worst-case search involves looking for leaf nodes in the tree and therefore the number of comparisons is determined by the height of the tree which is $O(log_2 n)$. Therefore, the worst-case complexity of the solution to the problem is $O(log_2 n)$.

PROBLEM 19.4.–

Let v and w be two n-bit numbers where, for simplicity, n is a power of 2. A Divide and Conquer-based algorithm splits the bit numbers into two parts, i.e. a and b for bit number v and c and d for bit number w, as shown in Figure P19.4. The product of the two-bit numbers v and w is recursively computed as,

$$v.w = \left(a.2^{n/2} + b \right).\left(c.2^{n/2} + d \right)$$
$$= a.c.2^n + \left(a.d + b.c \right).2^{n/2} + b.d$$

where the multiplications of the split bit numbers $a.c$, $a.d$, $b.c$ and $b.d$ are done recursively. The base case is reached when $n=2$, at which stage these bit number multiplications turn into element multiplications.

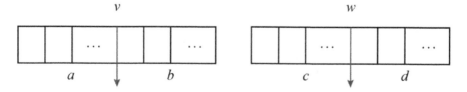

Figure P19.4. *Splitting the bit numbers v and w into two parts*

Determine the computing time of the above Divide and Conquer-based procedure for bit number multiplication. Assume that $n = 2^k$ for simplicity.

Solution:

Let $T(n)$ be the time complexity of the algorithm to multiply two-bit numbers of length n recursively, using the Divide and Conquer-based approach. The algorithm involves four recursive multiplications and three additions of bit numbers of length $\lceil \frac{n}{2} \rceil$. The recurrence relation is therefore given by,

$$T(n) = \begin{cases} 4.T\left(\dfrac{n}{2}\right) + c.n, & n > 2 \\ b, & n = 2 \end{cases}$$

Here $c.n$ is the upper bound for the three bit number additions.

Solving the recurrence relation in the usual manner yields the following in the $k\text{-}1^{th}$ step.

$$T(n) = 4^{k-1}T(n/2^{k-1}) + c.n.(1+2+2^2 +....+2^{k-2})........(step\ k-1)$$

$$= \frac{n^2}{4}.T(2) + c.n.(2^{k-1} - 1)$$

$$= d.n^2 + c.n.(\frac{n}{2} - 1)$$

$$\leq s.n^2$$

$$\cong O(n^2)$$

Hence, the time complexity of the Divide and Conquer-based bit number multiplication algorithm is $O(n^2)$.

PROBLEM 19.5.–

For the Divide and Conquer-based bit number multiplication algorithm discussed in illustrative problem 19.4, what is the computing time if $(a.d+b.c)$ is computed as $(a+b).(c+d)-ac-bd$? Assume that $n = 2^k$ for simplicity.

Solution:

The transformation in the computation of *(a.d+b.c)* as *(a+b).(c+d)-ac-bd* results in the algorithm performing only three multiplications but six additions of two-bit numbers of length $\left[\frac{n}{2}\right]$. The recurrence relation, therefore, is given by,

$$T(n) = \begin{cases} 3.T\left(\dfrac{n}{2}\right) + c.n, & n > 2 \\ b, & n = 2 \end{cases}$$

Solving the equation in the usual manner yields the following in the *k-1th* step.

$$T(n) = 3^{k-1} T(n/2^{k-1}) + c.n.(1 + (3/2) + (3/2)^2 + ... + (3/2)^{k-2}).........(step\ k-1)$$

$$= \frac{3^k}{3}.T(2) + c.n.2.((3/2)^{k-1} - 1)$$

$$= d.n^{\log_2^3} + e.n.(\frac{n^{\log_2^3}}{n} - 1)$$

$$\leq s.n^{\log_2^3}$$

$$\cong O(n^{\log_2^3}) = O(n^{1.59})$$

Review questions

1) Why do Divide and Conquer-based algorithms inherently advocate recursion during their implementation?

2) Justify the Divide and Conquer approach adopted in quick sort, merge sort and binary search algorithms. Comment on the "Divide" strategies used by them.

3) Show that $3.\frac{n}{2} - 2$ comparisons are required to find the minimum and maximum elements of a list *L* with *n* elements.

4) Demonstrate the Divide and Conquer-based bit number multiplication methods discussed in illustrative problems 19.4 and 19.5 on the following two-bit numbers:

   v: 0101 w: 1000

5) What is the time complexity of multiplying two *n*-bit numbers using the traditional method?

Programming assignments

1) Implement the Divide and Conquer-based "high school" method to multiply two square matrices A_{nXn}, B_{nXn}.

2) Implement Strassen's method of matrix multiplication over two square matrices.

3) Implement the Divide and Conquer-based algorithm to find the minimum and maximum elements in a list L of n elements.

Greedy Method

This chapter discusses the greedy method and demonstrates the strategy over the *Knapsack problem*, *Prim's* and *Kruskal's spanning tree extraction algorithms* and *Dijkstra's Single Source Shortest Path problem*.

20.1. Introduction

The greedy method is an algorithm design technique, which is applicable to problems defined by an *objective function* that needs to be *maximized* or *minimized*, subject to some *constraints*. Given n inputs to the problem, the aim is to obtain a *subset of n*, that satisfies all the constraints, in which case it is referred to as a *feasible solution.* A feasible solution that serves to obtain the best objective function value (maximal or minimal) is referred to as the *optimal solution*.

The greedy method proceeds to obtain the feasible and optimal solution, by considering the inputs one at a time. Hence, an implementation of the greedy method-based algorithm is always *iterative* in nature. Contrast this with the implementation of Divide and Conquer based algorithms discussed in Chapter 19, which is always recursive in nature.

20.2. Abstraction

The abstraction of the greedy method is shown in Figure 20.1. Here, the function SELECT(A) makes a prudent selection of the input depending on the problem. Function FEASIBLE() ensures that the solution satisfies all constraints imposed on the problem and AUGMENT() augments the current input which is a feasible solution to the solution set. Observe how the **for** loop ensures consideration of inputs one by one, justifying the iterative nature of greedy algorithms.

```
procedure GREEDY(A,n)
/* array A of size n represents the inputs to the
problem */
  solution = {};
  for i = 1:n do
      x = SELECT(A);
      if FEASIBLE(solution, x) then
          solution = AUGMENT(solution, x)
  end
  return (solution)
end GREEDY
```

Figure 20.1. *Abstraction of the greedy method*

The application of the greedy method in the design of solutions to the knapsack problem, extraction of minimum cost spanning trees using Prim's and Kruskal's algorithms and Dijkstra's single source shortest path problem, are discussed in the ensuing sections.

20.3. Knapsack problem

The *knapsack problem* is a classic problem to illustrate the greedy method. The problem deals with n objects with weights ($W_1, W_2, ...W_n$) and with profits or prices ($P_1, P_2, ...P_n$). A knapsack with a capacity of M units is available. In other words, the knapsack can handle only a maximum weight of M, when objects with varying weights are packed into it. A person is allowed to own as many objects, on the conditions that (i) the total weight of all objects selected cannot exceed the capacity of the knapsack and (ii) objects can be dismantled and parts of them can be selected.

From a practical standpoint, a person while selecting the objects would try to choose those that would fetch high profits, hoping to maximize the profit arising out of owning the objects. Thus, *maximizing profit* is the *objective function* of the problem. The fact that objects selected can be dismantled and that their total weight cannot exceed the capacity of the knapsack are the *constraints*.

Let $(O_1, O_2, \ldots O_n)$ be n objects, and $(p_1, p_2, \ldots p_n)$ and $(w_1, w_2, \ldots w_n)$ be their profits and weights, respectively. Let M be the capacity of the knapsack and $(x_1, x_2, \ldots x_n)$ be the proportion of objects which are selected. The mathematical formulation of the knapsack problem is as follows:

$$max \left(\sum_{i=1}^{n} p_i . x_i \right)$$

subject to

$$\sum_{i=1}^{n} w_i . x_i \leq M$$

$$0 \leq x_i \leq 1 \qquad\qquad\qquad\qquad\qquad\qquad [20.1]$$

The objective function describes the maximization of the total profits. The constraints describe the total weight of the objects selected to be bound by M and the proportion of objects selected to lie between [0,1], where $x_i = 0$ denotes rejection, $x_i = 1$ denotes the selection of the whole object and anything in between [0, 1] denotes the selection of a part of the object after dismantling it.

20.3.1. *Greedy solution to the knapsack problem*

20.3.1.1. *Strategy 1*

A greedy solution to the knapsack problem involves selecting the objects one by one such that the addition of each object into the knapsack increases the profit value, subject to the capacity of the knapsack. This could mean *ordering the objects in the non-increasing order of their profits* and selecting them one by one until capacity M is exhausted. Will this strategy yield the optimal solution?

20.3.1.2. *Strategy 2*

Another "more-the-merrier" strategy could insist on *ordering the objects in the non-decreasing order of their weights* and pack as many objects as possible into the knapsack, subject to the capacity M, hoping to maximize profit by a larger selection of objects. Will this strategy yield the optimal solution?

20.3.1.3. *Strategy 3*

A third strategy could be to *order the objects according to the non-increasing order of profit per unit weight* (profit/weight), that is $\left(\frac{p_1}{w_1} \right) \geq \left(\frac{p_2}{w_2} \right) \geq \ldots \left(\frac{p_n}{w_n} \right)$, and select objects one by one until the capacity M of the knapsack is exhausted. Will this strategy yield the optimal solution?

It can be observed that all the three strategies are greedy method based since they revolve around selecting the object one by one while trying to satisfy the constraints and aiming to maximize the objective function. Let us explore these strategies over an example knapsack problem.

EXAMPLE 20.1.–

Consider three objects O_1, O_2, O_3 with $(p_1, p_2, p_3) = (25, 36, 34)$ and $(w_1, w_2, w_3) = (20, 28, 25)$ describing their profits and their weights, respectively. Let $M = 30$ be the capacity of the knapsack and (x_1, x_2, x_3) be the proportion of objects which are selected. The optimal solutions delivered by the three strategies described above are as given below:

Greedy method	(x_1, x_2, x_3)	M	$\left(\sum_{i=1}^{n} p_i \cdot x_i \right)$
Strategy 1	(0, 1, 2/25)	30	38.72
Strategy 2	(1, 0, 10/25)	30	38.6
Strategy 3	(0, 5/28, 1)	30	40.43

Of the three strategies, it can be seen that strategy 3 which selects objects based on the highest profit per unit weight value, obtains the optimal solution.

In strategy 3, the greedy method orders the objects according to the profit per unit weight value and selects the objects or their proportions such that the capacity M of the knapsack is not exceeded, thereby satisfying the constraints imposed and therefore turning out a feasible solution. The optimal solution arrived at after evaluating the objective function value for the selected x_i s is 40.43, which is the best. It can be proved that a greedy method that works by selecting the objects based on their profit per unit weight value, for a given instance of the knapsack problem, will always yield the optimal best solution. The proof for this can be seen in illustrative problem 20.1.

Algorithm 20.1 (**Procedure** GREEDYMETHOD_KNAPSACK()) illustrates the working of strategy 3.

```
procedure GREEDYMETHOD_KNAPSACK(p, w, x, M, n)
/*  objects  are  first  arranged  in  the  order  where
```
$$\left(\frac{p_1}{w_1}\right) \geq \left(\frac{p_2}{w_2}\right) \geq \ldots \left(\frac{p_n}{w_n}\right) */$$
```
/*  p[1:n] : profit vector of the n objects
    w[1:n] : weight vector of the n objects
    x[1:n] : proportion of objects selected, 0 ≤ x_i ≤ 1,
             which is the solution vector
        M: capacity of the knapsack
*/
  balance_capacity = M;

  for i = 1:n do
     if (w[i]  > balance_capacity) then exit()
     x[i] = 1;
     balance_capacity = balance_capacity - w[i]
  end

  if (i≤n) then x[i] = balance_capacity/w[i]

end GREEDYMETHOD_KNAPSACK.
```

Algorithm 20.1. *Greedy method*
solution for the knapsack problem

20.4. Minimum cost spanning tree algorithms

Given a connected undirected graph $G = (V, E)$, where V is the set of vertices and E is the set of edges, a subgraph $T = (V, E')$, where $E' \subseteq E$ is a *spanning tree* if T is a tree.

It is possible to extract many spanning trees from a graph G. When G is a connected, weighted and undirected graph, where each edge involves a cost, then a *minimum cost spanning tree* is a spanning tree that has the minimum cost. Section 9.5.2 of Chapter 9, Volume 2, details the concepts and construction of minimum spanning trees using two methods, which are, Prim's algorithm (Algorithm 9.4) and Kruskal's algorithm (Algorithm 9.5).

Both the algorithms adopt the greedy method of algorithm design, despite differences in their approach to obtaining the minimum cost spanning tree.

20.4.1. *Prim's algorithm as a greedy method*

Prim's algorithm selects the *minimum cost edge* one by one, to *optimize the cost of the spanning tree* and proceeds to construct the spanning tree after ensuring that the inclusion of the edge does not violate the *constraints* of (i) edge forming a cycle and (ii) edge staying connected, with the spanning tree under construction. Once all the vertices V have made their appearances in the constructed spanning tree, the algorithm abruptly terminates discarding any leftover edges, while declaring the minimum cost spanning tree as its output.

Thus, in the case of Prim's algorithm, the objective function is the minimization of the cost of the spanning tree and the constraints ensure the connectedness and acyclicity of the spanning tree, when each edge is added to the tree. The algorithm adopts the greedy method of design by selecting the edges one by one while working to obtain the feasible solution at every stage until the optimal solution is arrived at in the final step.

The time complexity of Prim's algorithm is $O(n^2)$, where n is the number of vertices in the graph.

20.4.2. *Kruskal's algorithm as a greedy method*

Kruskal's algorithm, on the other hand, selects a *minimum cost edge* one by one, just as Prim's algorithm does, but with a huge difference in that, the selected edges build a *forest* and not necessarily a tree, during the construction. However, the selection of edges ensures that no cycles are formed in the forest.

Kruskal's algorithm, therefore, works over a forest of trees until no more edges can be considered for inclusion and the number of edges in the forest equals $(n-1)$, at which stage, the algorithm terminates and outputs the minimum cost spanning tree that is generated.

Thus, in the case of Kruskal's algorithm, the objective function is the minimization of the cost of the spanning tree and the constraint ensures the acyclicity of trees in the forest. The algorithm also adopts the greedy method of design where the edges are selected one by one, obtaining the feasible solution at each stage until the optimal solution, which is the minimum cost spanning tree is obtained in the final stage.

The time complexity of Kruskal's algorithm is $O(e.\ log\ e)$, where e is the number of edges.

20.5. Dijkstra's algorithm

The *single source shortest path problem* concerns finding the shortest path from a node termed *source* in a *weighted digraph*, to all other nodes connected to it. For example, given a network of cities, a single source shortest path problem defined over it proceeds to find the shortest path from a given city (source) to all other cities connected to it.

Dijkstra's algorithm obtains an elegant solution to the single source shortest path problem and has been detailed in section 9.5.1 of Chapter 9, Volume 2, Algorithm 9.3, illustrates the working of Dijkstra's algorithm. The algorithm works by selecting nodes that are closest to the source node, one by one, and ensuring that ultimately the shortest paths from the source node to all other nodes are the minimum. Thus, Dijkstra's algorithm adopts the greedy method to solve the single source shortest path problem and reports a time complexity of $O(N^2)$, where N is the number of nodes in the weighted digraph.

Summary

– The greedy method works on problems which demand an optimal solution, as defined by an objective function, subject to constraints that determine the feasibility of the solution.

– The greedy method selects inputs one by one ensuring that the constraints imposed on the problem are satisfied at every stage. Hence, the greedy method based algorithms are conventionally iterative.

– The knapsack problem, construction of minimum spanning trees using Prim's and Kruskal's algorithms and Dijktra's algorithm for the single source shortest path problem are examples of greedy methods at work.

20.6. Illustrative problems

PROBLEM 20.1.–

The greedy method of solving the knapsack problem (**procedure GREEDYMETHOD_KNAPSACK**) discussed in section 20.3.1, selected the objects ordered on their non-increasing order of profits per unit weight, that is, $\left(\frac{p_1}{w_1}\right) \geq$ $\left(\frac{p_2}{w_2}\right) \geq ... \left(\frac{p_n}{w_n}\right)$, where $(p_1, p_2, ... p_n)$ are the profits and $(w_1, w_2, ... w_n)$ are the weights.

Prove that the greedy method obtains the optimal solution to the knapsack problem.

Solution:

Following the notations used for the knapsack problem in section 20.3.1, let $X = (x_1, x_2, ... x_n)$ be the solution arrived at by the greedy method. It can be easily inferred that the greedy solution would have the pattern $(1, 1, 1, ... x_k, 0, ...0)$, where $x_k \leq 1$.

To explain, the greedy solution keeps selecting whole objects so long as the knapsack can accommodate them. Hence, the sequence of 1s is in the prefix of the solution vector. At the point when the selected object cannot be accommodated wholly in the knapsack, the object is dismantled and the appropriate part of the object alone is pushed into the knapsack. Hence, $x_k \leq 1$. All other objects thereafter are rejected, and therefore, a sequence of 0s representing $(x_{k+1}, x_{k+2}, ... x_n)$ follows as the suffix of the solution vector.

Let $Y = (y_1, y_2, ... y_n)$ be an optimal solution for the knapsack problem. Without loss of generality, let us suppose that $\sum_{i=1}^{n} w_i. y_i = M$ We need to prove that the greedy solution X is as much an optimal solution as Y is.

To do this, let us compare X with Y. Let us suppose that x_t is the first point of difference between the two solution vectors. Now, we claim that $y_t < x_t$. Why?

Case 1: If $(t = k)$, then since $\sum_{i=1}^{n} w_i. x_i = M$, either $y_t < x_t$ or $\sum_{i=1}^{t} w_i. y_i > M$. Since the latter is not possible, we claim $y_t < x_t$ for this case.

Case 2: If $(t < k)$ then $x_t = 1$ and $y_t \neq x_t$ therefore $y_t < x_t$.

Case 3: If $(t > k)$, then $x_t = 0$, implying that $\sum_{i=1}^{t} w_i. y_i > M$, which is not possible. Hence this case cannot happen.

Thus, we assert that given the greedy solution X and the optimal solution Y, the first point of difference between the two vectors, x_t and y_t, satisfies the relation $y_t < x_t$.

Now, let us increase y_t to x_t and decrease $(y_{t+1}, y_{t+2}, ... y_n)$ so that the capacity of the knapsack used stays at M.

Let $Z = (z_1, z_2, ... z_t, ... z_n)$ be the modified vector where $z_i = x_i, 1 \le i \le t$ and
$$\sum_{t<i\le n} (y_i - z_i).w_i = (z_t - y_t).w_t$$

Now,

$$\sum_{1\le i\le n} p_i.z_i = \sum_{1\le i\le n} p_i.y_i + (z_t - y_t).w_t.\frac{p_t}{w_t} - \sum_{t<i\le n}(y_i - z_i).w_i.\frac{p_i}{w_i}$$

$$\ge \sum_{1\le i\le n} p_i.y_i + \left((z_t - y_t).w_t - \sum_{t<i\le n}(y_i - z_i).w_i\right).\frac{p_t}{w_t}$$

$$= \sum_{1\le i\le n} p_i.y_i$$

If $\sum_{1\le i\le n} p_i.z_i > \sum_{1\le i\le n} p_i.y_i$ then Y loses its optimal solution status and therefore they have to be equal, rendering $Z = X$ where X is optimal or $Z \ne X$, due to another point of difference. In the latter case, we repeat the procedure that was adopted for the first point of difference until Y gradually transforms itself into X, thereby rendering X to be the optimal solution.

Therefore, the greedy method for the knapsack problem, which orders the objects according to their non-increasing order of profit per unit weight, does obtain the optimal solution to the problem.

PROBLEM 20.2.–

[Optimal merge pattern]

The principle of merging two sorted files was elaborated in section 17.5 of Chapter 17.

If the two files $F1$ and $F2$ have n, m records then the number of comparisons undertaken to merge the two files is given by $(n + m)$. If there are k files F_1, F_2, ...F_k, with n_1, n_2, n_3, ...n_k records, then merging the files into one file can be undertaken by repeatedly merging the files in pairs until the final merge yields one file in $\sum_{i=1}^{k} n_i$ comparisons. The problem of an optimal merge pattern is to find the sequence in which the files should be *pairwise* merged so that the number of comparisons undertaken is minimized. Adopting the greedy method to the problem yields a solution that is elegant and optimal.

When the merge pattern involves pairwise merging, it can be described by means of a binary tree, known as a **two-way merge tree**, where the leaf nodes indicate the individual files F_1, F_2, ...F_k to be merged and the non-leaf nodes denote the pairwise merging of the files represented by the left child node and the right child node.

Let $(F_1, F_2, F_3, F_4, F_5)$ be five sorted files with lengths (2, 7, 3, 4, 6, 5).

i) Adopt a merge pattern that merges the files pairwise in the order of their appearance in the list. What is the total number of comparisons done to merge them into a single file?

ii) Devise a greedy method to merge the sorted files pairwise, so that the total number of comparisons undertaken to merge them into a single file is minimal.

Solution:

i) Figure P20.2(a) illustrates the binary merge tree that undertakes the merging of the files in the order of their appearance in the list. The files are indicated by square nodes and the merged files are indicated by circular nodes. The total number of comparisons is given by adding the sizes of the merged files, which is $9 + 12 + 16 + 22 + 27 = 86$.

ii) Since the total number of comparisons needs to be minimal, a greedy method would naturally look to merge files with the *smallest lengths* so that the increase in the total number of comparisons progresses slowly. Thus, the pair-wise merging of those files with the smallest lengths is sequenced first. Figure P20.2(b) shows the merge pattern that contributes to the optimal number of comparisons given by $5 + 9 + 11 + 16 + 27 = 68$.

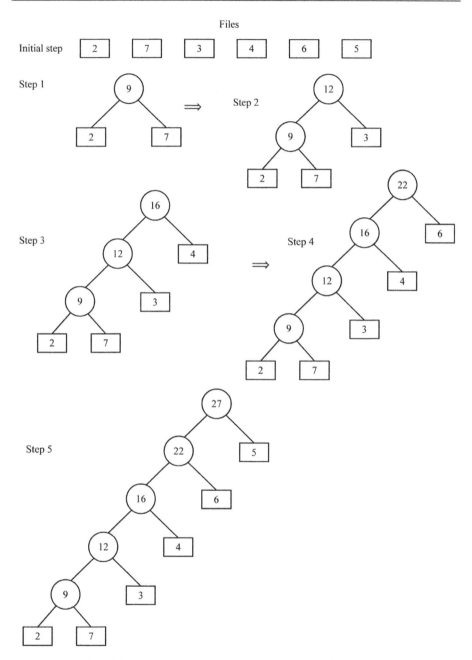

Figure P20.2(a). *The binary merge tree that undertakes the merging of the files in the order of their appearance in the list shown in illustrative problem 20.2*

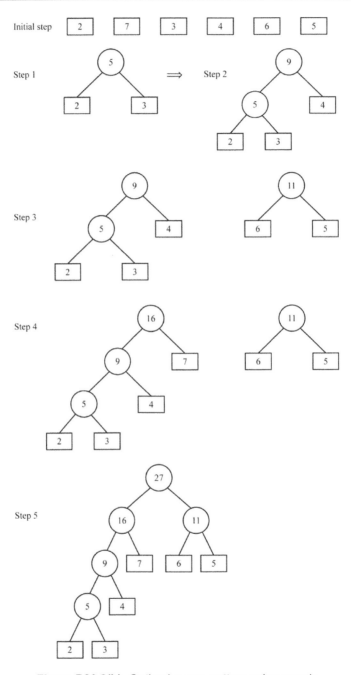

Figure P20.2(b). *Optimal merge pattern using greedy method for the list shown in illustrative problem 20.2*

PROBLEM 20.3.–

[Job sequencing using deadlines]

Let us suppose that there are n jobs (J_1, J_2, ... J_n) each of which takes a unit of time to be processed by a machine and there is just one single machine to process the jobs. Let us suppose that (d_1, d_2, d_3, ...d_n) are the deadlines in units of times to complete the jobs and (p_1, p_2, p_3, ...p_n) are the profits earned if the jobs are processed within the deadline. The objective is obviously to select those jobs and complete them within their deadlines so that maximum profit is earned.

Design a greedy method to obtain the optimal sequence of jobs that will earn maximum profits. Demonstrate it on the case where there are four jobs, with $n = 4$, deadlines given by ($d_1 = 2$, $d_2 = 1$, $d_3 = 3$, $d_4 = 1$) and profits earned as ($p_1 = 100$, $p_2 = 20$, $p_3 = 50$, $p_4 = 40$).

Solution:

A greedy method to solve this problem would sequence the jobs according to the order of their non-increasing profits since the objective is to maximize the profits. Thus, each job earning high profits is selected and checked to see if it can be completed within the deadline, to earn the profit concerned. Thus, those jobs which satisfy the constraint of their deadlines will be the feasible solution and those that do not, are discarded. The optimal solution to the problem will be the sequence of jobs all of which are executed within their deadlines and thereby yield maximum profit.

For the case given, the jobs (J_1, J_2, J_3, J_4) are arranged in the non-increasing order of profits, (J_1, J_4, J_3, J_2). Now, J_1 is selected and executed and a profit of 100 is earned. The next job J_4 fails its deadline and therefore is not a feasible solution and hence is discarded. J_3 with 3 units of deadline is a feasible solution and hence is executed and a profit of 50 is earned. The last job within its deadline of 1 is not a feasible solution and hence is rejected. Thus, the optimal profit earned by the greedy method is (100 + 50 = 150) with the jobs sequenced as (J_1, J_3).

Review questions

1) Why do greedy methods advocate iteration during their implementation?

2) Find the optimal solution for the instance of the knapsack problem shown below, using the greedy method:

Number of objects, $n = 7$, knapsack capacity $M = 20$, profits $(p_1, p_2, p_3, p_4, p_5 p_6, p_7) = (20, 10, 30, 5, 15, 25, 18)$ and weights $(w_1, w_2, w_3, w_4, w_5, w_6, w_7) = (4, 2, 6, 5, 4, 3, 3)$.

3) Demonstrate how Kruskal's algorithm and Prim's algorithm, adopting greedy methods, obtain the minimum cost spanning tree of the graph shown below.

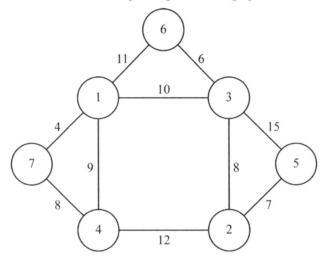

4) Let us suppose that n binary trees describe n files to be optimally merged using the greedy method, as explained in illustrative problem 20.2. The structure of the nodes of the binary trees is shown below:

LCHILD	SIZE	RCHILD

where LCHILD and RCHILD denote links to the left and right child nodes respectively, and SIZE denotes the number of records in the files.

Initially, all the binary trees possess just a single node (root node) that indicates the size of the file.

Write an algorithm, which begins with the list of n binary trees comprising single nodes and builds a forest of binary trees following the optimal merge pattern and eventually outputs a single binary tree that describes the complete two-way merge tree.

5) For the job sequencing using the deadlines problem, detailed in illustrative problem 20.3, an instance of which has been described below, find the optimal solution using the greedy method.

Number of jobs $n = 5$, profits $(p_1, p_2, p_3, p_4, p_5) = (110, 50, 70, 100, 30)$ and deadlines in time units $(d_1, d_2, d_3, d_4, d_5) = (2, 2, 3, 1, 4)$, with each job requiring a unit of time for completion.

Programming assignments

1) The GREEDYMETHOD_KNAPSACK() procedure was discussed in section 20.3.1. Implement the procedure and test it over the instance of the knapsack problem as discussed in review question 2.

2) Implement the algorithm constructed for the optimal merge pattern problem discussed in review question 4 using a programming language that supports the pointers.

21

Dynamic Programming

In this chapter, the algorithm design technique of *Dynamic Programming* is detailed. The technique is demonstrated over *0/1 Knapsack Problem, Traveling Salesperson Problem, All-Pairs Shortest Path Problem* and *Optimal Binary Search Tree Construction*.

21.1. Introduction

Dynamic Programming is an effective algorithm design technique built on *Bellman's Principle of Optimality* which states that '*an optimal sequence of decisions has the property that whatever the initial state and decisions are, the remaining decisions must constitute an optimal decision sequence with regard to the state resulting from the first decision*'.

The dynamic programming strategy is applicable to optimization problems, which comprise an *objective function* that needs to be maximized or minimized, subject to *constraints* that need to be satisfied. A candidate solution that satisfies the constraints is termed a *feasible solution* and when a feasible solution results in the best objective function value, it is termed an *optimal solution*.

The greedy method (discussed in Chapter 20) also works over problems whose characteristics are as defined above and obtains optimal solutions to these problems. How then is a greedy method different from dynamic programming?

A greedy method works in an iterative fashion, selecting objects constituting the solution set one by one and constructing a feasible solution set, which eventually turns into an optimal solution set. However, there are problems where generating a single optimal decision sequence is not always possible and therefore, a greedy method might not work on these problems.

It is here that dynamic programming finds its rightful place. Dynamic programming, unlike the greedy method, generates *multiple decision sequences using Bellman's principle of optimality* and eventually delivers the best decision sequence that leads to the optimal solution to the problem. Also, dynamic programming ensures that any decision sequence that is being enumerated but does not show promise of being an optimal solution is not generated. Thus, to favor the enumeration of multiple decision sequences, dynamic programming algorithms are always *recursive in principle*.

Let $P(1, n)$ denote a problem, which demands an optimal sequence of n decisions as its solution, with an initial problem state S_0. Let $(x_1, x_2,...x_n)$ be the n decision variables with regard to the problem. Let us suppose that from among a set of k decisions $\{d_1, d_2,...d_k\}$ available for decision variable x_1, a decision $x_1 = d_j$ was taken, which results in a problem state S_1. According to the principle of optimality, whatever be the decision d_j taken on x_1, the remaining decision sequence pertaining to decision variables $(x_2, x_3, ...x_n)$ must constitute an optimal sequence with regard to the problem state S_1.

Generalizing, if S_i is the respective problem state following each of the decisions $d_i, 1 \leq i \leq k$, for the decision variable x_1, and Γ_i are the optimal decision sequences with regard to the rest of the decision variables, for the problem states S_i, then according to the principle of optimality the final optimal decision sequence with regard to the problem whose initial state is S_0, is the *best of the decision sequences*, $d_i\Gamma_i, 1 \leq i \leq k$.

It is therefore quite obvious that dynamic programming generates many decision sequences, but the strategy employing the principle of optimality ensures that those sequences which are sub-optimal are not generated, as far as possible. In the worst case, if there are n decision variables each of which has d choices for their respective decisions, then the total number of decision sequences generated would be d^n, which is exponential in nature. Despite this observation, dynamic programming algorithms for most problems have reported polynomial time complexity considering the fact that the sub-optimal decision sequences are not generated by the strategy.

It is prudent to apply the principle of optimality in a *recursive fashion* considering the large sequence of decisions that are generated, each with regard to the problem states arising out of the earlier decisions that are taken. Hence, dynamic programming algorithms are always governed by *recurrence relations*, solving which one can easily attain the optimal decision sequence for the problem concerned. Adhering to the norms of recursion, the *base cases for the recurrence relations* need to be constructed from the respective problem definitions.

The solution of the recurrence relations defining a dynamic programming algorithm can be undertaken in two ways, viz., ***forward approach*** and ***backward approach***.

In the forward approach, if $(x_1, x_2, ...x_n)$ are the n decision variables on which an optimal decision sequence has to be constructed, then the decision on x_i is made in terms of the optimal decision sequences for $x_{i+1}, x_{i+2}, ...x_n$. On the contrary, in the backward approach, the decision on x_i is made in terms of the optimal decision sequences for $x_1, x_2, ...x_{i-1}$. Thus, the forward approach deals with "look ahead" decision making and the backward approach deals with "look back" decision making.

In practice, formulating the recurrence relation for a problem works out easier, when a backward approach is followed. The recurrence relation, however, is solved forwards. For a forward approach based on recurrence relation, the solution of the relation becomes easier when backward solving is undertaken beginning with the last decision.

Another important characteristic of dynamic programming strategy is that the solutions to sub-problems obtained by the respective optimal decision subsequence are preserved thereby avoiding re-computation of values. Therefore, in most cases, the values computed by the recurrence relations can be tabulated, which permits the effective transformation of a recursive process into iterative program code, while implementing dynamic programming algorithms. Thus, *most dynamic programming algorithms can be expressed as iterative programs*.

The ensuing sections demonstrate the application of dynamic programming to the problems of 0/1 knapsack, traveling salesperson, all-pairs shortest paths and optimal binary search trees.

21.2. 0/1 knapsack problem

The 0/1 knapsack problem is similar to the knapsack problem discussed in section 20.2 of Chapter 20, but with the difference that none of the objects selected may be dismantled while pushing them into the knapsack. In other words, x_i the proportion of objects selected could be either 1 when the object is fully selected for inclusion in the knapsack, or 0, when the object is rejected for it does not completely fit into the knapsack.

The 0/1 knapsack problem is therefore defined as:

$$max\left(\sum_{i=1}^{n} p_i \cdot x_i\right)$$

subject to

$$\sum_{i=1}^{n} w_i \cdot x_i \leq M \qquad\qquad\qquad [21.1]$$

$$x_i = 0 \quad \text{or} \quad 1, \quad 1 \leq i \leq n$$

where, $O_1, O_2, \ldots O_n$ indicate n objects, and $(p_1, p_2, \ldots p_n)$ and $(w_1, w_2, \ldots w_n)$ represent their profits and weights, respectively. Here, M is the capacity of the knapsack and $(x_1, x_2, \ldots x_n)$ are the proportion of objects selected, which can be either 0 or 1. The objective is to determine the sequence of objects which will fit into the knapsack and yield maximum profits.

How does dynamic programming work to obtain the recurrence relation that will help obtain the optimal decision sequence?

21.2.1. *Dynamic programming-based solution*

Let KNAP0/1 (1, n, M) indicate the 0/1 knapsack problem instance, which demands n optimal decisions with regard to its selection of objects that fit into a knapsack whose capacity is M. With regard to x_1, there can only be two decisions. If $(x_1 = 0)$ then the first object is rejected and therefore the optimal decision sequence involves solving the sub-problem KNAP0/1(2, n, M). If $(x_1 = 1)$ then the first object is selected and therefore the optimal decision sequence involves solving the sub-problem KNAP0/1(2, n, M-w$_1$).

Let $g_j(y)$ be the optimal solution (maximal profits) to the sub-problem KNAP0/1(j+1, n, y). The objective is to obtain the optimal solution $g_0(M)$ to the original problem KNAP0/1 (1, n, M). There can only be two decisions with regard to the first decision on x_1, viz., $x_1 = 0$ or $x_1 = 1$. Following the principle of optimality, $g_0(M)$ can be computed as:

$$g_0(M) = \max(g_1(M), \ g_1(M - w_1) + p_1) \qquad\qquad [21.2]$$

Here $g_1(M)$ denotes the optimal solution to the rest of the sub-problem, with no profits accrued so far and with M intact, on account of the first decision $x_1 = 0$. $g_1(M-w_1) + p1$ denotes the optimal solution to the rest of the sub-problem with a profit of p_1 gained already and a decreased capacity of $M-w_1$, on account of the first decision $x_1 = 1$. Generalizing to accommodate the optimal solutions with regard to intermediary sequences for the sub-problems concerned:

$$g_i(y) = max(g_{i+1}(y), g_{i+1}(y - w_{i+1}) + p_i) \qquad [21.3]$$

It can be seen that the recurrence relation [21.3] models a forward approach and the base cases can be framed using the knowledge that $g_n(y) = 0, \forall y$, since n decisions have already been taken by then and therefore there are no profits to be earned.

Solving backward beginning with $g_n(y)$, we obtain $g_{n-1}(y)$ by substituting $i = n-1$ in equation [21.3], from $g_{n-1}(y)$ we obtain $g_{n-2}(y)$ and so on until we finally arrive at $g_0(M)$ that yields the optimal solution to the 0/1 knapsack problem.

A backward approach to the dynamic programming algorithm for the 0/1 knapsack problem, would try to compute $g_n(M)$ as the optimal solution to the problem KNAPO/1(1, n, M), yielding the following recurrence relation:

$$g_i(y) = max(g_{i-1}(y), g_{i-1}(y - w_i) + p_i) \qquad [21.4]$$

$$g_0(y) = 0, \forall y, \quad y \geq 0$$
$$g_0(y) = -\infty, \forall y, y < 0$$

EXAMPLE 21.1.–

Let us consider the following 0/1 knapsack problem instance:

$n = 3$, $(w_1, w_2, w_3) = (20,30,40)$, $(p_1, p_2, p_3) = (10,20,50)$, and $M = 60$.

Adopting the backward approach described in [21.4], $g_3(60)$ would yield the optimal solution to the 0/1 knapsack problem instance. The first step yields:

$g_3(60) = max(g_2(60), g_2(60-w3)+p_3)$

$= max(g_2(60), g_2(20)+50)$

Progressing with the computations of $g_2(60)$ and $g_2(20)$ in a similar fashion, making use of the base cases at the appropriate steps to terminate computations and backtracking to return the results to the calling recursive functions, results in $g_3(60) = max(g_2(60), g_2(20) + 50) = max(30, 10 + 50) = 60$, which is the optimal solution to the problem instance.

Tracking which among the two decisions gave the maximum value can help fix the value of the decision variable x_i concerned. Thus, $g_3(60)$ obtains its maximum value from $g_2(20) + 50$, which decides on including the object $w_3 = 40$ into the knapsack and therefore sets $x_3 = 1$. Proceeding in a similar way, the optimal values of the decision variables turn out to be $(x_1, x_2, x_3) = (1,0,1)$. The maximum profit earned is 60 with the knapsack capacity utilized to be 60.

21.3. Traveling salesperson problem

The traveling salesperson problem deals with finding the optimal cost of undertaking a *tour* that begins with a city, visiting all other cities charted out in the tour once, without revisiting any one of them again, before returning to the city from where the tour started.

Let $G = (V, E)$ where V is the set of vertices and E is the set of edges, be a weighted digraph with c_{ij} indicating the *cost* (weight) of edge $<i, j>$. Let $|V| = n$, $n > 1$ be the number of vertices. The cost matrix $(c_{ij})_{n \times n}$ is defined as $c_{ij} > 0$, for all i and j, and $c_{ij} = \infty$, if edge $<i, j>$ does not exist in E.

A *tour* of G is a directed cycle that begins from a vertex S and includes all other vertices of G before it ends in vertex S. The *cost of the tour* is the sum of the costs of all the edges. A *minimum cost tour* is a tour that reports the minimal cost. The traveling salesperson problem concerns finding the minimum cost tour from a source node S.

EXAMPLE 21.2.–

Figure 21.1(a) illustrates a weighted digraph and Figure 21.1(b) the cost matrix of the graph. Given node {1} to be a source node, the cycle {1, 3, 4, 2, 1} represents a tour whose cost is 46 and the cycle {1, 2, 4, 3, 1} represents a minimum cost tour whose cost is 40, that shall be obtained using dynamic programming.

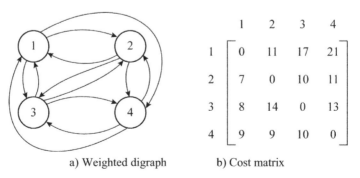

a) Weighted digraph   b) Cost matrix

Figure 21.1. *Traveling salesperson problem – an example*

21.3.1. *Dynamic programming-based solution*

The recurrence relation of the dynamic programming-based solution for the traveling salesperson problem can be framed as follows.

Let $g(x, y)$ denote the minimum cost of the tour undertaken from node x, traveling through all other nodes in y before ending the tour at the source node S. Without loss of generality, let us suppose that $V = \{1, 2, 3, ...n\}$ are the n nodes in the weighted digraph and node $\{1\}$ is the source node.

Following the principle of optimality, the recurrence relation to obtaining the minimum cost tour is given by:

$$g(1, \ V - \{1\}) = \min_{2 \leq k \leq n} \left(c_{1k} + g(k, V - \{1, k\}) \right) \qquad [21.5]$$

To obtain $g(1, V\text{-}\{1\})$, a series of decision sequences with regard to the tour moving over to the next node k, $2 \leq k \leq n$ from the source node, need to be recursively computed.

Generalizing, for $i \notin T$:

$$g(i, T) = \min_{j \in T} \left(c_{ij} + g(j, T - \{j\}) \right) \qquad [21.6]$$

Equation [21.6] can now be used to undertake recursive computations for the intermediary decision sequences. The base case is reached when there are no more nodes to visit during the tour before ending the tour at the source node $\{1\}$. The base cases are therefore given by:

$$g(i, \varphi) = c_{i1} \quad \forall i \in T - \{1\} \qquad [21.7]$$

EXAMPLE 21.3.–

The dynamic programming-based computation of the minimum cost tour for the traveling salesperson problem defined in example 21.2, using equations [21.5]–[21.7] is detailed below.

Using equation [21.5] that adopts a forward approach,

$$g(1, V - \{1\})) = g(1, \{2,3,4\}) = \min_{2 \le k \le 4} \{c_{1k} + g(k, V - \{k, 1\})\}$$

$$= \min \begin{Bmatrix} c_{12} + g(2, \{3,4\}) \\ c_{13} + g(3, \{2,4\}) \\ c_{14} + g(4, \{2,3\}) \end{Bmatrix} = \min \begin{Bmatrix} 11 + g(2, \{3,4\}) \\ 17 + g(3, \{2,4\}) \\ 21 + g(4, \{2,3\}) \end{Bmatrix}$$

Using equation [21.6] to recursively compute the intermediary decision functions of $g(2, \{3,4\})$, $g(3, \{2, 4\})$, $g(4, \{2, 3\})$ yields:

$$g(2, \{3,4\}) = \min \begin{Bmatrix} c_{23} + g(3, \{4\}) \\ c_{24} + g(4, \{3\}) \end{Bmatrix} = \min \begin{Bmatrix} 10 + g(3, \{4\}) \\ 11 + g(4, \{3\}) \end{Bmatrix}$$

$$g(3, \{2,4\}) = \min \begin{Bmatrix} 14 + g(2, \{4\}) \\ 13 + g(4, \{2\}) \end{Bmatrix}$$

$$g(4, \{2,3\}) = \min \begin{Bmatrix} 9 + g(2, \{3\}) \\ 10 + g(3, \{2\}) \end{Bmatrix}$$

Progressing further:

$$g(3, \{4\}) = c_{34} + g(4, \phi) = c_{34} + c_{41} = 13 + 9 = 22$$
$$g(4, \{3\}) = c_{43} + g(3, \phi) = c_{43} + c_{31} = 10 + 8 = 18$$
$$g(2, \{4\}) = c_{24} + g(4, \phi) = c_{24} + c_{41} = 11 + 9 = 20$$

and similarly:

$$g(4, \{2\}) = 16$$
$$g(2, \{3\}) = 18$$
$$g(3, \{2\}) = 21$$

It can be seen that the base cases of the recurrence relation are defined by equation [21.7] which are $g(2, \phi) = c_{21} = 7$, $g(3, \phi) = c_{31} = 8$, $g(4, \phi) = c_{41} = 9$ have been made use of to terminate recursion and initiate backtracking to finally yield the value:

$$g(1, V - \{1\})) = g(1, \{2,3,4\}) = \min \begin{Bmatrix} 11 + g(2, \{3,4\}) \\ 17 + g(3, \{2,4\}) \\ 21 + g(4, \{2,3\}) \end{Bmatrix} = \min \begin{Bmatrix} 11 + 29 \\ 17 + 29 \\ 21 + 27 \end{Bmatrix} = 40$$

The solution to the traveling salesperson problem, therefore, yields a minimum cost of 40. To trace the path, one merely needs to find the node k at which the minimum cost was attained during the intermediary decisions. Thus, $g(1, V\text{-}\{1\})$ found its minimum when k was 2, therefore the path traced is $1 \rightarrow 2$. Next, $g(2, \{3,4\})$

found its minimum when k was 4, resulting in path $1 \rightarrow 2 \rightarrow 4$. Finally, $g(4, \{3\})$ results in the path $1 \rightarrow 2 \rightarrow 4 \rightarrow 3$, at which stage all the nodes have been visited and hence the tour terminates at node 1 resulting in the minimum cost tour of $1 \rightarrow 2 \rightarrow 4 \rightarrow 3 \rightarrow 1$.

21.3.2. *Time complexity analysis and applications of traveling salesperson problem*

The number of $g(i, T)$ functions that are computed before equation [21.5] is used to compute $g(1, V-\{1\})$ is given by:

$$\sum_{k=0}^{n-2} (n-1).\left({}^{n-2}C_k \right) = (n-1).2^{n-2}$$

This is so since for each set T during the intermediary computations, there are $(n-1)$ choices for i. Therefore, the number of distinct sets of T, excluding 1 and i is ${}^{n-2}C_k$. Each $g(i, T)$ requires $(k-1)$ comparisons when the cardinality of the set T is k. Hence, the time complexity is given by $\Theta(n^2. 2^n)$.

The traveling salesperson problem finds its application in areas such as planning, scheduling, vehicle routing, logistics and packing, robotics and so forth.

21.4. All-pairs shortest path problem

The ***all-pairs shortest path problem*** deals with finding the shortest path between any pair of cities given a network of cities.

Let $G = (V, E)$ be a weighted digraph with n vertices represented by V and edges $<i, j>$ represented by E. Let $(C)_{n \times n}$ denote the cost (weight) matrix where $C_{ij} = 0$, for $i = j$ and $C_{ij} = \infty$, for $<i.j> \notin E$. The all-pairs shortest path problem concerns such a graph $G = (V, E)$ where the vertices V represent cities and the edges E represent the connectivity between the cities, and the cost matrix $(C)_{n \times n}$ represents the distance matrix between the cities. Thus, C_{ij} denotes the distance between the cities represented by vertices i and j.

It is possible that the distance between two cities i, j connected by a direct edge, can be longer than a path $i \rightarrow k \rightarrow j$, where k is an intermediate city between i and j. The solution to the all-pairs shortest path problem is to obtain a matrix S which gives the minimum distance between cities i and j.

It is possible to solve the all-pairs shortest path problem by repeatedly invoking Dijkstra's single source shortest path algorithm (discussed in section 9.5.1 of Chapter 9, Volume 2) n times, with each city i as the source, thereby obtaining the shortest paths from city i to all other cities. However, *Floyd's algorithm* which will be introduced in the ensuing section employs the principle of optimality over the cost matrix $(C)_{n \times n}$ and obtains the optimal matrix S which obtains the minimum distance between any two cities, in one run.

21.4.1. *Dynamic programming-based solution*

Floyd's algorithm adopts dynamic programming to solve the all-pairs shortest path problem. Let $S^k(i,j)$ represent the length of the shortest path from node i to node j passing through no vertex of index greater than k. Then the paths from i to k and k to j must also be shortest paths not passing through a vertex of index greater than $(k\text{-}1)$. Making use of this observation, the recurrence relation is framed as:

$$S^k(i,j) = min(S^{k-1}(i,j), \quad S^{k-1}(i,k) + S^{k-1}(k,j)), \text{ for } \quad k \geq 1$$
$$= C_{ij}, 1 \leq i \leq n, \quad 1 \leq j \leq n, \quad \text{for } k = 0 \qquad \qquad [21.8]$$

```
procedure FLOYD (n, C)
/* n is the number of vertices (cities) labelled as
{1,2, 3, ..n} and C is the cost matrix denoting the
distances between the cities connected by edges E, where
Cᵢᵢ =0 and Cᵢⱼ = ∞, when edge <i, j> ∉ E */
        for i = 1 to n do
          for j = 1 to n do
              S[i, j] = C[i,j]
          end
        end

        for k = 1 to n do
          for i = 1 to n do
            for j = 1 to n do
                if (S[i, k]+S[k, j]) < S[i, j] then
                    S[i, j] = S[i,k]+S[k, j]
            end
          end
        end

end FLOYD
```

Algorithm 21.1. *Floyd's algorithm for the all-pairs shortest path problem*

The shortest path from i to j that does not go through a vertex higher than k, either goes through a vertex k or it does not. If it goes through k, then $S^k(i,j) = S^{k-1}(i,k) + S^{k-1}(k,j)$ and if it does not go through k, then $S^k(i,j) = S^{k-1}(i,j)$, which explains the recurrence relation for $k \geq 1$.

On the other hand, when $k = 0$, the shortest path is given by the edges connecting i and j, for all i and j, that is C_{ij}, which are the base cases for the recurrence relation.

Algorithm 21.1 illustrates Floyd's algorithm, which employs the recurrence relation described in equation [21.8] to obtain the optimal distance matrix S, which is the solution to the all-pairs shortest path problem.

EXAMPLE 21.4.–

Let the weighted digraph $G = (V, E)$, illustrated in Figure 21.2, represent a network of cities $V = \{1, 2, 3\}$ and E the set of edges connecting the cities. The cost matrix C represents the distances between cities directly connected by an edge. As pointed out earlier, $C_{ii} = 0$ and $C_{ij} = \infty$, if edge $<i, j> \notin E$.

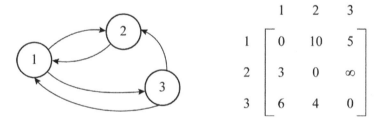

$$
\begin{array}{c@{\quad}ccc}
 & 1 & 2 & 3 \\
1 & 0 & 10 & 5 \\
2 & 3 & 0 & \infty \\
3 & 6 & 4 & 0
\end{array}
$$

Figure 21.2. *An all-purpose shortest path problem instance*

The execution of Floyd's algorithm illustrated in Algorithm 21.1 yields the following snapshots of the optimal distance matrix $S[i, j]$.

Initialization: $S^0[i, j] = C[i, j], \ 1 \leq i, j \leq 3 = \begin{bmatrix} 0 & 10 & 5 \\ 3 & 0 & \infty \\ 6 & 4 & 0 \end{bmatrix}$.

The shortest paths passing through the vertex with the highest index $k = 1$, to obtain $S^1[i, j]$ needs to be worked upon. Tabulation of the computations for $k = 1$ yield:

i	j	$S^0[i, j]$	$S^0[i, k]+S^0[k, j]$	$Min(S^0[i, j], S^0[i, k]+S^0[k, j])$
1	1	0	0+0	Min(0, 0) = 0
1	2	10	0+10	Min(10, 10) = 10
1	3	5	0+5	Min(5, 5) = 5
2	1	3	3+0	Min(3, 3) = 3
2	2	0	3+10	Min(0, 13) = 0
2	3	∞	3+5	Min(∞, 8) = 8
3	1	6	6+0	Min(6, 6) = 6
3	2	4	6+10	Min(4, 16) = 4
3	3	0	6+5	Min(0, 11) = 0

$$\text{Thus, } S^1[i, j] = \begin{bmatrix} 0 & 10 & 5 \\ 3 & 0 & 8 \\ 6 & 4 & 0 \end{bmatrix}$$

Progressing, in a similar way, for finding all shortest paths passing through the vertex with the highest index $k = 2$, followed by finding all shortest paths passing through the vertex with the highest index $k = 3$ yields

$$S^2[i, j] = \begin{bmatrix} 0 & 10 & 5 \\ 3 & 0 & 8 \\ 6 & 4 & 0 \end{bmatrix} \text{ and } S^3[i, j] = \begin{bmatrix} 0 & 9 & 5 \\ 3 & 0 & 8 \\ 6 & 4 & 0 \end{bmatrix}$$

Therefore, $S^3[i, j]$ yields the optimal shortest path matrix between any two cities i, j.

21.4.2. Time complexity analysis

Floyd's algorithm illustrated in Algorithm 21.1, is an iterative implementation of its governing recurrence relations described by equation [21.8]. It is therefore easy to see that the three **for** loops each running from 1 to n, yield a time complexity of $\Theta(n^3)$. However, while Algorithm 21.1 is a naïve rendering of the recurrence relations as they are, it is possible to achieve a speed up by cutting down on the computations and comparisons, in the innermost loop.

21.5. Optimal binary search trees

Binary search trees were detailed in Chapter 10, Volume 2. To recall, a binary search tree is a binary tree that can be empty or if non-empty, comprises *distinct* identifiers representing nodes that satisfy the property of the left child node identifier being less than its parent node identifier and the right child node identifier being greater than its parent node identifier. This leads to the characteristic that all the identifiers in the left subtree of the binary search tree are less than the identifier in the root node and all the identifiers in the right subtree of the binary search tree are greater than the identifier in the root node.

Figure 21.3 illustrates an example binary search tree representing the keys {*h, r, e, k, a, f, c, z*}. It can be observed that with *h* as the root node, the keys {*a, c, e, f*} which form the left subtree are less than key *h* of the root node and the keys {*k, r, z*} which form the right subtree are greater than the key *h* of the root node. Besides, each parent node key is such that the left child node key is less than itself and the right child node key is greater than itself.

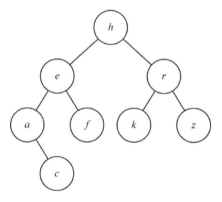

Figure 21.3. *An example binary search tree*

Given a set of keys, for each permutation or arrangement of the keys in the list, a binary search tree can be constructed resulting in a variety of binary search tree structures each with its own behavioral characteristics. Thus, each binary search tree could be associated with a *cost* with regard to successful/unsuccessful searches performed on them, as discussed in illustrative problem 10.4, in Chapter 10, Volume 2. To recollect, if $S = \{a_1, a_2, a_3, \ldots a_n\}$ is a set of keys and T_k are the set of associated binary search trees that can be constructed out of S, then the cost of a binary search tree is given by:

$$\sum_{1 \le i \le n} p_i. \, level(a_i) + \sum_{0 \le j \le n} q_j. \, (level(e_j) - 1) \tag{21.9}$$

where $p_i, 1 \le i \le n$, is the probability with which a_i is searched for (***probability of successful search***) and $q_j, 0 \le j \le n$, is the probability with which a key X,

$a_j \leq X \leq a_{j+1}$ is unsuccessfully searched for (**probability of unsuccessful search**) on a binary search tree T_k.

The cost of the binary search tree can also be defined in terms of the depth of the nodes as:

$$\sum_{i=1}^{n} p_i \cdot \left(depth(a_i) + 1\right) + \sum_{i=0}^{n} q_i \cdot \left(depth(i)\right) \qquad [21.10]$$

where *depth(i)* indicates the depth of the external nodes indicated as squares, at which the unsuccessful search logically ends (see section 10.2, Chapter 10, Volume 2, for more details).

An *optimal binary search tree* is a tree $T \in T_k$ such that $cost(T)$ is the minimum.

Dynamic programming helps to obtain the optimal binary search tree by working over decision sequences and applying the principle of optimality, to select the right node at each stage which will ensure minimal cost.

21.5.1. Dynamic programming-based solution

Given the list of keys $S = \{a_1, a_2, a_3, \dots a_n\}$ and the probabilities $p_i, 1 \leq i \leq n$, and $q_j, 0 \leq j \leq n$, the objective is to obtain the optimal binary search tree using dynamic programming.

Let T_{ij} be the minimum cost tree for the subset of keys $S_{ij} = \{a_{i+1}, a_{i+2}, a_{i+3}, \dots a_j\}$ with cost C_{ij} and root R_{ij}. By this description and notation, T_{ii} denotes an empty tree with cost $C_{ii} = 0$. Let the weight W_{ij} of T_{ij} be defined as:

$$W_{ij} = q_i + (p_{i+1} + q_{i+1}) + (p_{i+2} + q_{i+2}) + \dots + (p_j + q_j) \qquad [21.11]$$

The weight W_{ii} of the empty tree T_{ii} would be q_i.

The tree T_{ij} consists of a root $a_k, i \leq k \leq j$ with its left subtree T_{ik-1} representing the minimum cost tree for keys $S_{ik-1} = \{a_{i+1}, a_{i+2}, a_{i+3}, \dots a_{k-1}\}$ and right subtree T_{kj} representing the minimum cost tree for keys $S_{kj} = \{a_{k+1}, a_{k+2}, a_{k+3}, \dots a_j\}$, as shown in Figure 21.4.

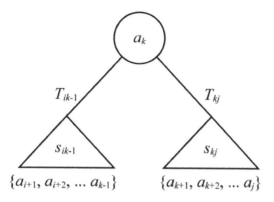

Figure 21.4. *Composition of minimum cost tree T_{ij}*

It can be inferred that when ($i = k-1$) the left subtree is empty and when ($k = j$) the right subtree is empty.

The construction of T_{ij} with a_k, T_{ik-1} and T_{kj}, results in the depth of nodes in the left and right subtrees of T_{ij} increasing by 1, in respect of their earlier depths when they belonged to T_{ik-1} and T_{kj}. The cost C_{ij} of T_{ij} defined by equation [21.10], can now be written as:

$$C_{ij} = C_{ik-1} + C_{kj} + p_k + W_{ik-1} + W_{kj}$$

[21.12]

Since:

$$W_{ij} = p_k + W_{ik-1} + W_{kj}$$

[21.13]

we obtain:

$$C_{ij} = C_{ik-1} + C_{kj} + W_{ij}$$

[21.14]

To find the optimal cost tree T_{ij}, we need to choose the root node $a_k, i < k \leq j$ with T_{ik-1} and T_{kj} as the left and right subtrees, compute the cost and then select the tree with the minimal cost. Therefore, the recurrence relation that computes the minimal cost tree is given by:

$$C_{ij} = \min_{i < k \leq j} \left(C_{ik-1} + C_{kj} \right) + W_{ij}$$

[21.15]

The minimum cost tree T_{0n} for the list $S = \{a_1, a_2, \dots a_n\}$ can be obtained by solving for C_{0n} from the equation [21.15]. The base cases for the recurrence relation are given by $C_{ii} = 0$ and $W_{ii} = q_i$, $0 \leq i \leq n$. To compute W_{ij} in equation [21.15] easily, the following equation derived from equation [21.11] by mere manipulation of the terms, can be used effectively.

$$W_{ij} = p_j + q_j + W_{ij-1} \qquad\qquad [21.16]$$

21.5.2. *Construction of the optimal binary search tree*

The optimal binary search tree T_{0n} for n keys can be easily constructed by tracking that index k at which point $\min_{i<k\leq j}(C_{ik-1} + C_{kj})$ attains its minimum value in equation [21.15], while computing the cost C_{ij} for the subtree T_{ij}. Thus, the root R_{ij} for the subtree T_{ij} is a_k. This means that the left subtree T_{ik-1} of a_k shall comprise the keys $\{a_{i+1}, a_{i+2}, \dots a_{k-1}\}$ and the right subtree $T_{k, j}$ shall comprise the keys $\{a_{k+1}, a_{k+2}, \dots a_{kn}\}$, whose root nodes concerned will be arrived at, following similar arguments and computations. Eventually, when C_{0n} is computed, $R_{0n} = a_k$ denotes the root node of the optimal binary search tree represented by T_{0n}.

Algorithm 21.2 illustrates the procedure to obtain the optimal binary search tree, given the list of keys $S = \{a_1, a_2, a_3, \dots a_n\}$ and the probabilities $p_i, 1 \leq i \leq n$ and $q_j, 0 \leq j \leq n$.

```
procedure Optimal_BST(a, p, q, n)
/* a[1:n] is the vector of keys, p[1:n] and q[1:n] are
the probabilities of successful search and unsuccessful
search respectively and n is the input size*/
/* C[i, j] denotes the minimum cost of the subtree  T[i,
j]*/
/*W[i, j] denotes the weight of the subtree T[i, j]*/
/*R[i, j] stores the  root nodes for the minimum cost
subtrees T[i, j], concerned*/


   for i = 0 to n do
     W[i,i] = q[i]
     C[i,i]=0
   end
   for t = 1 to n do
     for i = 0 to n-t do
       j = i + t;
       W[i, j] = W[i, j-1]+p[j] + q[j];
       Obtain l, the value of k, i<k≤j,  for which
                     C[i, k-1]+C[k,j] is minimum;
```

```
      C[i, j]  =  C[i, 1-1]+C[1, j]+W[i, j];
      R[i, j]  =  a[1]
   end
end

end Optimal_BST.
```

Algorithm 21.2. *Dynamic programming-based*
solution to optimal binary tree construction

The demonstration of **procedure** Optimal_BST on a list of keys with known probabilities of successful search and unsuccessful search has been illustrated in example 21.5. It can be seen that the computations with regard to the recurrence relation described by equation [21.15] have been organized in the increasing order of value of $j - i$, as specified in the algorithm.

EXAMPLE 21.5.–

Let $n = 4$, $(a_1, a_2, a_3, a_4) = (e, g, m, v)$, $(p_1, p_2, p_3, p_4) = (4/17, 2/17, 1/17, 1/17)$ and $(q_0, q_1, q_2, q_3, q_4) = (1/17, 2/17, 1/17, 2/17, 3/17)$. The dynamic programming-based construction of the optimal binary search tree following **procedure** Optimal_BST proceeds as follows. For the ease of computations, we consider $(p_1, p_2, p_3, p_4) = (4, 2, 1, 1)$ and $(q_0, q_1, q_2, q_3, q_4) = (1, 2, 1, 2, 3)$.

Here, $W_{00} = 1$, $W_{11} = 2$, $W_{22} = 1$, $W_{33} = 2$, $W_{44} = 3$ and $C_{00} = C_{11} = C_{22} = C_{33} = C_{44} = 0$. The root node R_{ii} of the empty tree T_{ii} is null.

The computations sequenced in the increasing order of $(j - i)$ yield Table 21.1.

i $j-i$	0	1	2	3	4
0	$W_{00} = 1$ $C_{00} = 0$ $R_{00} = -$	$W_{11} = 2$ $C_{11} = 0$ $R_{11} = -$	$W_{22} = 1$ $C_{22} = 0$ $R_{22} = -$	$W_{33} = 2$ $C_{33} = 0$ $R_{33} = -$	$W_{44} = 3$ $C_{44} = 0$ $R_{44} = -$
1	$W_{01} = 7$ $C_{01} = 7$ $R_{01} = a_1$	$W_{12} = 5$ $C_{12} = 5$ $R_{12} = a_2$	$W_{23} = 4$ $C_{23} = 4$ $R_{23} = a_3$	$W_{34} = 6$ $C_{34} = 6$ $R_{34} = a_4$	
2	$W_{02} = 10$ $C_{02} = 15$ $R_{02} = a_1$	$W_{13} = 8$ $C_{13} = 12$ $R_{13} = a_2$	$W_{24} = 8$ $C_{24} = 12$ $R_{24} = a_4$		

3	$W_{03} = 13$ $C_{03} = 24$ $R_{03} = a_2$	$W_{14} = 12$ $C_{14} = 23$ $R_{14} = a_3$			
4	$W_{04} = 17$ $C_{04} = 36$ $R_{04} = a_2$				

Table 21.1. *Computations in the dynamic programming-based construction of the optimal binary search tree following* **procedure** `Optimal_BST`

For example, $W_{24} = p_4 + q_4 + W_{23} = 1 + 3 + 4 = 8$, using the equation [21.16] that has been coded in **procedure** `Optimal_BST`. All other W_{ij}s can be computed in a similar fashion.

For the computation of C_{ij} s, equation [21.15] is used and the same can be observed in **procedure** `Optimal_BST`. For example, C_{14} is computed as follows:

$$C_{14} = \min_{1<k\leq4} \begin{Bmatrix} C_{11} + C_{24} \\ C_{12} + C_{34} \\ C_{13} + C_{44} \end{Bmatrix} + W_{14}$$

$$= \min_{1<k\leq4} \begin{Bmatrix} 12 \\ 11 \\ 12 \end{Bmatrix} + 12$$

$$= 23$$

Similarly, all other C_{ij} s can be computed to ultimately yield $C_{04} = 36$. The optimal cost of the binary search tree represented as T_{04}, is given as 36/17.

The root node R_{ij} s for the corresponding subtrees following the discussion in section 21.5.2 are shown in the table.

The building of the optimal binary search tree using the R_{ij} s is illustrated in Figure 21.5.

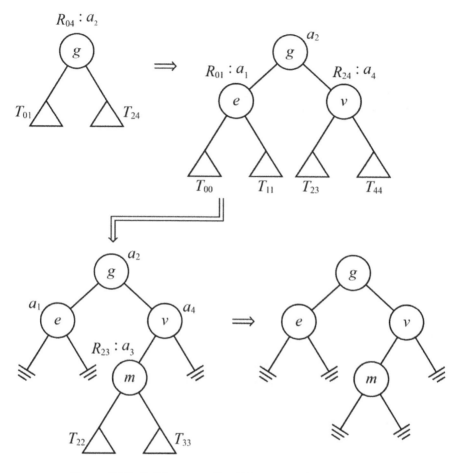

Figure 21.5. *Building an optimal binary search tree using R_{ij}, the root nodes of the optimal subtrees shown in Table 21.1*

21.5.3. Time complexity analysis

The time complexity of the optimal binary search tree construction can be easily arrived at by observing the loops in the **procedure** Optimal_BST. The major portion of the time is consumed at the point where the recurrence relation of the dynamic programming-based solution is executed. This concerns finding that k which minimizes $C_{ik-1} + C_{kj}$, $1 < k \leq j$. The loop executing this requires $O(j-i)$ time. The outer loop in the second **for** statement works n times and the inner loop works at most n times for each iteration of the outer loop. Hence, the time complexity of the construction of an optimal binary search tree is $O(n^3)$.

Summary

– Dynamic programming works over Bellman's Principle of Optimality.

– The method works over optimization problems defined by an objective function and constraints. It obtains the optimal solution to the problem.

– Dynamic programming unlike the greedy method, generates many decision sequences before the optimal decision sequence is delivered as the solution. The greedy method, in contrast, generates only one decision sequence.

– Dynamic programming is governed by recurrence relations which can be solved by adopting a backward approach or a forward approach.

– The method has been demonstrated over the problems of 0/1 knapsack, traveling salesperson, all-pairs shortest path and optimal binary search tree construction.

21.6. Illustrative problems

Problem 21.1.–

Solve the following traveling salesperson problem where the cost matrix of the vertices $V = \{1, 2, 3, 4, 5\}$ are as given below and the tour begins and ends at vertex 1:

$$\begin{bmatrix} 0 & 3 & 1 & 4 & 6 \\ 2 & 0 & 3 & 5 & 6 \\ 4 & 4 & 0 & 1 & 2 \\ 5 & 5 & 4 & 0 & 6 \\ 6 & 3 & 2 & 4 & 0 \end{bmatrix}$$

Solution:

Adopting the forward approach to solve the recurrence relation (equations [21.5]–[21.7]) related to the dynamic programming-based solution of the traveling salesperson problem, yields the following computations.

$$g\left(1,\{2,3,4,5\}\right) = \min \begin{cases} c_{12} + g\left(2,\{3,4,5\}\right) \\ c_{13} + g\left(3,\{2,4,5\}\right) \\ c_{14} + g\left(4,\{2,3,5\}\right) \\ c_{15} + g\left(5,\{2,3,4\}\right) \end{cases}$$

Progressing further:

$$g\left(2,\{3,4,5\}\right) = \min \begin{cases} c_{23} + g\left(3,\{4,5\}\right) \\ c_{24} + g\left(4,\{3,5\}\right) \\ c_{25} + g\left(5,\{3,4\}\right) \end{cases}$$

and on similar lines $g(3, \{2, 4, 5\})$, $g(4, \{2, 3, 5\})$ and $g(5, \{2, 3, 4\})$ can be framed.

This further leads to:

$$g\left(3,\{4,5\}\right) = \min \begin{cases} c_{34} + g(4,\{5\}) \\ c_{35} + g(5,\{4\}) \end{cases}$$

and on similar lines $g(4, \{3, 5\})$, $g(5, \{3, 4\})$, $g(2, \{4, 5\})$, $g(4, \{2, 5\})$, $g(5, \{2, 4\})$, $g(2, \{3, 5\})$, $g(3, \{2, 5\})$, $g(5, \{2, 3\})$, $g(2, \{3, 4\})$, $g(3, \{2, 4\})$ and $g(4, \{2, 3\})$ can be framed.

Now:

$$g\left(4,\{5\}\right) = c_{45} + g\left(5,\phi\right) = 6 + 6 = 12$$

and on similar lines, $g(5,\{4\}) = 9$, $g(3,\{5\}) = 8$, $g(5,\{3\}) = 6$, $g(3, \{4\}) = 6$, $g(4, \{3\}) = 8$, $g(5, \{2\}) = 5$, $g(3, \{2\}) = 6$, $g(4, \{5\}) = 12$, $g(2, \{5\}) = 12$, $g(2, \{4\}) = 10$, $g(2, \{3\}) = 7$ can be computed.

Backtracking the computations appropriately, the optimal cost of the traveling salesperson's tour yields $g(1, \{2,3,4,5\}) = 13$.

To track the path, we pin the nodes (vertex k) at which the minimum costs were attained during the computations of the function $g(x, y)$. This yields the results shown in Table P21.1:

The tour begins from vertex 1 and since vertex 3 yields the minimum cost node for $g(1, \{2, 3, 4, 5\})$ the next stopover is at vertex 3. The minimum cost node for

$g(3, \{2, 4, 5\})$ is 4 and hence the next stopover is at vertex 4. Now, $g(4, \{2, 5\})$ attains its minimum cost at vertex 5 and, therefore, the next stopover is at vertex 5. Finally, $g(5, \{2\})$ leads to vertex 2 before the tour returns to vertex 1, which was the source. The path is therefore given by, $1 \rightarrow 3 \rightarrow 4 \rightarrow 5 \rightarrow 2 \rightarrow 1$.

$g(x,y)$	Minimum cost	Vertex k which yields the minimum cost
$g(1, \{2, 3, 4, 5\})$	13	3
$g(2, \{3, 4, 5\})$	14	3, 5
$g(3,\{2, 4, 5\})$	12	4
$g(4, \{2, 3, 5\})$	11	3
$g(5, \{2, 3, 4\})$	10	3
$g(3, \{4, 5\})$	11	5
$g(4, \{3, 5\})$	12	3, 5
$g(5, \{3, 4\})$	8	3
$g(2,\{4, 5\})$	15	5
$g(4, \{2, 5\})$	11	5
$g(5, \{2, 4\})$	11	4
$g(2, \{3, 5\})$	11	3
$g(3, \{2, 5\})$	7	5
$g(5, \{2,3\})$	8	3
$g(2, \{3,4\})$	9	3
$g(3, \{2, 4\})$	8	4
$g(4, \{2, 3\})$	10	3

Table P21.1. *Tracking the path for the traveling salesperson problem detailed in illustrative problem 21.1*

PROBLEM 21.2.–

Trace Floyd's algorithm for the all-pairs shortest path problem defined over a digraph with vertices $V = \{1, 2, 3, 4\}$ and whose cost matrix is given below:

$$\begin{bmatrix} 0 & 11 & 2 & 20 \\ 4 & 0 & \infty & 6 \\ \infty & \infty & 0 & 3 \\ 2 & 1 & 5 & 0 \end{bmatrix}$$

Solution:

Tracing Floyd's algorithm yields the following optimal distance matrices for the respective values of k, during the iterations:

→ $k = 1$

$$S^1 = \begin{bmatrix} 0 & 11 & 2 & 20 \\ 4 & 0 & 6 & 6 \\ \infty & \infty & 0 & 3 \\ 2 & 1 & 4 & 0 \end{bmatrix}$$

→ $k = 2$

$$S^2 = \begin{bmatrix} 0 & 11 & 2 & 17 \\ 4 & 0 & 6 & 6 \\ \infty & \infty & 0 & 3 \\ 2 & 1 & 4 & 0 \end{bmatrix}$$

→ $k = 3$

$$S^3 = \begin{bmatrix} 0 & 11 & 2 & 5 \\ 4 & 0 & 6 & 6 \\ \infty & \infty & 0 & 3 \\ 2 & 1 & 4 & 0 \end{bmatrix}$$

→ $k = 4$

$$S^4 = \begin{bmatrix} 0 & 6 & 2 & 5 \\ 4 & 0 & 6 & 6 \\ 5 & 4 & 0 & 3 \\ 2 & 1 & 4 & 0 \end{bmatrix}$$

S^4 is the optimal distance matrix.

PROBLEM 21.3.–

For the binary search tree instance described below (already discussed in illustrative problem 10.4 of Chapter 10, Volume 2) construct an optimal binary search tree, tabulating the computations as shown in Table 21.1 for the problem instance discussed in Example 21.5.

Set $S = \{a_1, a_2, a_3, a_4\} = \{\textbf{\textit{end, goto, print, stop}}\}, \{p_1, p_2, p_3, p_4\} = \left\{\frac{1}{20}, \frac{1}{5}, \frac{1}{10}, \frac{1}{20}\right\}$ and $\{q_0, q_1, q_2, q_3, q_4\} = \left\{\frac{1}{5}, \frac{1}{10}, \frac{1}{5}, \frac{1}{20}, \frac{1}{20}\right\}$.

Solution:

Table P21.3 illustrates the computations undertaken to construct the optimal binary search tree following the same method illustrated in example 21.5, and Figure P21.3 illustrates the building of the optimal binary search tree.

$\dfrac{i}{j-i}$	0	1	2	3	4
0	$W_{00} = 4$ $C_{00} = 0$ $R_{00} = -$	$W_{11} = 2$ $C_{11} = 0$ $R_{11} = -$	$W_{22} = 4$ $C_{22} = 0$ $R_{22} = -$	$W_{33} = 1$ $C_{33} = 0$ $R_{33} = -$	$W_{44} = 1$ $C_{44} = 0$ $R_{44} = -$
1	$W_{01} = 7$ $C_{01} = 7$ $R_{01} = a_1$	$W_{12} = 10$ $C_{12} = 10$ $R_{12} = a_2$	$W_{23} = 7$ $C_{23} = 7$ $R_{23} = a_3$	$W_{34} = 3$ $C_{34} = 3$ $R_{34} = a_4$	
2	$W_{02} = 15$ $C_{02} = 22$ $R_{02} = a_2$	$W_{13} = 13$ $C_{13} = 20$ $R_{13} = a_2$	$W_{24} = 9$ $C_{24} = 12$ $R_{24} = a_3$		
3	$W_{03} = 18$ $C_{03} = 32$ $R_{03} = a_2$	$W_{14} = 15$ $C_{14} = 27$ $R_{14} = a_2$			
4	$W_{04} = 20$ $C_{04} = 39$ $R_{04} = a_2$				

Table P21.3. *Computations in the dynamic programming-based construction of the optimal binary search tree for the problem instance given in illustrative problem 21.3*

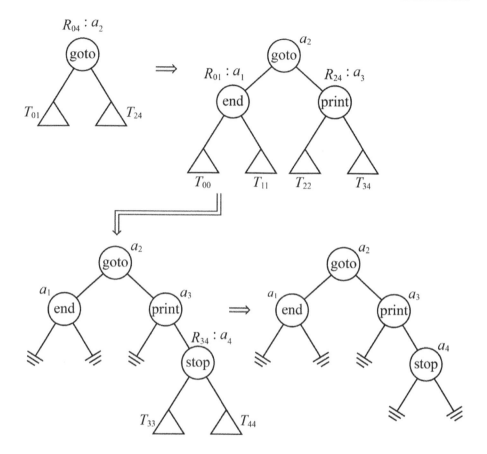

Figure P21.3. *Building of the optimal binary search tree for the problem instance given in illustrative problem 12.3*

Review questions

1) Define the principle of optimality.

2) Distinguish between dynamic programming and greedy method ways of problem-solving.

3) The backward approach to solving the 0/1 knapsack problem has been defined by equation [21.4] in this chapter. Trace the approach over the 0/1 knapsack instance discussed in example 21.1 of this chapter.

4) Obtain the recurrence relation of the dynamic programming-based solution to the traveling salesperson problem.

5) Solve the following traveling salesperson problem assuming that the cost matrix of the vertices $V = \{1, 2, 3, 4, 5\}$ is as given below:

$$\begin{bmatrix} 0 & 4 & 1 & 4 & 6 \\ 2 & 0 & 3 & 5 & 7 \\ 5 & 3 & 0 & 1 & 2 \\ 5 & 5 & 4 & 0 & 6 \\ 8 & 3 & 2 & 4 & 0 \end{bmatrix}$$

6) Outline the dynamic programming-based algorithm for the all-pairs shortest path problem.

7) Obtain the solution to the all-pairs shortest path problem with four cities $\{a, b, c, d\}$ whose distance matrix is as given below:

$$\begin{array}{c} & a & b & c & d \\ a & \begin{bmatrix} 0 & 8 & 2 & 18 \\ b & 4 & 0 & 10 & 6 \\ c & 9 & \infty & 0 & 3 \\ d & 2 & 1 & 5 & 0 \end{bmatrix} \end{array}$$

8) Construct an optimal binary search tree for the keys $\{l, u, w, m\}$ with probabilities of successful and unsuccessful search given by $(p_1, p_2, p_3, p_4) = (4/20, 3/20, 5/20, 1/20)$ and $(q_0, q_1, q_2, q_3, q_4) = (1/20, 2/20, 1/20, 2/20, 1/20)$, respectively.

Programming assignments

1) Implement Algorithm 21.1 **procedure** FLOYD and test it over the problem instance shown in review question 7.

2) Implement Algorithm 21.2 **procedure** Optimal BST and test it over the problem instance shown in review question 8.

22

P and NP Class of Problems

22.1. Introduction

A galaxy of computational problems exists in various disciplines, and researchers and scientists in general have striven hard or are still striving hard to solve these problems on a computer, by discovering or toiling hard to discover efficient algorithms for their solutions. Many of these problems have even offered them opportunities to discover an array of algorithms, one surpassing the other, in terms of efficiency or implementation.

There is a big class of problems that have been solved using algorithms having *polynomial time complexity*. For example, the time complexity $T(n)$ of the best-known algorithms for the problems of finding the max/min element in a list or matrix multiplication or finding the first positive element in a list, to quote a well-known few, report polynomial time complexity. Such algorithms report $T(n) = O(f(n))$ or $T(n) = \Omega(f(n))$ or $T(n) = \Theta(f(n))$, where $f(n)$ is a polynomial of a small degree and $O(f(n))$, $\Omega(f(n))$ and $\Theta(f(n))$ denote the upper bound, lower bound and both upper and lower bound, respectively, for $T(n)$. The definitions and details pertaining to $O(f(n))$, $\Omega(f(n))$ and $\Theta(f(n))$ can be found in Chapter 2, Volume 1. Thus, the best-known algorithm to find the max/min element in a list reports $\Theta(n)$, the high school method of matrix multiplication reports $O(n^3)$ and the best case complexity for finding the first positive element in a list of real numbers reports $\Omega(1)$.

Such a class of problems is theoretically referred to as the *Polynomial time class* or *P class* of problems. However, a formal definition of P class includes only *decision problems*, which are problems that can be answered with yes/no type questions on the inputs specified.

Problems that can be solved in polynomial time are known as *tractable* problems and those that cannot be solved in polynomial time are known as *intractable* problems.

Another category of problems exists, which to date has failed to reveal the existence of any polynomial time algorithm to solve them. The best-known algorithms for these problems to date report *exponential time complexity*. Thus, if $T(n)$ is the time complexity of such an algorithm, then $T(n) = O(g(n))$ or $T(n) = \Omega(g(n))$ or $T(n) = \Theta(f(n))$, where $g(n)$ is larger than any polynomial. For example, the traveling salesperson problem discussed in section 21.3 reports an exponential time complexity of $\Theta(n^2.2^n)$ when a dynamic programming strategy is applied to solve the problem. That exponential time complexity algorithms can turn unwieldy when due to their rapid growth rate they tend to consume humongous proportions of time even for moderate-sized problem inputs, was discussed and demonstrated in Chapter 2, Volume 1. Such a class of problems whose best-known algorithms report exponential time complexity and for which no polynomial time algorithms have been developed exists.

Some of these problems are decision problems and a vast majority of these decision problems are computationally difficult to solve and that is why they yield exponential time complexity solutions. However, when an oracle or somebody let us suppose, randomly calls out a solution, *verification of the solution turns out to be computationally easy*. In other words, verification of the solution can be done in polynomial time.

For example, a Hamiltonian circuit of a graph was defined in Chapter 9, Volume 2. To recall, a Hamiltonian circuit in a graph is a path that starts from a vertex, traverses through all other vertices exactly once, and returns to the start vertex. Given a graph with n vertices, finding a Hamiltonian circuit can be computationally difficult. However, given an ordered list of vertices by an oracle let us say, it is easy to check if the list describes a Hamiltonian circuit. All that it calls for is to check if there are $(n+1)$ vertices with the starting and ending vertices being the same, whether the in-between vertices are all distinct, and lastly, every consecutive pair of vertices is connected by an edge.

This concept of "guessing" a solution and "verifying" it led to the concept of *nondeterministic algorithms*. The definition of *NP class* or *Nondeterministic Polynomial class*, which relies on nondeterministic algorithms, shall be detailed in the next section.

The concept of *NP-completeness* that evolved out of the *NP* class of problems will be the subject matter of this chapter.

So, what are we driving at?

Assume that a developer was assigned the task of designing an efficient algorithm for a problem that solves it within a reasonable time. Discovering a polynomial time algorithm should help the developer accomplish the task successfully. Let us suppose that the developer, despite all the efforts put forth, fails to obtain an algorithm that has reasonable performance. The developer has two options now, either to accept defeat saying that he/she is unable to find a polynomial time algorithm or assert with confidence that the given problem belongs to the *NP* class and is typically "*hard*" or *intractable,* and therefore no polynomial time algorithm exists for the said problem! The latter assertion could possibly lead to the developer being assigned the task of finding efficient algorithms for either special cases of the original problem or compromised versions of the problem or finding approximate solutions rather than exact solutions or employing *heuristics* to find near-optimal or acceptable solutions to the problem. Thus, a knowledge of *NP*-completeness is essential for algorithm designers and developers to rightly interpret their failures with regard to finding efficient algorithms for certain problems.

Garey and Johnson (Garey and Johnson, 1979) in their treatise on *NP*-completeness summed up aptly when they wrote "*...In short, the primary application of the theory of NP-completeness is to assist algorithm designers in directing their problem-solving efforts towards those approaches that have the greatest likelihood of leading to useful algorithms.*"

The aim of this chapter is therefore to enlighten the reader on *NP*-completeness and its associated concepts.

22.2. Deterministic and nondeterministic algorithms

Deterministic algorithms exhibit the property of uniquely defined operations that produce a distinct output for a given input when executed on a computer, which is a *deterministic machine* or, theoretically, a *deterministic Turing machine*.

Nondeterministic algorithms, on the other hand, describe a theoretical framework where the restriction that a distinct output needs to be produced for a given input is removed and in its place, the generation of a specified set of possible outputs with a degree of randomness is allowed. From a deterministic standpoint, nondeterministic algorithms can be thought of as a deterministic algorithm that replicates itself in parallel as many times as to produce the specified set of possibilities as output, randomly! A theoretical machine capable of executing such a phenomenon is termed a *nondeterministic machine*.

A nondeterministic algorithm for practical reasons is seen as a procedure that takes a decision problem X and does (i) *nondeterministic guessing* of random candidate solutions to the problem instances of X and (ii) with *unbounded parallelism proceeds to verify* each of the candidate solutions to the problem instances concerned, emitting a success signal if it is a solution (the decision problem instance reports "yes") and a failure signal if it is not a solution (the decision problem instance reports "no").

If the nondeterministic algorithm emits *at least one success signal* during the verification, then we claim that the nondeterministic algorithm has successfully solved the decision problem. On the other hand, if the nondeterministic algorithm *emits a failure signal during the verification of each of the randomly generated candidate solution sets*, then we claim that the nondeterministic algorithm is unsuccessful in solving the decision problem.

A nondeterministic algorithm is said to be a ***nondeterministic polynomial time algorithm*** if the verification of the randomly generated candidate solution sets can be done in polynomial time by the algorithm.

A nondeterministic algorithm can be theoretically described by augmenting the following function and statements to a deterministic framework:

i) **Choice (S)**: Given a set S of possibilities or inputs, the function arbitrarily chooses any element of S. This function executes the guessing stage.

ii) **Failure**: Signals unsuccessful termination of a process or computation.

iii) **Success**: Signals successful termination of a process or computation

Function **choice**($[1:n]$), for example, indicates a random choice of any $x \in [1:n]$ with no rule to explain why the value was chosen. The function undertakes arbitrary choices during its execution. **failure** and **success** functions play a significant role in determining the successful completion or termination of the nondeterministic algorithm. A nondeterministic algorithm terminates successfully, if any one set of choices has triggered a **success** signal on its completion. On the other hand, a nondeterministic algorithm terminates unsuccessfully, if and only if there exists no set of choices that can trigger a **success** signal.

All the three algorithm components are assumed to have a time complexity of $O(1)$ when executed on a nondeterministic machine, which is still utopian to date!

Example 22.1 illustrates a nondeterministic algorithm to find an element X in an unordered array $A[1:n]$.

EXAMPLE 22.1.–

On a nondeterministic machine, the nondeterministic algorithm to find an element X in an unordered array $A[1:n]$ would work with unbounded parallelism replicating itself to find if any of $A[i]$ is X, as shown below. If for a specific choice i of $[1:n]$ the algorithm "copy" finds X and terminates with a **success**, then the nondeterministic algorithm is deemed to have completed its task successfully. On the other hand, if X was not found in array $A[1:n]$, then all the algorithm "copies" terminate with **failure** and hence the nondeterministic algorithm terminates with a failure, but not before printing a message to this effect.

```
i = choice([1:n])
if (A[i] == X) then
    print( ' element X found'); success
print('element X not found')
failure.
```

For a given input, if there exists a sequence of choices that leads to the successful completion of a nondeterministic algorithm, then the minimum number of steps or operations required to reach the successful completion determines the time taken by a nondeterministic algorithm. If the nondeterministic algorithm completes unsuccessfully, then the time taken is $O(1)$.

A nondeterministic algorithm reports a complexity of $O(f(n))$, if for all inputs of size $n, n \geq n_0$, which yields a successful completion of the algorithm, the time required is at most $c.f(n)$, for some constants c and n_0.

Going by the theoretical interpretation of a nondeterministic algorithm making several copies of itself every time a choice is made, the nondeterministic search for X in the unordered array $A[1:n]$ reports $O(1)$ time complexity. Contrast this with a deterministic algorithm which would report $O(n)$ considering a **for** loop that would work through the unordered array $A[1:n]$, one element at a time to check if it is X.

So the idea behind the theoretical concept of nondeterministic algorithms and their superior performance on a nondeterministic machine, when compared to deterministic algorithms, helps rephrase the definition of many problems belonging to the *NP* class. Thus, there exist many *NP* class problems whose best-known deterministic algorithms that yield exponential time complexity, are solvable on a nondeterministic machine using nondeterministic algorithms having polynomial time complexity.

If *the P* class alludes to problems with deterministic algorithms having polynomial time complexity when run on deterministic machines, *the NP* class alludes to problems with nondeterministic algorithms having polynomial time complexity when run on nondeterministic machines.

In light of the above, P class and NP class are defined as below:

P class

This is a class of decision problems that can be solved in *polynomial time* by *deterministic algorithms.*

NP class

This is a class of decision problems that can be solved by *nondeterministic polynomial time algorithms*, where verification of the solution can be done in polynomial time.

Most decision problems are in NP and $P \subseteq NP$, since the deterministic algorithm that solves the problem belonging to the P class can be used to verify the solution in polynomial time after ignoring the nondeterministic guessing of the candidate solution, both of which are hallmarks of nondeterministic algorithms.

22.3. Satisfiability problem

The satisfiability problem picked from the domain of logic, typically *propositional logic* or *propositional calculus*, is a simple problem that has found itself significantly linked to the concept of NP-completeness. The problem and its nondeterministic algorithm are detailed here.

Let $x_1, x_2, \ldots x_n$ indicate logical variables with truth values *true* or *false*, but not both. The logical variables are termed *propositions* in propositional logic and are defined as a statement, that is, either true or false but not both. Thus, the statement x_1: water boils at 50°C denoted by the proposition or logical variable x_1, is *false*, while the statement x_2: the sun rises in the east denoted by the proposition or logical variable x_2, is *true*.

To model real-world knowledge as logical formulae, *connectives* are required and propositional logic provides a set of them, for example, $\neg, \wedge, \vee, \rightarrow$ and $=$, named *negation, conjunction, disjunction, implication* and *equality*, respectively, and referred to as *not, and, or, implies* and *equals*.

If x_1, x_2 are two logical variables, then the syntax of the logical connectives is given by $\neg x_1, x_1 \wedge x_2, x_1 \vee x_2, x_1 \rightarrow x_2$ and $x_1 = x_2$ and the semantics of the connectives is defined using a ***truth table***. Table 22.1 illustrates the truth table that defines the connectives of propositional logic.

x_1	x_2	$\neg x_1$	$x_1 \wedge x_2$	$x_1 \vee x_2$	$x_1 \rightarrow x_2$	$x_1 = x_2$
true	true	false	true	true	true	true
true	false	false	false	true	false	false
false	true	true	false	true	true	false
false	false	true	false	false	true	true

Table 22.1. *Definition of logical connectives*

A logical formula with n variables $x_1, x_2, \dots x_n$ will evoke a truth table with 2^n ***interpretations***, where an interpretation is a row in a truth table that evaluates the truth value of the logical formula for a set of truth values assigned to the variables. For example, the truth table for the logical formula $(x_1 \wedge x_2) \vee \neg x_3$ shown in Table 22.2 evokes $2^3 = 8$ interpretations.

A logical formula that obtains the truth value *true* for *all its interpretations* in its truth table is called a ***tautology*** and if it obtains the truth value *false* for *all its interpretations* in its truth table, then it is called a ***contradiction***.

x_1	x_2	x_3	$x_1 \wedge x_2$	$\neg x_3$	$(x_1 \wedge x_2) \vee \neg x_3$
true	true	true	true	false	true
true	false	true	false	false	false
false	true	true	false	false	false
false	false	true	false	false	false
true	true	false	true	true	true
true	false	false	false	true	true
false	true	false	false	true	true
false	false	false	false	true	true

Table 22.2. *Interpretation of the logical formula $(x_1 \wedge x_2) \vee \neg x_3$*

22.3.1. Conjunctive normal form and Disjunctive normal form

A *literal* in propositional logic is a variable (proposition) or its negation. Thus, $\neg x_3$ or x_1 are examples of literals. A *clause* is a disjunction of literals. Thus, $x_1 \lor \neg x_2 \lor x_3$ is an example of a clause.

A logical formula is in **Conjunctive normal form** (**CNF**) if it is represented as $\bigwedge_{i=1}^{n} (D_i)$ where each D_i is a clause.

Examples

$(x_1 \lor \neg x_2) \land (x_3 \lor x_4) \land \neg x_5$ is a CNF.

$\neg(x_1 \lor \neg x_2) \land (x_3 \lor x_4)$ is not a CNF.

A logical formula is in **Disjunctive normal form** (**DNF**) if it is represented as $\bigvee_{i=1}^{n} (C_i)$ where each C_i is a conjunction of literals.

Examples

$(x_1 \land \neg x_2) \lor (x_3 \land x_4) \lor \neg x_5$ is a DNF.

$\neg(x_1 \land \neg x_2) \lor \neg(x_3 \lor x_4)$ is not a DNF.

22.3.2. Definition of the satisfiability problem

A *satisfiability problem* concerns determining interpretations for which a logical formula would be rendered true. In other words, what truth values (*true/false*) when assigned to the variables in the logical formula will compute it to be *true* or if no such assignment of values exists, then prove that none exists.

For example, the logical formula $(x_1 \land x_2) \lor \neg x_3$ whose truth table is shown in Table 22.2 is satisfiable for the following set of truth values assigned to its variables, since the formula is rendered *true* for these assignments.

i) $x_1 = true$, $x_2 = true$ and $x_3 = true$

ii) $x_1 = true$, $x_2 = true$ and $x_3 = false$

iii) $x_1 = true$, $x_2 = false$ and $x_3 = false$

iv) $x_1 = false$, $x_2 = true$ and $x_3 = false$, and

v) $x_1 = false$, $x_2 = false$ and $x_3 = false$

If the logical formula is a *CNF*, then the problem is called **CNF-satisfiability**. The *CNF*-satisfiability problem is abbreviated as **SAT** in the literature.

If the *CNF* involves clauses with k literals, then it is known as **k-CNF** or **k-conjunctive normal form**. In such a case, the satisfiability problem is known as **k-CNF-satisfiability**. When $k = 2$, it is called **2-CNF-satisfiability**, and when $k = 3$, it is called **3-CNF-satisfiability (3-CNF SAT)**.

Examples

$(x_1 \vee x_2) \wedge (\neg x_3 \vee x_1) \wedge (\neg x_2 \vee \neg x_1)$ is a *2-CNF* and the assignment $(x_1 = true, x_2 = false, x_3 = true)$ is a solution to the *2-CNF*-satisfiability problem.

$(x_1 \vee \neg x_2 \vee x_3) \wedge (\neg x_3 \vee x_1 \vee \neg x_2) \wedge (\neg x_2 \vee \neg x_1 \vee x_4)$ is a *3-CNF* and the assignment $(x_1 = true, x_2 = false, x_3 = true, x_4 = false)$ is a solution to the *3-CNF*-satisfiability problem.

22.3.3. Construction of CNF and DNF from a logical formula

Given a logical formula F of n variables $x_1, x_2, ... x_n$, the *CNF* and *DNF* equivalences to F can be constructed by making use of the truth table *T(F)* of logical formula F.

To construct a *CNF C* from formula F:

i) Consider those interpretations I (rows) in the truth table *T(F)*, which yield $T(F) = 0(false)$. Each row I yields a formula of the type $C_i: (L_1 \vee L_2 \vee L_3 \vee ... \vee L_n)$, where $L_i = x_i$, if $t(x_i) = 0\,(false)$ and $L_i = \neg x_i$, if $t(x_i) = 1(true)$ and $t(x_i)$ is the truth value of x_i in the corresponding interpretation I.

ii) Combine all C_i s as $C: C_1 \wedge C_2 \wedge C_3 \wedge ... C_n$. C is a *CNF* equivalent to logical formula F.

To construct a *DNF D* from formula F:

i) Consider those interpretations I (rows) in the truth table $T(F)$, which yield $T(F) = 1(true)$. Each row I yields a formula of the type $D_i: (L_1 \wedge L_2 \wedge L_3 \wedge ... \wedge L_n)$, where $L_i = x_i$, if $t(x_i) = 1(true)$ and $L_i = \neg x_i$, if $t(x_i) = 0(false)$ and $t(x_i)$ is the truth value of x_i in the corresponding interpretation I.

ii) Combine all D_is as $D: (D_1 \vee D_2 \vee D_3 \vee ... \vee D_n)$. D is a *DNF* equivalent to logical formula F.

The construction of *CNF* and *DNF* for a logical formula F has been demonstrated in illustrative problem 22.4.

22.3.4. *Transformation of a CNF into a 3-CNF*

A *3-CNF* is a *CNF C: $C_1 \wedge C_2 \wedge C_3 \wedge ... C_n$*, where each C_i is a clause that is a disjunction of *exactly* 3 literals.

To transform a *CNF C* into its equivalent *3-CNF*, the following procedure, which serves to reduce each of the clauses C_i to have exactly 3 literals, needs to be followed:

i) If the clause C_i has only a single literal l, that is, $C_i = l$, then introduce two auxiliary variables p, q such that the clause C_i is now represented as $C_i' = (l \vee p \vee q) \wedge (l \vee \neg p \vee q) \wedge (l \vee p \vee \neg q) \wedge (l \vee \neg p \vee \neg q)$. It can be observed that C_i' is satisfiable iff C_i is satisfiable.

ii) If clause C_i has two literals l_1, l_2, that is, $C_i = (l_1 \vee l_2)$, then introduce an auxiliary variable p such that the clause C_i is now represented as $C_i' = (l_1 \vee l_2 \vee p) \wedge (l_1 \vee l_2 \vee \neg p)$. It can be observed that C_i' is satisfiable iff C_i is satisfiable.

iii) If the clause C_i has more than three literals, for example, $l_1, l_2, l_3, ... l_k$, that is, $C_i = (l_1 \vee l_2 \vee l_3 \vee ... l_k)$, then introduce auxiliary variables $p_1, p_2, p_3, ... p_{k-3}$ such that the clause C_i is now represented as

$$C_i' = (l_1 \vee l_2 \vee p_1) \wedge (l_3 \vee \neg p_1 \vee p_2) \wedge (l_4 \vee \neg p_2 \vee p_3) \wedge ...$$
$$... \wedge (l_{k-2} \vee \neg p_{k-4} \vee p_{k-3}) \wedge (l_{k-1} \vee l_k \vee \neg p_{k-3}).$$

It can be observed that C_i' is satisfiable iff C_i is satisfiable.

The construction of *3-CNF* from *CNF* has been demonstrated in illustrative problem 22.5.

22.3.5. *Deterministic algorithm for the satisfiability problem*

It was discussed earlier that a logical formula with n variables generates 2^n interpretations, where each interpretation defines the assignment of truth values to the variables concerned and the evaluation of the formula for those values, to ultimately yield the corresponding truth value as the result.

A straightforward deterministic algorithm for the satisfiability problem, therefore, involves looping through the 2^n interpretations to find out which of these interpretations yields the truth value *true* for the logical formula concerned. Hence the deterministic algorithm for the satisfiability problem has a time complexity of $O(2^n)$, which belongs to the category of exponential time complexity algorithms.

22.3.6. *Nondeterministic algorithm for the satisfiability problem*

The nondeterministic algorithm for satisfiability problem adopting the functions and statements exclusive to nondeterministic machine discussed in section 22.2, is as described in algorithm ND_SATISFIABILITY () shown in Figure 22.1. As described earlier, the function **choice ({true, false})** triggers parallelism on the nondeterministic machine with the algorithm replicating itself and therefore the time complexity of the algorithm is $O(n)$.

Thus, the satisfiability problem, which has exponential time complexity over a deterministic machine, reports polynomial time complexity on a nondeterministic machine. Therefore, the satisfiability problem belongs to *the NP* class.

22.4. NP-complete and NP-hard problems

The *NP* class was introduced as a class of problems to which the best-known algorithms to date report exponential time complexity. Also, these problems do not show evidence that polynomial time algorithms do not exist for them either. However, the best thing is that many of the problems for which no polynomial time algorithm exists, seem to be computationally related establishing two classes of problems, for example, *NP-complete* and *NP-hard*.

```
procedure ND_SATISFIABILITY (L, n)
/* L is a logical formula involving n variables xᵢ, i=
1, 2, 3, …n */

for i  = 1 to n do
  xᵢ = choice ({ true, false})
end
if  L(x₁, x₂, … xₙ) is true then success
else failure

end ND_SATISFIABILITY
```

Figure 22.1. *Nondeterministic algorithm for the satisfiability problem*

An *NP*-complete problem is one that can be solved in polynomial time if all other *NP*-complete problems can also be solved in polynomial time. An *NP*-hard problem is one which, if solvable in polynomial time, then all other *NP*-complete problems can be solved in polynomial time. Thus, all *NP*-complete problems are *NP*-hard but all *NP*-hard problems are not *NP*-complete.

The formal definitions that describe *NP*-completeness are listed in the next section.

22.4.1. *Definitions*

22.4.1.1. *Problem reducibility*

Let X and Y be two problems. X *reduces to* Y, denoted as $X \propto Y$ if there is a method to solve X by a deterministic polynomial time algorithm using a deterministic algorithm that solves Y in polynomial time.

It can be proved that problem reducibility satisfies the ***transitivity property***. Thus, if $X \propto Y$ and $Y \propto Z$ then $X \propto Z$.

22.4.1.2. *NP-hard problem*

The problem X is *NP-hard* if the satisfiability problem reduces to X, that is, $SAT \propto X$.

22.4.1.3. *NP-complete problem*

A problem X is *NP-complete* if X is *NP*-hard and X $\in$ *NP*.

It can be inferred from the definitions that there are *NP*-hard problems that are not *NP*-complete. If problem classes, in general, can be categorized as *decision class* and *optimization class*, only decision problems can be *NP*-complete. The optimization class of problems, however, may belong to *the NP*-hard class. Also, if *D* is a decision problem and *O* is an optimization problem then D $\propto$ O is quite possible.

For example, let us consider the 0/1 knapsack optimization problem discussed in section 21.2. The 0/1 knapsack decision problem concerns the 0/1 assignment of values to variables $x_i, 1 \leq i \leq n$ such that $\sum p_i x_i \geq P$ and $\sum w_i x_i \leq M$, $1 \leq i \leq n$, where *P* and *M* are given numbers denoting an expected profit and capacity of the knapsack respectively, and nonnegative numbers p_i s and w_i s indicate profits and weights respectively. It can be trivially established that the 0/1 knapsack decision problem is reducible to the 0/1 knapsack optimization problem.

In general, decision problems can be *NP*-complete but optimization problems cannot be *NP*-complete. However, there do exist *NP*-hard decision problems that are not *NP*-complete. The **halting problem** from the theory of computation is a classic example of an *NP*-hard problem that is not *NP*-complete.

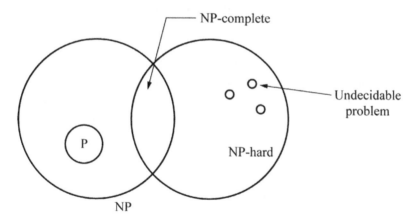

Figure 22.2. *Relationship between P, NP, NP-hard, NP-complete and undecidable problems*

Given an arbitrary computer program and its input, the halting problem tries to determine whether the program will finish running and thereby come to a halt or keep on running forever. Alan Turing adopted the concept of a Turing machine to describe a computer and a program and went on to prove that a general algorithm that will determine the program-input combinations for which the machine will halt, does not exist. Therefore, the halting problem is termed an *undecidable problem* and hence halting problem $\notin NP$. Therefore, the halting problem is not an *NP*-complete problem.

Figure 22.2 illustrates the relationship between the problem classes P, NP, *NP*-hard, *NP*-complete and undecidable problems.

22.4.1.4. Polynomial equivalence of problems

Two problems X and Y are said to be *polynomially equivalent* if $X \propto Y$ and $Y \propto X$.

In order to show that a problem Z is *NP*-hard, it is enough to show that $X \propto Z$, where X is a problem already known to be *NP*-hard. This can be easily inferred, since problem reducibility ($\propto$) satisfies transitivity property and X is already *NP*-hard, we have satisfiability $\propto X$ and $X \propto Z$ implying satisfiability $\propto Z$, which declares Z to be *NP*-hard.

To show that an *NP*-hard decision problem is *NP*-complete, it only needs to be shown that a nondeterministic algorithm that runs in polynomial time exists for it.

Therefore, to show that a problem M is *NP*-hard:

i) select a problem L that is already *NP*-hard, that is, $SAT \propto L$;

ii) show how to obtain in deterministic polynomial time an instance $I^{(M)}$ of problem M, from any instance $I^{(L)}$ of problem L, such that from the solution of instance $I^{(M)}$, the solution to instance $I^{(L)}$ can be obtained in deterministic polynomial time;

iii) establish that $L \propto M$ from condition (ii);

iv) establish from (i) and (iii) and the transitivity property of $\propto$, that $SAT \propto M$. Hence M belongs to *the NP*-hard class.

22.5. Examples of NP-hard and NP-complete problems

There are numerous problems which are *NP*-hard only or *NP*-complete. A few of the well-known problems to serve as examples for the concepts discussed earlier has been given below.

i) *Circuit satisfiability problem (CIRCUIT-SAT)* finds if a *Boolean combination circuit* made up of AND, OR and NOT gates as illustrated and defined by means of their respective truth tables in Figure 22.3 is *satisfiable*.

A circuit is satisfiable if it produces an output of 1. The circuit satisfiability problem surfaces in the domain of computer-aided hardware optimization problem, where a sub-circuit that always produces a 0 as output can be eliminated to reduce the clutter and be replaced by a simpler circuit that constantly outputs a 0. An instance of the *CIRCUIT-SAT* problem has been discussed in illustrative problem 22.2. *CIRCUIT-SAT* is an *NP*-complete problem.

ii) **Satisfiability problem (SAT)** and **3-CNF satisfiability problem (3-CNF SAT)** are *NP*-complete. Both the problems belong to *NP* class and are *NP*-hard, for it is possible to find an *NP*-hard problem that reduces to it. It can be shown that *CIRCUIT-SAT* $\propto$ SAT and *SAT* $\propto$ *3-CNF SAT*, where both *CIRCUIT-SAT* and *SAT* are *NP*-hard problems.

Illustrative problem 22.3 demonstrates *CIRCUIT-SAT* $\propto$ *SAT* and illustrative problem 22.6 demonstrates *SAT* $\propto$ *3-CNF SAT*.

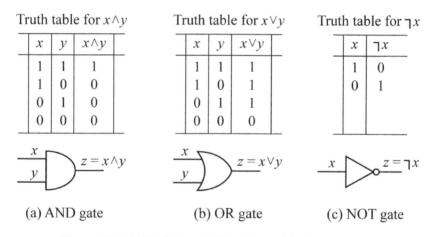

Figure 22.3. *AND, OR and NOT gates and their truth tables*

iii) **Directed Hamiltonian circuit problem (DHC)** finds if a digraph has a directed Hamiltonian cycle, which is a path that begins from a vertex of the graph, traverses through all other vertices once and returns to the starting vertex.

This problem is *NP*-hard since it can be shown that *SAT* $\propto$ *DHC*. Also, *DHC* $\in$ *NP* since verification of a candidate solution for the problem can be done in polynomial time. Hence *DHC* is an *NP*-complete problem.

iv) **Traveling salesperson decision problem (TSP-decision)** finds whether the cost of undertaking a tour of n cities, beginning from a city, visiting all other cities once without revisiting any one of them again, before returning to the starting city from where the tour started, can be at most M. Note that this problem is a decision problem and not an optimization problem as was discussed in section 21.3, where a dynamic programming based algorithm was evolved to solve it.

The *TSP*-decision problem is *NP*-hard since it is possible to show that the Directed Hamiltonian Cycle problem which is *NP*-hard can be reduced to the *TSP*-decision problem, that is, *DHC* $\propto$ *TSP*-decision. Also, *TSP*-decision $\in$ NP and therefore the *TSP*-decision problem is *NP*-complete.

v) **Chromatic number (CN) decision problem** is associated with the **graph coloring problem**, where, given a graph, the **chromatic number**, that is the smallest number of colors required to color the graph in such a way that no two adjacent vertices are assigned the same color, needs to be found. The *CN* problem is a decision problem that only tries to determine if the graph has a coloring for a given chromatic number k.

CN is *NP*-hard since *3-CNF SAT*, which is a restricted version of the *CNF* satisfiability problem, is *NP*-hard and it can be shown that *3-CNF SAT* $\propto$ *CN*. Also, *CN* $\in$ *NP* and hence *CN* is an *NP*-complete problem.

22.6. Cook's theorem

It is now understood that P class refers to the set of all decision problems solvable by deterministic algorithms in polynomial time and *NP* class refers to the set of all decision problems solvable by nondeterministic algorithms in polynomial time.

As illustrated in Figure 22.1, deterministic algorithms are a subclass of nondeterministic algorithms and therefore $P \subseteq NP$. The question of whether $P = NP$ or $P \neq NP$ has intrigued researchers for many years now. Is it possible to obtain deterministic algorithms that run in polynomial time for all the problems in *NP*, thereby rendering $P = NP$? The answer seems elusive for now, despite all the tremendous efforts that have been put in this direction, giving rise to the now famous unsolved problem $P \overset{?}{=} NP$.

However, thanks to the efforts of S. Cook, who formulated *Cook's theorem*, that has served to make a breakthrough in the solution of the original problem. Cook asserted that there does exist a problem in *NP* which if showed to be in P would automatically imply that $P = NP$ and that special problem was none other than the satisfiability problem!

The statement of Cook's theorem is as below:

Theorem: Satisfiability is in P if and only if $P = NP$.

An informal proof to the theorem is as described below:

Let us suppose that $P = NP$. To show that satisfiability is in P.

It is already known that satisfiability is in NP. Hence if $P = NP$ then satisfiability is in P.

Let us suppose that satisfiability is in P. To show that $P = NP$.

To show that $P = NP$, we need to show that $P \subseteq NP$ and $NP \subseteq P$. That $P \subseteq NP$ is trivial and known.

To show that $NP \subseteq P$, it can be proved that from any nondeterministic polynomial time algorithm A and an input I, a logical formula $Q(A, I)$ can be obtained such that Q is satisfiable if A terminates successfully for input I. It is possible to obtain a deterministic algorithm Z to determine the outcome of A on any input instance I. Z merely computes Q and then uses the deterministic algorithm for the satisfiability problem to determine whether or not Q is satisfiable. This construction only shows that every problem in NP reduces to satisfiability. Since satisfiability is in P, we have $NP \subseteq P$.

Therefore, from $P \subseteq NP$ and $NP \subseteq P$, we have $P = NP$.

22.7. The unsolved problem $P \overset{?}{=} NP$

The now famous $P \overset{?}{=} NP$ problem just depends on whether a deterministic polynomial time algorithm can be found for the satisfiability problem. Not an easy one though, for it is one among 7 Millennium Problems listed by the Clay Mathematical Institute, with a standing offer of $1 million for anyone who can prove or disprove it.

However, a lot of research efforts are under way to obtain *SAT* solvers and, in certain cases, they have even matured to the point of being commercially exploited in industrial applications. Malik and Zhang (2009) present a good review of *SAT* solvers and their effective deployment for practical problems and applications.

Summary

– The Polynomial class or P class refers typically to decision problems that can be solved in polynomial time by deterministic algorithms and are known as tractable problems.

– Nondeterministic Polynomial class or NP class refers to decision problems that can be solved using nondeterministic polynomial time algorithms, where the verification of the solution can be done in polynomial time. NP class problems are termed hard or intractable.

– The satisfiability problem (SAT) is an important problem that is associated with NP-completeness.

– A problem X is NP-hard if $SAT \propto X$ or if it is possible to select a problem L which is NP-hard such that $L \propto X$.

– A problem X is NP-complete if $X \in NP$ and X is NP-hard.

– There are NP-hard problems that are not NP-complete and the halting problem which is termed as an undecidable problem is an example.

– Cook's theorem states that satisfiability is in P if $P = NP$. To date $P \overset{?}{=} NP$ is an unsolved problem.

– SAT, 3-CNF SAT, Directed Hamiltonian Circuit problem, Traveling Salesperson Decision problem and Chromatic Number decision problem are examples of NP-complete problems.

22.8. Illustrative problems

PROBLEM 22.1.–

In order to show that a problem L2 is NP-hard, it is adequate to show that L1 $\propto$ L2, where L1 is an NP-hard problem. Justify.

Solution:

Since problem L1 is NP-hard by definition, SAT (satisfiability problem) $\propto$ L1. If it can be shown that L1 $\propto$ L2, then by transitivity property, we have $SAT \propto$ L1 and L1 $\propto$ L2, implying $SAT \propto$ L2, which is the condition for L2 to be NP-hard.

Hence, it is adequate to show that L1 $\propto$ L2, where L1 is an NP-hard problem, to prove that L2 is NP-hard.

PROBLEM 22.2.–

Test if an instance of the *CIRCUIT-SAT* problem shown in Figure P22.2 is satisfiable?

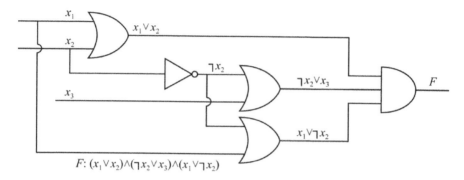

Figure P22.2. *An instance of the CIRCUIT-SAT problem*

Solution:

The Boolean combination circuit shown in Figure P22.2 illustrates the logical formula F: $(x_1 \vee x_2) \wedge (\neg x_2 \vee x_3) \wedge (x_1 \vee \neg x_2)$. A truth table for the formula is as shown in Table P22.2.

It can be seen that for three interpretations of F, where $(x_1 = 1, x_2 = 1, x_3 = 1)$, $(x_1 = 1, x_2 = 0, x_3 = 1)$ and $(x_1 = 1, x_2 = 0, x_3 = 0)$, the circuit is satisfiable and produces an output of 1.

x_1	x_2	x_3	$\neg x_2$	$x_1 \vee x_2$	$\neg x_2 \vee x_3$	$x_1 \vee \neg x_2$	F
1	1	1	0	1	1	1	1
1	1	0	0	1	0	1	0
1	0	1	1	1	1	1	1
1	0	0	1	1	1	1	1
0	0	0	1	0	1	1	0
0	0	1	1	0	1	1	0
0	1	0	0	1	0	0	0
0	1	1	0	1	1	0	0

Table P22.2. *Truth table for F:* $(x_1 \vee x_2) \wedge (\neg x_2 \vee x_3) \wedge (x_1 \vee \neg x_2)$

PROBLEM 22.3.–

Show that the circuit satisfiability problem reduces to the satisfiability problem, that is, $CIRCUIT\text{-}SAT \propto SAT$.

Solution:

To show that $CIRCUIT\text{-}SAT \propto SAT$, we need to show that an instance I' of SAT can be obtained in deterministic polynomial time from an instance I'' of $CIRCUIT\text{-}SAT$, such that from the solution of I' the solution of I'' can be determined in deterministic polynomial time.

Obtaining an instance I of SAT which is a logical formula F, from an instance I'' of $CIRCUIT\text{-}SAT$ which is a Boolean combination circuit C, can be easily obtained by a straightforward procedure that works in deterministic polynomial time.

Also, if an assignment of values renders formula F of SAT satisfiable, then the same set of values renders the circuit C of $CIRCUIT\text{-}SAT$ satisfiable.

Hence CIRCUIT-SAT $\propto SAT$.

PROBLEM 22.4.–

Construct a CNF and DNF for the logical formula F: $(x_1 \vee \neg x_2) \wedge (\neg x_2 \rightarrow x_1)$.

Solution:

The construction of CNF C and DNF D for the logical formula F, following procedures discussed in section 22.3.3, is as shown below.

x_1	x_2	$\neg x_2$	$x_1 \vee \neg x_2$	$\neg x_2 \rightarrow x_1$	F
1	1	0	1	1	1
1	0	1	1	1	1
0	1	0	0	1	0
0	0	1	1	0	0

Table P22.4. Truth table for the logical formula F: $(x_1 \vee \neg x_2) \wedge (\neg x_2 \rightarrow x_1)$

The truth table $T(F)$ for the logical formula F is illustrated in Table P22.4, where the truth values *false* and *true* are represented by Boolean values 0 and 1 respectively.

Construction of *CNF* involves the last two rows (interpretations) of $T(F)$ and the construction of *DNF* involves the first two rows of $T(F)$.

The *CNF* *C* following the construction procedure is given by
$C: \left(x_1 \vee \neg x_2\right) \wedge \left(x_1 \vee x_2\right).$

The *DNF* *D* following the construction procedure is given by
$D: \left(x_1 \wedge x_2\right) \vee \left(x_1 \wedge \neg x_2\right)$

PROBLEM 22.5.–

Transform the following logical formulae into a *3-CNF*.

a) $F: \left(x_1 \vee \neg x_2\right) \wedge \left(\neg x_2 \rightarrow x_1\right)$

b) $G: \left(X\right) \wedge \left(\neg U \vee \neg V \vee W \vee \neg X\right)$

Solution:

a) The procedure to obtain the *CNF* for the logical formula F has already been discussed in illustrative problem 22.4 and is given by $C: \left(x_1 \vee \neg x_2\right) \wedge \left(x_1 \vee x_2\right).$

To obtain the *3-CNF*, we follow the procedure discussed in section 22.3.5. Since both the clauses of the *CNF* have only two literals, two auxiliary variables, p, q, one each for the clauses in *C*, are introduced. The *3-CNF* is given by,
$C: \left(x_1 \vee \neg x_2 \vee p\right) \wedge \left(x_1 \vee \neg x_2 \vee \neg p\right) \wedge \left(x_1 \vee x_2 \vee q\right) \wedge \left(x_1 \vee x_2 \vee \neg q\right).$

b) The formula G is a *CNF*. Following the procedure, the *3-CNF* equivalent to G is given by,

$$\left(X \vee p \vee q\right) \wedge \left(X \vee p \vee \neg q\right) \wedge \left(X \vee \neg p \vee q\right) \wedge \left(X \vee \neg p \vee \neg q\right) \wedge$$
$$\left(\neg U \vee \neg V \vee r\right) \wedge \left(W \vee \neg X \vee \neg r\right)$$

where p, q, r are auxiliary variables. It can be observed that since clause (X) comprises a single literal, two auxiliary variables p, q need to be introduced. Clause $\left(\neg U \vee \neg V \vee W \vee \neg X\right)$ on the other hand, needs only one auxiliary variable r.

PROBLEM 22.6.–

Show that the *CNF*-satisfiability problem (*SAT*) reduces to the *3-CNF SAT* problem.

Solution:

To show that *SAT* ∝ *3-CNF SAT*, we need to show that an instance *I* of *3-CNF SAT* can be obtained from an instance *I'* of *SAT* in deterministic polynomial time such that using the solution for *I*, the solution to *I'* can be found in deterministic polynomial time. An instance *I* of *3-CNF SAT* is a *3-CNF* formula, which can be obtained from an instance *I'* of *SAT*, which is a *CNF*, in deterministic polynomial time. The solution for *I*, a *3-CNF* formula, is only assignment of values to variables that render it satisfiable. The same assignment of values to variables will render *I'*, which is a *CNF*, satisfiable. This can be easily accomplished in deterministic polynomial time. Hence, *SAT* ∝ *3-CNF SAT*.

PROBLEM 22.7.–

Show that the *3-CNF* satisfiability problem (*3-CNF SAT*) is *NP*-complete.

Solution:

To show that *3-CNF SAT* is *NP*-complete, we need to show that (i) *3-CNF SAT* ∈ NP and (ii) *3-CNF SAT* belongs to *the NP*-hard class, to accomplish which there needs to be an *NP*-hard problem *L* that reduces to *3-CNF SAT*, that is, *L* ∝ *3-CNF SAT*.

Now, *3-CNF SAT* ∈ *NP*, since verification of the solution to the *3-CNF SAT* problem, which involves testing the satisfiability of the *3-CNF* for an assignment of values to its variables, can be easily accomplished in polynomial time.

To show that *3-CNF SAT* is *NP*-hard, we choose *L = SAT*, which is an *NP*-hard problem. It can be proved that SAT ∝ *3-CNF SAT* (see illustrative problem 22.6).

Hence *3-CNF SAT* is *NP*-complete.

Review questions

1) Define *P* class and *NP* class of problems.

2) When is a problem said to be *NP*-hard?

3) When is a problem said to be *NP*-complete?

4) Give an example of an *NP*-hard decision problem that is not *NP*-complete. Explain.

5) Which of the following problems is not *NP*-complete?

a) Traveling Salesperson decision problem.

b) Direct Hamiltonian circuit problem.

c) Chromatic number decision problem.

d) Halting problem.

6) What is the satisfiability problem (*SAT*) and why is it *NP*-complete?

7) State Cook's theorem and discuss an informal proof for it.

8) State which of the following statements are true or false:

i) Every *NP*-complete problem is *NP*-hard.

ii) Every *NP*-hard problem is *NP*-complete.

a) (i) true, (ii) true   b) (i) true (ii) false

c) (i) false (ii) true   d) (i) false (ii) false

9) Outline a nondeterministic polynomial time algorithm for the satisfiability problem.

10) When are two problems said to be polynomially equivalent?

References

Aragon, C.R. and Seidel, R. (1989). Randomized search trees. In *Proc. 30th Symp. Foundations of Computer Science (FOCS 1989)*. IEEE Computer Society Press, Washington, DC.

Donald, K. (1998). *Art of Computer Programming, Vol. III*. 2nd edition. Addison-Wesley Professional, Reading, MA.

Garey, M.R. and David, S.J. (1979). *Computers and Intractability: A Guide to the Theory of NP-Completeness*. W.H. Freeman, New York.

Hoare, C.A.R. (1962). Quick sort. *The Computer Journal*, 5(1), 10–16.

Knuth, D.E. (1973). *The Art of Computer Programming, Volume 1: Fundamental Algorithms*. 2nd edition. Addison-Wesley, Reading, MA.

Malik, S. and Lintao, Z. (2009). Boolean satisfiability, from theoretical hardness to practical success. *Communications of the ACM*, 52(8), 76–82.

Perlis, A.J. and Thornton, C. (1960). Symbol manipulation by threaded lists. *Communications of the ACM*, 3(4), 195–204.

Pugh, W. (1990). Skip lists: A probabilistic alternative to balanced trees. *Communications of the ACM*, 33(6), 668–676.

Shell, D.L. (1959). A high-speed sorting procedure. *Communications of the ACM*, 2(7), 30–32.

Index

Summary of Volume 1

Chapter 6. Linked Lists

Chapter 7. Linked Stacks and Linked Queues

References

Index

Summary of Volume 2

References

Index

Other titles from

in

Computer Engineering

2022

MEHTA Shikha, TIWARI Sanju, SIARRY Patrick, JABBAR M.A.
Tools, Languages, Methodologies for Representing Semantics on the Web of Things

SIDHOM Sahbi, KADDOUR Amira
Systems and Uses of Digital Sciences for Knowledge Organization (Digital Tools and Uses Set – Volume 9)

ZAIDOUN Ameur Salem
Computer Science Security: Concepts and Tools

2021

DELHAYE Jean-Loic
Inside the World of Computing: Technologies, Uses, Challenges

DUVAUT Patrick, DALLOZ Xavier, MENGA David, KOEHL François, CHRIQUI Vidal, BRILL Joerg
Internet of Augmented Me, I.AM: Empowering Innovation for a New Sustainable Future

HARDIN Thérèse, JAUME Mathieu, PESSAUX François,
VIGUIÉ DONZEAU-GOUGE Véronique
Concepts and Semantics of Programming Languages 1: A Semantical Approach with OCaml and Python
Concepts and Semantics of Programming Languages 2: Modular and Object-oriented Constructs with OCaml, Python, C++, Ada and Java

MKADMI Abderrazak
Archives in The Digital Age: Preservation and the Right to be Forgotten (Digital Tools and Uses Set – Volume 8)

TOKLU Yusuf Cengiz, BEKDAS Gebrail, NIGDELI Sinan Melih
Metaheuristics for Structural Design and Analysis (Optimization Heuristics Set – Volume 3)

2020

DARCHE Philippe
Microprocessor 1: Prolegomena – Calculation and Storage Functions – Models of Computation and Computer Architecture
Microprocessor 2: Core Concepts – Communication in a Digital System
Microprocessor 3: Core Concepts – Hardware Aspects
Microprocessor 4: Core Concepts – Software Aspects
Microprocessor 5: Software and Hardware Aspects of Development, Debugging and Testing – The Microcomputer

LAFFLY Dominique
TORUS 1 – Toward an Open Resource Using Services: Cloud Computing for Environmental Data
TORUS 2 – Toward an Open Resource Using Services: Cloud Computing for Environmental Data
TORUS 3 – Toward an Open Resource Using Services: Cloud Computing for Environmental Data

LAURENT Anne, LAURENT Dominique, MADERA Cédrine
Data Lakes
(Databases and Big Data Set – Volume 2)

OULHADJ Hamouche, DAACHI Boubaker, MENASRI Riad
Metaheuristics for Robotics
(Optimization Heuristics Set – Volume 2)

SADIQUI Ali
Computer Network Security

VENTRE Daniel
Artificial Intelligence, Cybersecurity and Cyber Defense

2019

BESBES Walid, DHOUIB Diala, WASSAN Niaz, MARREKCHI Emna
Solving Transport Problems: Towards Green Logistics

CLERC Maurice
Iterative Optimizers: Difficulty Measures and Benchmarks

GHLALA Riadh
Analytic SQL in SQL Server 2014/2016

TOUNSI Wiem
Cyber-Vigilance and Digital Trust: Cyber Security in the Era of Cloud Computing and IoT

2018

ANDRO Mathieu
Digital Libraries and Crowdsourcing
(Digital Tools and Uses Set – Volume 5)

ARNALDI Bruno, GUITTON Pascal, MOREAU Guillaume
Virtual Reality and Augmented Reality: Myths and Realities

BERTHIER Thierry, TEBOUL Bruno
From Digital Traces to Algorithmic Projections

CARDON Alain
Beyond Artificial Intelligence: From Human Consciousness to Artificial Consciousness

PÉTROWSKI Alain, BEN-HAMIDA Sana
Evolutionary Algorithms
(Metaheuristics Set – Volume 9)

PAI G A Vijayalakshmi
Metaheuristics for Portfolio Optimization
(Metaheuristics Set – Volume 11)

2016

BLUM Christian, FESTA Paola
Metaheuristics for String Problems in Bio-informatics
(Metaheuristics Set – Volume 6)

DEROUSSI Laurent
Metaheuristics for Logistics
(Metaheuristics Set – Volume 4)

DHAENENS Clarisse and JOURDAN Laetitia
Metaheuristics for Big Data
(Metaheuristics Set – Volume 5)

LABADIE Nacima, PRINS Christian, PRODHON Caroline
Metaheuristics for Vehicle Routing Problems
(Metaheuristics Set – Volume 3)

LEROY Laure
Eyestrain Reduction in Stereoscopy

LUTTON Evelyne, PERROT Nathalie, TONDA Albert
Evolutionary Algorithms for Food Science and Technology
(Metaheuristics Set – Volume 7)

MAGOULÈS Frédéric, ZHAO Hai-Xiang
Data Mining and Machine Learning in Building Energy Analysis

RIGO Michel
Advanced Graph Theory and Combinatorics

2015

BARBIER Franck, RECOUSSINE Jean-Luc
COBOL Software Modernization: From Principles to Implementation with the BLU AGE® Method

CHEN Ken
Performance Evaluation by Simulation and Analysis with Applications to Computer Networks

CLERC Maurice
Guided Randomness in Optimization
(Metaheuristics Set – Volume 1)

DURAND Nicolas, GIANAZZA David, GOTTELAND Jean-Baptiste, ALLIOT Jean-Marc
Metaheuristics for Air Traffic Management
(Metaheuristics Set – Volume 2)

MAGOULÈS Frédéric, ROUX François-Xavier, HOUZEAUX Guillaume
Parallel Scientific Computing

MUNEESAWANG Paisarn, YAMMEN Suchart
Visual Inspection Technology in the Hard Disk Drive Industry

2014

BOULANGER Jean-Louis
Formal Methods Applied to Industrial Complex Systems

BOULANGER Jean-Louis
Formal Methods Applied to Complex Systems:Implementation of the B Method

GARDI Frédéric, BENOIST Thierry, DARLAY Julien, ESTELLON Bertrand, MEGEL Romain
Mathematical Programming Solver based on Local Search

KRICHEN Saoussen, CHAOUACHI Jouhaina
Graph-related Optimization and Decision Support Systems

DELAHAYE Daniel, PUECHMOREL Stéphane
Modeling and Optimization of Air Traffic

FRANCOPOULO Gil
LMF — Lexical Markup Framework

GHÉDIRA Khaled
Constraint Satisfaction Problems

ROCHANGE Christine, UHRIG Sascha, SAINRAT Pascal
Time-Predictable Architectures

WAHBI Mohamed
Algorithms and Ordering Heuristics for Distributed Constraint Satisfaction Problems

ZELM Martin *et al.*
Enterprise Interoperability

2012

ARBOLEDA Hugo, ROYER Jean-Claude
Model-Driven and Software Product Line Engineering

BLANCHET Gérard, DUPOUY Bertrand
Computer Architecture

BOULANGER Jean-Louis
Industrial Use of Formal Methods: Formal Verification

BOULANGER Jean-Louis
Formal Method: Industrial Use from Model to the Code

CALVARY Gaëlle, DELOT Thierry, SÈDES Florence, TIGLI Jean-Yves
Computer Science and Ambient Intelligence

MAHOUT Vincent
Assembly Language Programming: ARM Cortex-M3 2.0: Organization, Innovation and Territory

MARLET Renaud
Program Specialization

SOTO Maria, SEVAUX Marc, ROSSI André, LAURENT Johann
Memory Allocation Problems in Embedded Systems: Optimization Methods

2011

BICHOT Charles-Edmond, SIARRY Patrick
Graph Partitioning

BOULANGER Jean-Louis
Static Analysis of Software: The Abstract Interpretation

CAFERRA Ricardo
Logic for Computer Science and Artificial Intelligence

HOMÈS Bernard
Fundamentals of Software Testing

KORDON Fabrice, HADDAD Serge, PAUTET Laurent, PETRUCCI Laure
Distributed Systems: Design and Algorithms

KORDON Fabrice, HADDAD Serge, PAUTET Laurent, PETRUCCI Laure
Models and Analysis in Distributed Systems

LORCA Xavier
Tree-based Graph Partitioning Constraint

TRUCHET Charlotte, ASSAYAG Gerard
Constraint Programming in Music

VICAT-BLANC PRIMET Pascale *et al.*
Computing Networks: From Cluster to Cloud Computing

2010

AUDIBERT Pierre
Mathematics for Informatics and Computer Science

BABAU Jean-Philippe *et al.*
Model Driven Engineering for Distributed Real-Time Embedded Systems

BOULANGER Jean-Louis
Safety of Computer Architectures

MONMARCHE Nicolas *et al.*
Artificial Ants

PANETTO Hervé, BOUDJLIDA Nacer
Interoperability for Enterprise Software and Applications 2010

SIGAUD Olivier *et al.*
Markov Decision Processes in Artificial Intelligence

SOLNON Christine
Ant Colony Optimization and Constraint Programming

AUBRUN Christophe, SIMON Daniel, SONG Ye-Qiong *et al.*
Co-design Approaches for Dependable Networked Control Systems

2009

FOURNIER Jean-Claude
Graph Theory and Applications

GUEDON Jeanpierre
The Mojette Transform / Theory and Applications

JARD Claude, ROUX Olivier
Communicating Embedded Systems / Software and Design

LECOUTRE Christophe
Constraint Networks / Targeting Simplicity for Techniques and Algorithms

2008

BANÂTRE Michel, MARRÓN Pedro José, OLLERO Hannibal, WOLITZ Adam
Cooperating Embedded Systems and Wireless Sensor Networks

MERZ Stephan, NAVET Nicolas
Modeling and Verification of Real-time Systems

PASCHOS Vangelis Th
Combinatorial Optimization and Theoretical Computer Science: Interfaces and Perspectives

WALDNER Jean-Baptiste
Nanocomputers and Swarm Intelligence

2007

BENHAMOU Frédéric, JUSSIEN Narendra, O'SULLIVAN Barry
Trends in Constraint Programming

JUSSIEN Narendra
A TO Z OF SUDOKU

2006

BABAU Jean-Philippe *et al.*
From MDD Concepts to Experiments and Illustrations – DRES 2006

HABRIAS Henri, FRAPPIER Marc
Software Specification Methods

MURAT Cecile, PASCHOS Vangelis Th
Probabilistic Combinatorial Optimization on Graphs

PANETTO Hervé, BOUDJLIDA Nacer
Interoperability for Enterprise Software and Applications 2006 / IFAC-IFIP I-ESA'2006

2005

GÉRARD Sébastien *et al.*
Model Driven Engineering for Distributed Real Time Embedded Systems

PANETTO Hervé
Interoperability of Enterprise Software and Applications 2005

Printed and bound by CPI Group (UK) Ltd, Croydon, CR0 4YY

27/10/2024

14580248-0003